W9-AVW-019

**A Voice From Afar**

The History of
Telecommunications
in Canada

## Books by Robert Collins

1962    The Legend of the Devil's Lode
1965    Rory's Wildcat
1968    East to Cathay
1969    A Great Way to Go
1972    The Medes and the Persians
1977    The Age of Innocence: 1870–1880
1977    A Voice from Afar

On the jacket:
*Front:* "It listens Good." (Bell Canada Telephone Historical Collection).
*Back, Clockwise:* Blake magneto telephone, 1880s (Bell Canada Telephone Historical Collection). Telephone exchange in Dr. Riddell's drugstore, about 1914 (Public Archives of Canada PA 70872). Launching of Anik satellite on NASA Delta rocket at Cape Canaveral (Telesat). Linemen in Stettler, Alta., 1909 (Provincial Archives of Alberta).

# A Voice From Afar

## The History of
## Telecommunications
## in Canada

# Robert Collins

**McGraw-Hill Ryerson Limited**

Toronto   Montreal   New York   St. Louis   San Francisco   Auckland
Bogotá   Düsseldorf   Johannesburg   London   Madrid   Mexico   New Delhi
Panama   Paris   São Paulo   Singapore   Sydney   Tokyo

1 2 3 4 5 6 7 8 9 0   BP   8 9 0 1 2 3 4 5 6 7

Printed and bound in Canada
Excerpt from *Collected Poems of Robert Service* reprinted by permission.


Canadian Cataloguing in Publication Data

Collins, Robert, 1924–
   A voice from afar

Also published in French under title: Une voix venue de loin.

Bibliography: p.
Includes index.
ISBN 0-07-082536-X

1. Telecommunication — Canada — History.   I. Title.

HE7814.C65      384'.0971      C77-001150-0

The text for this book was prepared with the support of a research grant from
the Canadian Telecommunications Carriers Association. The opinions
expressed, however, are those of the author. They do not necessarily represent
the views of the C.T.C.A. or of its member companies.

### MEMBERS OF THE C.T.C.A.

Alberta Government Telephones
Bell Canada
British Columbia Telephone Company
Canadian Independent Telephone
   Association
Canadian National Telecommunications
Canadian Pacific Telecommunications
edmonton telephones
The Island Telephone Company Limited
Manitoba Telephone System
Maritime Telegraph and Telephone
   Company Limited

The New Brunswick Telephone
   Company, Limited
Newfoundland Telephone Company
   Limited
Northern Telephone Limited
Okanagan Telephone Company
Ontario Northland Communications
Québec-Téléphone
Saskatchewan Telecommunications
Télébec Limitée
Teleglobe Canada
Telesat Canada
Trans-Canada Telephone System

For LESLEY and CATHY
who were sailing right behind me

# CONTENTS

# Acknowledgements

The bulk of this work was researched in public and private libraries and archives across Canada. I am particularly indebted to Elizabeth Geraghty, Bell Canada historian in Montreal, and to her superb staff and archives. Special thanks also go to Elfleda Wilkinson, British Columbia Telephone Company; Evelyn Murphy, New Brunswick Telephone Company; Joyce Robertson, Bell Canada in Toronto; Shirley Smith, CN Telecommunications, Toronto; and James Shields, Canadian Pacific, Montreal. Archivists, historians or librarians all, they were unfailingly patient and helpful.

The Public Archives of Canada, Newfoundland, Nova Scotia, Ontario, Saskatchewan, Alberta and British Columbia were rich sources of material. Archivists Margaret Mattson of PAC, Edwin Morgan of PAS and Dr. Bruce Fergusson and Allan C. Dunlop of PANS were especially generous with their time and suggestions. The reference facilities of Metropolitan Toronto Central Public Library were invaluable, as so often before in my writing career.

Private interviews and reminiscences were contributed by Dan Hanneberry, Victoria; A. J. Clark, Vancouver; Fred Waite, Delta, B.C.; Margaret Seens, Gold River, B.C.; Gillies McCormick, Regina; Harold Clarke, Toronto; Gen. Hugh Young, Col. William Lockhart and Reginald Gisborne, all of Ottawa; Don McKelvie, New Liskeard, Ont.; Doug Macleod, Lancaster, Ont.; Alex Lester, Montreal; and Ted O'Keefe, St. John's. Other individuals across Canada facilitated my research in a host of ways, among them: Robert LaRiviere, Newfoundland Telephone Company; Walter Auld, The Island Telephone Company; Furber Marshall, Maritime Tel and Tel; John Reid and H. B. Kee, New Brunswick Telephone Company; Louis Arsenault, Québec Téléphone; Hugh Seadon, of Québec Téléphone, on behalf of the Canadian Independent Telephone Association; Robert Spencer and Don Atkinson, Bell Canada; Jean-Claude Delorme and Hubert Potvin, Teleglobe; David Golden and Michael Steers, Telesat; James Forbes, Canadian Pacific; Anthony Kuhr and Mac Lawson, CN Telecommunications; Gordon Thompson, Bell Northern Research; Fred Kember, Manitoba Telephone System; Ted Cholod, SaskTel, and Max

Macdonald of the Regina *Leader-Post*. To all of them, much thanks.

I am indebted to Tony Cashman of Alberta Government Telephones for permitting me to draw from his excellent history, "Singing Wires." Tom Grindlay of the Ontario Telephone Commission kindly allowed me to read in manuscript his history of independent telephone companies in that province. Throughout this project, M. N. Davies, president of the Canadian Telecommunications Carriers Association, was unceasingly helpful with contacts and advice.

Several of the aforementioned read the manuscript and offered helpful suggestions, as did my brother Lawrence Collins, who also contributed research. My daughters, Lesley and Catherine Collins, shared in the research and cataloguing. Cathy Hayward, Susan Myers and Dorothy Wowk typed the manuscript in its various stages.

In any work of this magnitude and complexity, errors are almost inevitable. For these, I alone am responsible.

ROBERT COLLINS

# Foreword

Telecommunications means any transmission or reception of words, images or data of any other nature, by means of electronic signals. Under this book's terms of reference, however, I touch only on the beginnings of wireless and radio broadcasting and do not attempt a history of commercial radio or television. Radio and TV, like the rest of us, are customers of the telecommunications systems.

This, then, is primarily a story of the signal carriers — telegraph, telephone and satellite — and, more particularly, of the men and women whose labour and genius linked the solitudes of this country and helped make it a nation.

## A VOICE FROM AFAR

Faintly as from a star
Voices come o'er the line;
Voices of ghosts afar,
Not in this world of mine . . .

"The Telegraph Operator"
from *Ballads of a Cheechako*
by Robert W. Service


Telephone: (Gr.) — *tele* ("far") + *phone* ("sound")

# The Way It Was

Such blessed innocents they are, these two million denizens of British North America, yawning out of their cotton quilts and rope beds this Saturday morning. They have a date with history but who among them knows it? Today, December 19, the telegraph is coming. It will change their lives forever, beyond recognition. But because there *is* no telegraph, most British North Americans have never *heard* of it, or of any other current event. They are only as close to recent happenings as sailing ships and galloping steeds can carry the news, which is far away indeed.

They rise this day to sounds as basic and uncomplicated as their lives — birdsong, dogs' bark, clocks' tick, sleigh bells, the clatter of kitchen crockery, the hiss of runners in snow. They comb their beards, coil their braids, encase themselves in flannel undershirts or whale bone corsets, and tuck away stupefying breakfasts of hominy, toast, molasses, chops, fried potatoes and tea. Then, rumbling with dyspepsia, a common affliction of their time, they move heavily to their labours. Saturday is a working day. The six-day work week, 10 hours a day, is all they know.

No ringing bells, no urgent broadcasts, no instant messages of any kind will ruffle their routine. Distant loved ones may have died last week; kingdoms may have toppled; invaders may be marching toward their shores — these people have no way of knowing.

A promising young Kingston lawyer, John Alexander Macdonald, will be named Queen's Counsel today. The news will please the Scots of Red River, a thousand miles west in wild Rupert's Land, but it will not reach them until *next summer*, with the first Hudson's Bay Company canoe brigade. The Royal Mail steamer *Unicorn* docked in Newfoundland this week with English newspapers a *month* old. Fortunately, as the St. John's *Royal Gazette* reports, "The news is not of particular importance."

Two nights ago in Richmond Hill, a hamlet 15 miles north of Toronto, a jilted lover tried to kill himself, bungled the job and flung the pistol at his erstwhile sweetheart in a fit of pique. This juicy item will not get into the Toronto press for another three days. *Globe* readers are only now perusing the market reports of December 10.

And so it goes in all the isolated settlements, scattered thinly throughout this enormous land. The people of British North America are castaways on a vast, lonely ocean of distance.

What are they like, these human and geographical fragments of Canada-to-be on this day of the telegraph? At the eastern ramparts, 96,000 Newfoundlanders hunch their backs against the mainland and turn their faces to the sea. Storms, ice and water are their realities, not Canada. Even England, 10 days away by Samuel Cunard's fastest new coal-burning steamers, seems closer.

Across Cabot Strait a half-million Maritimers cock a snook at those frost-bitten Newfoundland faces, those puzzling French to the west, and those clodhoppers somewhere westerly still. Snug and smug, the Maritimers are, with their rich little farms, their shipyards fragrant with fresh-planed wood, and their universities (more than the rest of British North America put together). Why bother to commune with Toronto, two weeks distant by mail — a foreign land, almost — when friendly Boston is only two days off by sail?

As for the Province of Canada: it threatens to fly apart at any moment like a cracked goblet. The habitant farms of Canada East, stacked like dominoes against the St. Lawrence, and their villages with names that ring like chapel bells, inhabit a close and private world of God, work, song and family.

To them, Montreal upriver is a distant world — cosmopolitan, remote, a little frightening. Its 40,000 people make it twice the size of any other city in the land. Priests, merchant princes, scarlet-clad officers of the Queen; labourers eking out a squalid existence; English, French; mansions, slums — Montreal is all positives and negatives. There are no shades of grey. For the lucky ones, life is good this Christmas season. As in every mid-December, the Scottish settlers from backwoods Glengarry are streaming into town, bells tintinnabulating, 12-foot sleighs groaning with tubs of sweet butter, golden cheeses, chickens, turkeys, geese and hogs. Thrifty housewives and rich men's cooks are out at dawn to buy the best, and the Scots go home with pockets full of shillings and wide smiles cracking their square bearded faces.

The little capital of Canada West feels somewhat cowed by Montreal. Toronto a mere 12 years ago was Muddy York, which tends to make it shrill and mildly schizophrenic. Toronto is torn between sin and salvation. Its Bible-thumping Protestants honor the Sabbath with shades discreetly drawn. A day at the horse races will, they know, guarantee eternal hellfire, almost as surely as consorting with scarlet women. Righteous parents, with thin lips set like two halves of muffin, force their miserable offspring to memorize 10 verses of Scripture each week. Yet among these 20,000 God-fearing souls are enough tipplers to support 300 taverns and beer shops.

Toronto burghers boast of their "city" and so it is in name, yet somehow it still has the look of York. Beyond Yonge and a street that will be Dundas lie scattered plots of forest. The southeast corner of Spadina and College is dominated by the accursed race track. A mile north is Yorkville village. Not far beyond, Indians still pitch their tepees, docile, bewildered Indians but genuine enough to quicken the pulses of small city boys and set them dreaming of the west.

Yes! The west exists! It lies out there beyond the Red River, knee-deep in snow this day, speckled with buffalo herds pawing through the drifts for the nourishing "prairie wool." Every eastern boy, every man, yearns to journey there, where the Cree are still warring and the Metis ride wild in the everlasting wind.

Some greenhorns go there and die, for the west is cruel. Some survive the awful journey to reach solitary Fort Edmonton where, today, behind the palisades on the hill, hardy trappers, traders and the Hudson's Bay factor are readying their annual Christmas feast: dried moose nose, whitefish baked in buffalo marrow, buffalo tongues, beaver tails, roast wild goose, potatoes and turnips grown in their own good black earth.

Some travellers prevail for a thousand miles beyond, through snow-clogged passes raked with wind, to find the coastal sun shining on a bit of Empire. The traders, soldiers and British seamen of Fort Vancouver and new Fort Victoria, named for the beloved Queen, stare curiously at human creatures from the east. Out here, San Francisco is reality. Canada? The Maritimes? They are as vague as yesterday's dreams. Sometimes, but rarely, mail trickles in from the east with a Bay brigade (which charges $1 for transporting the first half-ounce, 25¢ for each additional ounce).

In all these leagues of distance, the only decent "highways" are rivers and lakes. There is only one railway, the Champlain and St. Lawrence — a toy train, really, with 13-foot engine and wooden track; a 14.5 mile portage between La Prairie and St. Jean, south of Montreal. A Montreal-Toronto railroad is 10 years away.

Canada West brags of 6,000 miles of post road but a recent British visitor who travelled them went home aghast, muttering words like "wretched" and "terrible." One rainy night less than a month ago, seven hapless stagecoach passengers left Hamilton at six o'clock for Niagara 50 miles away. They arrived at sunrise, mudcaked, drenched and exhausted. They had ridden and walked by turns all night.

The roads are passable in winter, when frozen and smoothed with snow. Six winters ago William Weller, stagecoach king of Canada — a sporty fellow, with coaches of buttercup hue drawn by matching bays — whisked the Governor-in-Chief, Lord Sydenham, from Toronto to Montreal in just under 36 hours. Weller drove nonstop, except to change horses every 15 miles. It was such an incredible feat that Sydenham gave him £100 and a gold watch. Ordinary mortals make this bone-shaking trip in four days, resting their bruised bodies every 70 miles or so and praying the driver is sober in the morning. (Five years hence, Canada will enact a maximum fine of £5 or one month "in Common Gaol" for drunken driving.)

The mails are no better than the roads. Newfoundland villagers get letters erratically, by relays of boat and saddle horse. Toronto merchants ordering goods from Montreal cannot expect delivery in less than three weeks. In Nova Scotia an investigation of mail theft this year revealed that thieves snatch newspapers from holes in the ragged mail bags while the postmen's backs are turned. Just why anyone would *want* to steal newspapers is a moot point. They exist on warmed-over gossip, wild opinion and weeks-old foreign news.

Lately, though, an uncommon timeliness has crept into the Toronto press. Two months ago, a deck of headlines over the foreign despatches in the *British Colonist* explained it:

ARRIVAL OF THE

GREAT WESTERN

Eight days later from England.
By Magnetic Telegraph from New York to
Buffalo; by Railroad from Buffalo to
Lewiston; and by the Steamer
*Admiral*, Capt. W. Gordon, from
Lewiston to Toronto

Incredible! By ship to telegraph to railroad to lake boat, trimming weeks off the normal relay of news from England! But what *is* the magnetic telegraph? The newspapers mention it sparingly, because they neither trust nor understand it. Today, December 19, the "talk by lightning," as the Toronto *Examiner* terms it, will begin between Toronto and Hamilton. Does that mean the messages will be routed through Heaven?

Those few who have heard of the telegraph know only that the Yankees have had it for two years. The Yankees have nearly *everything* except Canada itself, and they plan to remedy that. Now, as always, the heavy shadow of the States hangs over this land. Only a year ago an American magazine voiced a common American desire: "the fulfillment of our manifest destiny to overspread the continent." Some British North Americans are almost ready to accept the inevitable, as they see it. Three years hence, 325 eminent Canadians — including John Abbott, a future prime minister — will sign their names to the Annexation Manifesto, urging union with the States.

Throughout the years ahead the telegraph and its successors will be tormented by the Canadian dichotomy. They will demand U.S. money and expertise, yet will bridle under U.S. ownership. Nonetheless, the seeds of identity are sprouting. On this day, even before the first "dot-dash" chatters over the wires, a Canadian communications story is taking shape.

Near Queenston Heights three-year-old Robbie McMicking plays on his father's farm, never dreaming of his role in the drama to come.

On another farm at St-Eustache, gangling 22-year-old Fred Gisborne falls asleep red-eyed each night beside his flickering candle, his head in a book on the new science of electricity. In Portsmouth, New Hampshire, 14-year-old schoolboy Charlie Sise knows nothing yet of the science that will lead him to Canada (*his* head is full of sailing ships).

In Edinburgh, a Scottish professor of elocution, Alexander Melville Bell, not long returned from Newfoundland, is fussing over his young wife, six months' pregnant with their second child. If it is a boy, he will be called Alex. The young man, the adolescent, the small boy, the baby yet unborn, and thousands more will build telegraph, telephone and other tools of communication more wondrous still, and so build a country.

Today, no one in British North America dreams this *will* be a country. But telegraph, telephone and the rest will shrink the distance and keep the dialogue flowing. They will help quell rebellions, build railways and open the mysterious north. They will mend the ravages of fire, wind, flood and war. And they will stitch this patchwork of wilderness into a nation.

# Chapter 1

## The Talk by Lightning

In the beginning was confusion. The telegraph had come to Canada. The shiny brass instruments waited mute in Hamilton and Toronto, this morning of December 19, 1846, ready to electrify the plodding colony with news, commerce, excitement, *progress*. But where were the welcoming committees, the speeches, the brass bands? Only a single operator in each city, a reporter from the *Examiner* in Toronto and a few hangers-on stood ready to witness the first "talk by lightning."

The weather did little for their spirits. It was murky grey and unseasonably warm, the mercury headed for 50 degrees F, not the nippy Christmas weather that outdoors lovers longed for. The telegraph watchers were stifling in their flannel underwear. Outside the Toronto office, a temporary room in the new City Hall, Front Street East was a quagmire of mud, melting snow and horse manure. Top-hatted men, their cuffs already soiled, and painfully corseted women, their trailing skirts hoisted prettily above the ankles, were slogging through the slush. Christmas was less than a week away. Sleigh bells were on sale at Thomas Rigney & Co. Riddel & McLean, Merchant Tailors, were offering bargains in "plain and fancy Trowserings and Vestings. . .Broad Cloths, Cassimeres and Doeskins." Whole succulent turkeys dangled in the market at only two shillings sixpence (about 60¢) each.

So the Saturday shoppers streamed by, oblivious to the vigil in new City Hall. Did they not know that history was about to explode in that little room?

Inside, telegraph operator Samuel Porter tossed back the tails of his frock coat and settled before a clutter of wires, batteries and brass. He flexed one hand over a pivoted lever called the "key." In the other he grasped a copy of the Morse code, a series of dots and dashes paired off with letters of the alphabet and numbers from one to ten.

But what next? Without official guidance, Toronto and Hamilton were stymied. Finally, just before noon, the talk by lightning in Canada began — no deathless phrases for posterity, just a puzzled exchange of trivia.

As current flowed over the wire from Hamilton, the Toronto receiver began to chatter. Electrical impulses, transmitted to a stylus, appeared as dots and dashes imprinted on a revolving paper tape. The Toronto operator copied them in longhand.

"Who is in your office?" said Hamilton. "Is Mr. Gamble [the president of the telegraph company] present?"

The Toronto operator tapped out a reply, alternately pressing and releasing his key, starting or stopping the flow of current. A short quick press formed a "dot"; a longer hold produced a "dash." A combination of these — with subtle variations in the spaces between, distinguishable only to the well-attuned ear — spelled out words across the distance.

"DASH space DOT space space space DOT space space DOT [NO]," came Toronto's answer.

H: "What o'clock is it?"

T: "Twenty-five minutes past eleven."

H: "You must mean twelve?"

T: "No, it is just half-past eleven."

H: "Is that the town time?"

T: "Yes."

H: "Well advise Mr. Gamble that Mr. Dawson will speak with him at half-past one."

Then the operators went home for a hot meal. Mankind had waited a half-million years for the telegraph. Toronto could wait until after lunch. . .

# "What Hath God Wrought?"

For centuries, men had passed messages by runner or horseman, and for almost as long they had sought a better way. Yet everything they devised — fire or smoke signals, drums, flags, sunlight flashed from mirrors, carrier pigeons — was limited by distance. Each was only as good as the eye could see, the ear could hear or a bird could fly.

By the late 18th century the signals were, at least, more sophisticated. In 1767 a sporty Englishman named Edgeworth rigged a system of open and closed shutters, high on hills, to relay the race results from Newmarket. In France, Claude Chappe went a step better; his towers, fitted with moveable arms, spelled out intricate messages. By 1852 more than 500 of them stretched 4,800 kilometers across France.

The British Admiralty and Army adopted variations of this "semaphore" (meaning literally: "a sign I see"). In the early 1800s a few went up along the St. Lawrence River. Habitants were paid two pounds sterling per year (about $10) to let the towers stand on their land.

Long before that, Canada's first communications line sprang up in Nova Scotia. Its builder was Prince Edward, Duke of Kent, a balding young man with pouty lips, a vicious disposition and hearty sexual appetites. His only other notable feat was fathering Queen Victoria.

As George III's son, Edward naturally joined the army but not as a buck private. By 1794 at age 24 he commanded the Nova Scotia forces. In his private fantasies, Edward's bold dark eyes beheld a distant vision: himself, the valiant prince, fighting off French invaders with the mightiest defence system in North America. That system, he decided, would need a semaphore line from Halifax to Annapolis, or beyond.

He built it rapidly, without benefit of coffee breaks or overtime pay. His terrified troops were motivated by floggings, courts-martial and the occasional execution. By 1799 a series of signal flags, pennants and wooden balls ran the full 130 miles. A six-mile branch line veered off to Bedford Basin. There the prince — when snuggled into the rural love nest of his mistress, Madame Julie de Montgenet de Saint Laurent — could always be on top of events. All together, it was his finest year. His father also made him commander of all British North American forces and the loyal

Maritimers named Prince Edward Island (formerly Ile Saint Jean) in his honor.

Had he remained in the colony, Edward might have pushed the line all the way to Quebec, although rough terrain and tricky fogs were already raising hob with his signals. Unfortunately for a united Canada, but to the enormous relief of the troops, George III shipped his son off to Gibraltar and the line fell into disuse. Edward's semaphore, like most others, was highly expensive (one reason his father plucked him out of British North America) and limited always by the range of men's vision. It was really just a glorified smoke signal. There had to be a better way.

Electricity, long known in its primitive forms of lightning and magnetism, was at last being understood. Suddenly all over Europe, from crude smelly laboratories lit by guttering candles, inventions showered like sparks, culminating in the telegraph.

In 1753 an unknown doctor in Greenock, Charles Morrison, sent an intriguing proposal to the *Scots Magazine*: why not fasten separate wires to terminals arranged along a gun barrel, each terminal representing a letter of the alphabet? Electrical discharges from the wires would spark at the appropriate letters, spelling out words. Morrison was on the right track, but dropped from sight.

Then came a dozen variations on his idea. A Swiss proposed a similar "telegraph" (from the Greek "to write afar") with wooden balls indicating each letter. Another Swiss used sparking wires to illuminate tinfoil letters on a glass plate. A German arranged 35 wires, each terminating in a gold electrode submerged in water; bubbles indicated the desired letter or number. England's Francis Ronalds invented a telegraph with clockwork mechanism; the appropriate letter clicked into view behind a slot in a circular dial.

Yet another scheme required the operator to place his fingers and thumbs on 10 terminals, each hitched to a live wire. The current was passed in short bursts by code; a simultaneous shock in the right thumb and left index finger might signify the letter "A." As might have been expected, there was no rush of applicants for operator.

Most of these experiments were powered by a Leyden jar — a glass container partly filled with water, with a metal spike piercing its cork stopper. One end of the spike touched the water. The exposed end could pick up and hold a charge of static electricity from any frictional device (much as the scuffing of one's feet on carpet on a dry winter day builds up a "shock"). The jars had neither the strength nor continuity needed for commercial telegraphy.

But other inventors, whose names would lend new words to electrical language, pushed the new science ahead. The Italian Volta, aided by the discoveries of his countryman Galvani, invented the first battery. Oersted, a Dane, in 1820 proved a long-suspected relationship between electricity and magnetism. Others found that magnetism itself creates a slight current. Ampere, in France, suggested that electromagnetism be used for signalling at a distance.

Others proved that the flow of current could be multiplied by passing that current through a coil of insulated wire. Out of this came the electromagnet — a soft iron bar, temporarily magnetized by passing electric current through wire coiled around it. Moreover, it could transform a weak current into a stronger one.

At this point an American, Harrison Bray Dyar, teetered on the brink of immortality. In 1827 he raised a telegraph line on Long Island, and sent signals with sparks that registered marks on litmus paper. Only his source of power — the erratic frictional electricity — was wrong. But before poor Dyar could study up on batteries and pursue his dream of building a line between New York and Philadelphia, he was served a writ for "conspiracy to carry on secret communication from city to city." It was enough to make a man quit telegraphy and flee the country, which Dyar did.

By the early 1830s all these patient probing men had amassed a solid sum of knowledge. They knew that electric current, generated from batteries, would flow along wires. Resistance eventually slowed it to a trickle but the current could be magnified along the way. The scientific groundwork was done. The time was right for the telegraph. It remained for a far-ranging mind to piece the puzzle together. Neither of the men who simultaneously produced workable models was a scientist.

William Cooke of England had been studying anatomy, but with a scientist partner, Charles Wheatstone, he produced a telegraph so reliable that the British railways used it for decades. It utilized needles, magnetized by current at the touch of a transmitter key, to point to letters of the alphabet at the receiving end. Every circuit required six wires, making the system expensive. It was also slow.

It remained for Samuel Morse, an American artist, to invent a recording telegraph that would sweep the world. His sole credentials were curiosity, mulish stubbornness and a rudimentary knowledge of general science. As a 20-year-old art student in London he once tossed out the kind of phrase that great men's biographers later savor.

"I wish that in one instant I could tell you of my safe arrival," he wrote his mother from England, "but we are 3,000 miles apart and must wait four long weeks to hear from each other."

Beyond that passing flirtation with the idea of communications, he thought only of painting for the next 20 years. That in itself was struggle enough. His work hung in the Royal Academy, but could not earn him a decent living.

In 1832, hollow-cheeked, downcast, trapped in a dead-end career at 41, Morse was sailing home from Europe, when a fellow passenger filled his ears with talk of electromagnets. Morse's dreamy eyes caught fire. If electricity could flash along a wired circuit, why couldn't intelligent messages follow the same route? He filled his sketchbook with technical doodles. Back home he abandoned a half-finished painting and plunged into his new lifework.

"The idea that I had made a brilliant discovery, that it was original in my mind, was the exciting cause and the perpetual stimulus to urge me forward," Morse wrote later. "Had I supposed that the thought had ever occurred to any other person I would never have pursued it."

He doggedly taught himself more about electricity. Employing the electromagnet principle he built a relay that boosted dwindling current. He also used the electromagnet in his receiving instrument or "sounder." When the current flowed, a magnetized bar attracted a lever with a sharp click. When the current ceased, the demagnetized bar released the spring-activated lever. Thus the dots and dashes of Morse code were transmitted to paper, first with a pen and later a stylus. (Some years after, a less complicated version of Morse's code was adopted for international use.)

He had help: a brilliant mechanical partner, Alfred Vail, and the first truly workable battery, invented by an English physicist, John Daniell. But Morse alone pulled all the elements together and he alone endured heart-breaking years of trying to interest an indifferent nation.

Although a Congressional committee saw and admired his invention in 1838, the U.S. voted no funds. Morse lived in his studio, sneaking groceries in at night so his friends would not know of his hand-to-mouth existence. In 1841 he admitted to Vail, "I have not a cent in the world." He eked out occasional food money by teaching art at New York University. Once he had to borrow $10 from a student to buy his first meal in 24 hours.

"Don't be an artist," he told the youth bitterly. "A house dog lives better."

At last in February 1843, with Morse down to exactly 37¢, the U.S. Congress by a narrow vote granted him $30,000 for an experimental line. It ran from Washington to Baltimore and successfully carried his historic words, "What hath God wrought?" In 1845 the Morse telegraph went commercial; a year later several principal American cities had it.

Science in British North America was nowhere near the capability of telegraphic experiments. But when the line reached Buffalo in July 1846, entrepreneurs in the Province of Canada recognized its possibilities. The "lightning" was exactly what this sprawling colony needed.

On October 2, a group met in the Toronto law offices of Clark Gamble, part-time railway promoter, to found the Toronto, Hamilton and Niagara Electro-Magnetic Telegraph Company. Gamble was president and the directors included two hardware merchants, a wharf proprietor, a sheriff and a cashier of the Bank of Upper Canada.

They formed a joint stock company, capitalized at £4,000 (British North America, although officially on dollar currency, still clung erratically to sterling) and showed their confidence by purchasing nearly half the stock themselves. Then they hired an experienced American contractor, insisting that their line be better — more poles per mile, stronger wire — than the trouble-plagued American telegraph systems. The work proceeded rapidly, although on December 8 the Hamilton *Spectator* reported a rumor that "some evil disposed person has cut the wires below Wellington Square and, if so, we hope the wretch will be found out and punished." The wretch went undiscovered but the 40-mile Toronto-Hamilton section was ready in two months.

## "The Thing's No Good"

. . . Sharp at 1:30 p.m. on December 19 the Hamilton and Toronto operators were back at their senders.

"I have just returned from dinner," telegraphed Hamilton.

T: "Is anyone with you in the office?"

H: "No. How does your machine work?"

T: "First rate. How does yours?"

H: "Rather stiff."

And then, mercifully, with small talk running dry, the Toronto and Hamilton dignitaries swept into their respective offices on a great wave of goodwill and cigar smoke: Clark Gamble, his directors, mayors, police chiefs, magistrates and leading merchants. After a round of intercity back-slapping by wire they threw the telegraph open to the common people, free.

Brotherly love instantly welled up in both cities. All afternoon the public clomped down the boardwalks to send greetings by lightning, enriching the small cluttered offices with smells of sweat, steaming woolens and bear grease pomade. One of the first users, a Hamilton businessman, tartly advised a Toronto customer that his bill was overdue.

As soon as the TH&N started *charging* for messages, business slumped. On Christmas Eve the telegraph flashed its first Canadian news story: the report of a nine-building fire that destroyed the Hamilton establishments of "Mullins, Farmers Inn, Jones, watchmaker, Tracy, shoemaker, Milligan, innkeeper, Lees, baker," among others. But the press, not at all attuned to carrying local spot news, used the wire mainly for market reports and European despatches.

The public hardly used it at all. For one thing it was expensive in its first year, from one shilling threepence up to three shillings sixpence — about 85 cents — for 10 words. That sum would buy four dozen eggs, or a large turkey, or five pounds of butter, or a bushel of potatoes.

Furthermore the telegraph was not fully understood or trusted. Many folk expected angels of the Lord, or at least a crackling thunderbolt, to usher messages across the sky. The media and telegraph company did nothing to enlighten them. The Buffalo *Express* reported in mid-January that the line was complete from Toronto to Buffalo and "the lightning will be let on today." Message blanks in offices around Niagara-Queenston bore the sonorous logo: "He directeth it under the whole Heaven and His lightnings unto the ends of the earth."

When the telegraph reached Napanee, Ontario, all the school children received a holiday to witness the miracle, and a man walked 20 miles to see if messages really *did* fly over the wires. He sat long and vigilant on a hill, his eyes riveted on the telegraph office. Finally he stomped down in disgust.

"The thing's no good," he said. "I waited two hours and the thing never went at all."

And in the autumn of 1847 a Picton minister named Macaulay penned a note, both melancholy and prophetic, to his mother in Kingston.

"The electric telegraph seems to be extending itself everywhere," he wrote. "The world will get all its news now at once, which will not be half as pleasant as when it came, driblet by driblet, after long expectation. Indeed, what with steamboats, rail cars, electric telegraphs, and so forth, the next generation will be altogether a different kind of race from our dull plodding generation."

# Chapter 2

## The Vindication of Montreal

ll the initial public coolness, all the early frustrations and financial setbacks of the Toronto, Hamilton and Niagara Electro-Magnetic Telegraph were as nothing when weighed against one instant and glorious dividend: the line's very existence sent waves of shock and humiliation through Montreal.

The financial, political and cultural capital of Canada was not used to playing second fiddle. Montreal boasted the Canadian Parliament building on Youville Square, just off McGill Street. Only four years earlier Charles Dickens, no less, had found Toronto "very flat," "bare of scenic interest" and full of "wild and rabid Toryism," while Montreal was "pleasantly situated" and "full of life and bustle." This very year a Lt.-Col. B. W. A. Sleigh had harrumphed his opinion that Montreal was a place of "vast commercial importance," and in 1846 an Army officer's wisdom and judgment were beyond reproach.

And yet. . .Toronto had a telegraph. Montreal had not even *started* one.

The Montreal Board of Trade hastily met the day after Christmas. A committee reported on several telegraphic alternatives. The Board opted for lines to Quebec City and Toronto, convened a general meeting three days later and issued 1,250 shares at £10 each. It was too late to avoid the jeers: already the Toronto *Examiner* was crowing, "It could hardly be believed that the public spirit of Toronto should outstrip that of Montreal." But Montreal vowed to salve its municipal ego by building the finest telegraph line in North America.

The company directors faced reality: the only expertise was in the United States. For superintendent they came up with the best, Orrin S. Wood, a tall, middle-aged telegrapher with receding hair worn curled above the ears. His contemporaries praised his "commanding presence"; it was the kind of sober mien they could trust and respect. Indeed, were it not for his spade beard, he would have been a dead ringer for George Washington.

Wood had studied telegraphy under Samuel Morse, and built telegraph lines with his brother-in-law, Ezra Cornell. He and the future founder of Cornell University had started at rock bottom, arriving broke in New York, lugging a single trunk between them up Broadway, and once paying for breakfast with a shilling picked up off the street. Before New York would permit them to string a mile of wire along that street, Cornell and Wood had to pay a scientist $50 to swear that the wire would not attract lightning. But those frugal and frustrating beginnings served them well in the telegraph-building orgy of 1844–46. Unlike most of their contemporaries they knew their business and got value for their dollar.

Most early American lines were cheap and shoddy. The poles fell down. Iron wires rusted. Wires of unannealed copper snapped in the first ice storms. Lines with too much slack crisscrossed in windstorms and garbled the transmission. Construction crews, ignorant of the principles of insulation, nailed the wires directly to the poles; at every such point the current was leached away until, over a distance, the message vanished.

The industry learned to wrap its wires around nonconductive insulators — everything from cows' horns to bureau drawer knobs. Small grooved glass cups fitted over pegs on the telegraph pole crossarms gave the best results. They also turned every line on the continent into a shooting gallery. Every male from 6 to 60, with rifle, slingshot or good right arm, had to have a crack at those twinkling targets atop the poles.

All of these early miseries were shared by the Toronto, Hamilton, Niagara and St. Catharines (as the first telegraph became known). The Toronto *Examiner* pointed out in 1847: "We entered into an arrangement Monday for Telegraphic reports and we will now give our readers an idea of the value we have received for our money. On Monday evening there was no report; Tuesday, the report was anticipated by mail; Wednesday there was about six lines of report; and Thursday the wires were broken!"

Not so with Montreal Telegraph. Superintendent Wood demanded thick cedar poles set five feet into the ground, crossarms of seasoned white oak, solid glass insulators — marksmen be damned — and the new #9 galvanized (zinc-coated) wire, best on the continent.

The company directors shopped for equally durable human goods. For the crucial post of secretary they struck gold in the person of James Dakers, a 36-year-old Scottish immigrant with law office experience. Dedicated and dead serious, with pale eyes and a bristle of chin whiskers fringing his steel-trap jaw, Dakers gave Montreal Telegraph his body and soul. When not tending the books with consummate thrift, he waited on customers at the counter, took a turn at the telegraph key or delivered handfuls of messages on his way home to supper. With such zeal emanating from the top, it was little wonder that the line, finished in August, grew to 9 offices, 35 employees, 540 miles of wire and had sent 33,000 messages by year's end. The message rates helped, too: as little as 31¢ for 10 words, under a distance of 100 miles.

Soon, Montreal Telegraph hired another star for its electrical department, Ben Toye of Toronto, inventor of one of North America's two best telegraph repeaters — devices that boosted the current along the line and kept the message strong. And soon Hugh Allan bobbed to the top of this company as he did in almost every other important enterprise in British North America. This self-made Scot, not yet 40 but already a shipping magnate, was destined to become the richest, most powerful tycoon in the land. He would one day head more than a dozen companies, be knighted by his Queen, and figure prominently in the Canadian Pacific Railway, in an aura of scandalous payoffs. He would survive that shame, accept the plaudits of his peers (for whom wealth and power excused most sins), and reign in truly regal fashion at Ravenscrag, his Montreal mansion. But for now he was still scrabbling upward, feeding his merciless ambition with one acquisition after another. When he became president of Montreal Telegraph in 1851 things began to happen.

For many a would-be captain of industry the initial stampede to telegraphy was beginning to backfire. Every community wanted to have the lightning. Starting a company was relatively easy, but most of them quickly foundered for lack of money or sound management. Allan watched them keenly, and pounced when the time was right.

In the late 1840s and early '50s, a line sprang from Montreal to Troy, New York; another from Montreal to Bytown; a third from Quebec to Montreal; a fourth from Quebec through Riviere du Loup to Woodstock, N.B.; a fifth from Montreal to Ogdensburg, N.Y. Soon Montreal Telegraph absorbed them all.

The Grand Trunk Telegraph strung wire from Quebec to Buffalo; in due course Montreal Telegraph took it over. In 1853 Allan plucked a particularly juicy plum: exclusive perpetual rights to conduct public telegraph business along the Grand Trunk Railway.

This was all the more gratifying because the telltale wires had recently carried across the land a tale of Montreal's crumbling prestige. In 1849 a mob burned the Parliament Building to the ground. Only Queen Victoria was saved, by proxy: four patriotic young men, one of them named Sandford Fleming, fled with her portrait. The Governor-General fared worse; a mob stoned him during a visit a few days later. As a result, Montreal lost its role as the capital which, for a few years, rotated between Toronto and Bytown.

No matter. Montreal Telegraph redeemed the city's pride. Within a dozen years of inception it virtually wiped out opposition, through excellent service and the predatory swoops of Hugh Allan. Its distinctive logo — a spectacularly muscular arm clutching a fistful of lightning bolts — was known throughout Canada. The company also settled the score with Canada West. In 1852 Allan bought out the Toronto, Hamilton, Niagara and St. Catharines Electro-Magnetic Telegraph. Montreal was vindicated. Telegraphically, Toronto was number two.

# Pony Express

The Maritime provinces, being deemed inconsequential by Hugh Allan, were permitted to enter the telegraph age at a leisurely stroll. In January, 1847, a report to New Brunswick's Lieutenant-Governor explained that the telegraph "can be made to convey intelligence in a few or in many words, on matters of trivial or of vital importance, openly or with secrecy, for one or one thousand miles, by night or day, in winter or summer, at a cost not greater than is incurred by the present post office system, and with a velocity which is only comparable to that of a thought or a flash of lightning.''

Be that as it might, Maritimers were not about to be bowled over by any nine-day wonder. Exactly two years later, at a little less than the speed of thought, New Brunswick opened a line between Saint John and Calais, Maine, 80 miles away. The usual curious crowds spilled out of the telegraph shack onto the boardwalk while operator James Mount, who'd learned his trade with the British Army, deciphered the first dots and dashes. Later that year the line went to Sackville and Amherst to await the Nova Scotia telegraph, which so far lived only in the mouths of politicians.

New Brunswick was in no hurry for that link, but the fretful editors of New York City's daily newspapers were. A new fiercely competitive journalism was seething through Manhattan, headed by James Gordon Bennett of the *Herald* and Horace "Go West, young man" Greeley of the *Tribune*. Rival publishers used carrier pigeons, hilltop semaphores, pony relays, anything to be first with the news and build circulation. Reporters would cheerfully lie, steal or cheat their grandmothers for a scoop.

Having recently discovered both the telegraph and British North America, the editors were eager to use these new tools. As American lines inched toward the international boundary, the newsmen reasoned that despatches snatched from a Cunard steamer at Halifax, and somehow relayed to the nearest telegraph, could be in New York hours or days before the same ship completed its normal journey to the U.S.

To confound their enemies — other U.S. newspapers, supported by Wall Street speculators and cotton brokers — six New York papers formed the Associated Press, a news-sharing partnership, and sank $20,000 into a pony express network. For nine months it gave New York the news and Nova Scotia a biweekly 146-mile Wild West show.

On February 21, 1849, the Cunard Royal Mail steamer *Europa* chugged into Halifax, 11 days out of Liverpool. A small boat scurried out, identifying itself with signal flags and lanterns. Over the side came a sealed canister of European news despatches.

On shore a waiting rider slammed the canister into his pouch, wheeled his mount (no "pony" but the finest horseflesh in Nova Scotia) and plunged off at the dead gallop.

A relay station stood on the alert every 12 miles. A half-mile from it, the rider threw out a shrill warning blast from the horn slung to his neck. As he sprang to the ground, a fresh horse trotted out and the groom — sometimes just a starry-eyed small boy — deftly transferred saddle and bridle. A deep breath, a stretch, a swig of water and the rider was away. At Kentville, the halfway mark, a partner took over.

Crowds lined the road at every village and hamlet, waving, cheering and making side bets. As a man from Lawrencetown in Annapolis County wrote years later, it was more fun than a general election. At Annapolis, within earshot of the Bay of Fundy, a cannon boomed as the foam-flecked horse pelted through town. At Victoria Beach, across the neck of water from Digby, the rider tossed his sealed despatches into a waiting boat. With muscular seamen bent to the oars, it darted out to a waiting packet, and so 40 miles across Fundy to Saint John. Within an hour after arrival the news was in New York, a good 36 hours before the *Europa* reached New England.

The next mail ship, *America*, reached Halifax on March 8. This time AP's rivals had their own rider waiting for their own despatches. The two couriers raced out of town, neck and neck, at a rate, said the Halifax *British Colonist*, "unprecedented in this country." A man named Hamilton, riding for AP, was well in the lead until he broke a stirrup crossing a bridge at Windsor. He crashed to the road and lay stunned for 20 minutes while his rival thundered past.

Hamilton crawled groggily back to the saddle and rode 25 miles with one stirrup. At Kentville his partner, Thaddeus Harris, galloping like a madman, covered the next 18 miles in 53 minutes, and pounded into Victoria Beach just 2½ minutes behind the opposition. Since the latter's Fundy steamer wasn't ready and AP's was, the New York papers won the round. The riders had covered the ground in 8 hours, 26½ minutes, averaging almost 18 miles an hour.

After three months the opposition gave up and left the field to AP. The express was now the talk of Nova Scotia. Its riders — Pat Doyle the Irish jockey, Corey Odell, John Pineo, Benjamin Chesley — were local folk heroes. They stood ready around the clock, for the Royal Mail could arrive at any hour. Some of them packed guns, for highwaymen still lurked the roads. All of them risked life and limb in the everyday run of events. Once a swing bridge on the route was accidentally left open. The rider, racing the mail through pitch dark, didn't see it, but his horse leaped the 18-foot gap without breaking stride. At the next relay station the rider found out how close he'd been to a broken neck.

The express, for all its charm and panache, offended Nova Scotia's civic fathers because it symbolized their backwardness. What kind of province would use horses when others had the telegraph? So the government built the Halifax-Amherst line to join New Brunswick, the first news bulletin chattered directly to AP on November 15, 1849, and the short rollicking life of the pony express was over. One of the Nova Scotia Electric Telegraph's founders was Hiram Hyde. He had operated the leading pony express; now, in a manner of speaking, he felt it wise to change horses.

There was little romance in the chaotic years that followed. With separate companies in Nova Scotia, New Brunswick, Maine, Portland and Boston, telegraph messages had to be transmitted anew at each change of line, wasting time and garbling the content. As in the Province of Canada, the Maritimes would soon be ripe for a takeover by one of the telegraphic giants. But for the moment, Nova Scotia, like New Brunswick and the Province of Canada, was wallowing in the joys of instant communication.

# Weaving a Nation

Sometimes the wires broke, sometimes message rates were exorbitant, but the telegraph was evolving from novelty to necessity, a revolution in Canadian life. By the mid-1850s, the wire began weaving the fragments of colony into a nation. Sad news, glad news, commercial and political news, sped from the Maritimes to Canada West. Niagara and Hamilton began to hear about, wonder about, even *care* about Halifax and Saint John.

Now a Toronto merchant could wire an order to Montreal and have it back on the new chuffing steam locomotive in three days. Travellers could telegraph news of safe arrival to anxious families back home — or avoid a trip altogether, doing business by wire. Relatives could be swiftly summoned to a sickbed, a deathbed or a childbirth. Chess and checkers fanatics played games by telegraph. Up-to-the-day market reports speeded the tempo of brokerage and banking, and helped farmers get better prices for their produce. In summer and fall, crowds of brokers gathered around the open windows of telegraph offices to hear grain quotations read aloud. Sometimes the jockeying for position led to fistfights.

By early 1848 the Bank of Montreal, which helped finance Montreal Telegraph, resolved that "the great facility of communications between Quebec and Montreal now existing, whereby reference can be made to the parent office with little delay, renders the continuance of a President and Board of Directors at the former place inexpedient and unnecessary." Henceforth a branch manager reported directly to head office, the beginning of centralization.

Election results sped over the wires as soon as the polls closed, instead of plodding through the mails. For $1.95 a Toronto politician could send 10 words of congratulations to a newly elected colleague in Halifax, although few Victorians and no politicians could confine a compliment to 10 words.

Lives were saved. Two sworn enemies set out from Quebec City with seconds and surgeons in 1856, determined to duel to the death as soon as they crossed the U.S. border (duelling was illegal in Quebec). A well-placed telegram to the High Constable of Sherbrooke netted them halfway there. They pleaded guilty, were released on their own recognizance, and amiably repaired to the nearest bar.

The press — including a spate of new journals named "Telegraph" — grew brisk and lively with columns of political news from seats of government. On publication days editors would crowd into the nearest telegraph office, around a long table especially installed for the press, to hear the telegrapher read the news off the tape. Current events were suddenly meaningful. When France's Third Empire fell before the Prussians, a Quebec cleric noted, "the echo of these frightful disasters, brought by the telegraph and re-echoed by the newspapers, spread grief and consternation among the French population of Canada."

Britain, always dear to English-Canadians, drew even closer. In September, 1855, the British in faroff Crimea finally wrested the fortress of Sevastopol from the Russians, after a year of bitter siege. When the news reached Sherbrooke, Que., crowds of cheering British railwaymen, in town to work on the Grand Trunk, milled around the telegraph office, bellowing patriotic songs at the top of their lungs as operator John Murray deciphered the code.

The telegrapher was nearly always at the heart of admiring throngs. He was the new hero of the age. He plucked mysterious sounds and symbols from the air and translated them into sense. Actually any bright young man could learn the trade, and many of them were mere boys, on their way to greater things. Telegrapher

Robert Easson, destined to be a famed press despatcher, started out as a messenger boy. Two or three times a day he trudged from the Toronto office on Front Street to the fort beyond Bathurst with telegrams for the military. Along the way, he amused himself by shooting snipe and plover. After Easson graduated to telegrapher, Sandford Fleming, the patriotic Scot who saved the Queen's portrait from the Montreal mob, dropped in one day.

"Weel, Bob, how are ye' getting on wi' the telegraph?" he beamed. "Can ye' wind up the muckle weight yet?" And Easson showed how he could hoist the heavy metal weight that turned the rollers, feeding a ribbon of telegraph paper through the machine.

Lewis McFarlane, third president of Bell Canada, William Van Horne, a prime architect of the CPR, and Thomas Ahearn, builder of Canada's first electric street railway, all started out as telegraphers. Poet William Drummond gathered inspiration for "Leetle Bateese" and his other French-Canadian verse while tapping the key in a lumbering community northwest of Montreal.

It was a lean existence. William and Samuel Peck, the first telegraphers in Napanee, Ont., were so poor they had to run a toy shop on the side. In Amherst, N.S., the telegrapher also sold tea. Lewis McFarlane, as manager of the Prescott, Ont., office had to pay his rent, light, heat and operators' wages from the revenue, which left about $1 a day for himself.

But as the industry grew, good operators could earn $60–$75 a month, particularly for press work which demanded flawless transmission of long stories, often with strange technical or place names. A top operator could bang out 40–50 words a minute; 25–35 words was competent.

Most learned to "read by sound": decoding by ear from the dots and dashes rather than reading the tape; sometimes deftly amplifying the sound with an empty tobacco tin. At first their employers, fearing errors, thundered and stormed and threatened them with dismissal. But the technique was so much faster and the operators became so expert that reading by sound became the rule. This enhanced their mystique. Young telegraphers attending the opera in Montreal would spend intermissions "talking" in Morse over the heads of the crowd, with the toy metal clickers given as favours in popcorn boxes.

It was a sweet life for a picaresque bachelor. Job offers flowed steadily over the wires, railways offered free fare and telegraphers roamed careless as the breeze leaving a trail of broken hearts and empty bottles behind them. The itinerant life, odd hours and exacting work turned many of them into drunks. Office managers grew accustomed to fishing their star telegrapher out of his bed or favourite bar and drying him out in time for work.

A Sackville operator known as Spike had a huge iron nail hammered into his board. It was literally his anchor; even when sodden with booze, Spike stayed upright, clutching the nail with his left hand and tapping the key with his right. His messages were even more illegible than most. The typewriter was still years away. Messages were laboriously copied with pencil or pen. Making five or six carbon copies was like writing on a blanket and even a sober operator's hand was difficult to read.

Wherever there was action and money, telegraphers went. The U.S. Civil War in 1861, with its heavy demands on communications, drained Canada's telegraph offices. Britain and the U.S. almost went to war that year, after a Yankee warship plucked two Confederate agents off a British steamer. Mother England poured 10,000 troops into Canada, mostly through New Brunswick, and all winter 20 hours a day, a lone operator relayed military messages from Saint John.

Five years later the Fenians, mad Irishmen intent on driving the British out of Canada, or off the earth if possible, invaded from the U.S. It was a short-lived flurry but it kept telegraphers working around the clock in Cornwall, Prescott, Brockville, and Kingston. For days on end they snatched sleep beside their desks.

After the Civil War, yellow fever broke out in New Orleans. Lewis McFarlane, now a dapper blade with a rakish moustache and stylish part dividing his hairline into equal halves, answered the plea for telegraphers. He stayed a year and earned $1,500, more than the average Canadian labourer could amass in 10 years.

Telegraph dynasties grew up. Thomas Macleod fought for the North in the Civil War, then came home to Nova Scotia as telegrapher with the Intercolonial Railway. He taught his three sons the trade (any who were slow to learn Morse were locked in an office until they mastered it). One became a division superintendent for the railway. Another, Angus, became a railway telegrapher. He married telegrapher Minnie Peebles (whose sister and two brothers were also operators) and their son, Douglas, learned Morse code about the same time he learned English. By 17 he was earning a living "pounding the brass." In 1974 he retired as general manager of CP Telecommunications, rounding out a century of Macleod-Peebles telegraphy.

Throughout the eager 1860s the telegraph was an active agent of Confederation. One stipulation of union was that telegraphic communication between Prince Edward Island and the mainland would be maintained by the federal government. After the Charlottetown Conference of 1864, John A. Macdonald wired all interested parties that another conference to discuss union would be held in Quebec in October. Two years later, Leonard Tilley and Charles Tupper, premiers of New Brunswick and Nova Scotia respectively, wired John A. to meet them in England, with all haste, to prod the British North American Act past England's Parliament. The Maritimers wanted to get it over before they had to face their voters again. Macdonald, for devious political reasons, was in no hurry (he was called "Old Tomorrow" with good reason) and found it as easy to ignore a telegram as a letter.

The telegraph served him again in 1867 as he juggled his warring colleagues into an acceptable Cabinet. George Etienne Cartier insisted that three Quebec Catholics be on the roster. Protestants, Ontarians, Maritimers all had to be shoehorned in. With one week to go John A. was at his wits' end. Then Tupper graciously offered to step down and on June 24 Macdonald telegraphed an invitation to Edward Kenny, a Nova Scotia Catholic, thus balancing geography with religion. Thanks to the telegraph, John A. kept his date with the Dominion of Canada with a light heart and a full Cabinet.

# Perry Collins' Broken Dream

Apart from Sir John's desultory dreams of a nation from sea to sea, few Canadians even *knew* about the crown colony of British Columbia. America, on the other hand, was eyeing B.C. as a fox might ogle a plump hen. In the early sixties it became the route for an incredible telegraphic gamble — an effort to link North America, Asia and Europe. If that had happened, British Columbia might well have joined America.

By 1861 Western Union, a mere five years old, had a strong hold on U.S. telegraphy. Its wires stretched from coast to coast. (One of the beneficiaries was Ezra Cornell, who held two million shares of Western Union stock, and no longer had to salvage shillings from the street.) As the first messages flashed from New York to San Francisco, they triggered a preposterous thought in the busy brain of Perry McDonough Collins: why not build a telegraph *around the world?*

Collins, a slick-talking redheaded hustler, had lived by his wits for most of his 48 years. A friend claimed Collins could "sell a toupee to an African bushman." He had panned gold in California, survived a shaky banking enterprise in which duller-witted men would have lost their shirts, and landed a job as U.S. commercial agent to Russia.

There he proved that he was not all talk. He took a cram course in Russian, exerted his considerable charm on local officials and became the first North American to cross Siberia — an epic 3,545-mile journey, mostly by sleigh at temperatures to 50 below zero. Collins fortified himself for the trip with fur coats and robes, quantities of black bread and boiled eggs, and red pepper inside his socks to warm his feet.

In 35 days he slept under a roof only three times. He changed horses and drivers 21 times, met peasants and princes, and drank quantities of vodka and champagne. At a dinner in Kyachta, after innumerable toasts in which Collins excelled, he was accorded the ultimate honour: a circle of sturdy playful Russians repeatedly tossed him to the ceiling (catching him neatly on the way down). Throughout the journey Collins proved that the cold had not slowed his vital processes. His journal abounded with references to "buxom damsels with well formed bosoms" or "fine teeth, lively countenances and well turned busts."

Finally he reached the Pacific Coast. There, somewhere off through the mists to the northeast, lay Bering Strait and Russian America (now Alaska). Four years later, in 1861, he translated that memory into the most daring and heroic scheme in telegraph history: a line north from San Francisco, through British Columbia, the Yukon and Russian America, across Bering Strait and Russia to St. Petersburg (now Leningrad) on the Baltic Sea. Supersalesman Collins saw nothing unreasonable about 13,000 miles of line through the most inhospitable terrain on earth.

He went on a fund-raising visit to Sir George Simpson in Montreal. As governor of Rupert's Land and superintendent for the Hudson's Bay Company in North America, Sir George was virtually monarch of everything west of the Lakehead. A nod from his massive head sent fleets of canoes churning down rivers and turned grizzled Bay factors into groveling minions. Sir George, a Scot like so many builders of pioneer Canada, sometimes canoed through his domain with his personal piper skirling at his side. It awed the birds and the Indians. Sir George liked that.

His considerable ego did not, however, get in the way of his business sense. He thought he knew a charlatan when he saw one, and checked out Collins among his U.S. contacts. Although none of them could put a finger on any flimflammery, Sir George backed away from the Overland Telegraph. Yet the Bay, as Collins would discover, was not entirely disinterested in telegraphy.

Next, Collins petitioned the American government, winning much enthusiasm but no hard cash. Unperturbed, he tried the idea on an easier mark, Samuel Morse. Morse, now an oracle whose every murmur made headlines, saw "no serious obstacles" in the telegraph — but, of course, he didn't have to build it. Collins next loosed his golden tongue on Hiram Sibley, president of Western Union, a great, grey, barrel-chested man with a profile that seemed to have been chiselled from the side of a cliff. If Sibley liked the Overland, the battle was half won.

"The whole thing is entirely practicable," Sibley enthused in October 1861. "No work costing so little money was ever accomplished by man that will be so important in results. The benefit resulting to the world will pay its entire cost every year after completion so long as it is inhabited by civilized man!"

The benefit to Western Union was to be a tidy gross of $2.3 million a year, according to Collins' "conservative" estimate of 250 messages a day at $25 a message. Sibley's offhand reference to "so little money" — the estimated $5 million construction cost of the line — emphasized Western Union's enormous resources, after only five years in business.

Collins now verged on the biggest coup of his life — a million dollars worth of shares in the new company and $100,000 in cash, *if* he could get the necessary rights-of-way from governments. With this kind of incentive he needed no red pepper in his socks; his feet never stopped flying.

He swept into Russia and sweet-talked a deal from Czar Alexander II. The Russians would build 7,000 miles of line. But in London Collins ran into a mess of intrigue. The British Colonial office, nudged by private interests in Britain and Canada, had been pressuring the Hudson's Bay Company to open its western empire to a road and telegraph. Grudgingly, the Bay agreed after grumbling, "With regard to a telegraphic communication, it is scarcely necessary to point at the prairie fires, the depredation of natives and the general chapter of accidents as presenting almost insur-mountable obstacles."

The Atlantic and Pacific Transit and Telegraph Company, newly formed with English capital, now planned a line from Sault Ste. Marie through Fort Garry and Jasper House to Fort Langley, B.C. Orrin Wood of Montreal Telegraph would superintend the job and his company would provide the necessary link east of the Sault. The Bay itself then took an interest and sent John Rae, its most distinguished explorer, to survey a route. Rae returned to England in 1864, having trekked across the prairie, through the Rockies via the Yellowhead Pass and down the Fraser River to New Westminster. He reported that a mail road and telegraph were feasible.

So, the British-backed Atlantic and Pacific began stockpiling wire and other equipment, while Britain for a year vetoed any movement of the American-backed Collins Overland through British Columbia. (The B.C. legislature wanted the latter line but its opinion didn't count.)

In fact, the Overland telegraph to Russia and a line across Canada would not have been incompatible. But the latter was really just a pawn in a great power struggle between the Bay, clinging jealously to its fur-trade empire, and the proponents of wholesale western settlement. In the end the Atlantic and Pacific telegraph company was cast aside. Britain then nodded its imperial head to Perry Collins and the B.C. legislature: the Overland Telegraph could proceed.

At this point Collins evidently was given his money and told to stay from underfoot. His name rarely appeared again, except on the signboard of the Canadian head office, a two-storey frame building in New Westminster, the shack-town capital of B.C.

In late spring of 1865 an Overland flotilla sailed majestically out of San Francisco harbour, to extravagant fanfare in U.S. news-papers. Some called it the greatest exploration of all time. Others hinted, perhaps hoped, that the explorers would be swallowed up forever in the unknown North. Western Union, aware of the hazards, ran the expedition like a small war.

Engineer-in-chief Charles Bulkley, a superintendent of mili-tary telegraphs during the Civil War, was an Army colonel on leave. His senior men were all Civil War veterans, sporting army rank. Overall he would command 500 skilled workers plus a fluctuating legion of Indian, Siberian and Chinese labourers. He signed recruits for a minimum of one year's service and insisted on military discipline.

"Our very lives will be at stake," he warned.

He divided his private army into divisions, to work independently but simultaneously in B.C., the Yukon, Russian America and Siberia. The contingent included 150 pack horses and a few camels (Bactrian camels had been carrying cargo through the Fraser canyon since 1862) plus dozens of canoes and tons of wire. His planners briefed him in meticulous detail: "Fresh beef about 10¢ on Fraser"; "China Men $45 per month and feed themselves, or $30 per month and found"; "Trail to Comox cost $100 per mile." Bulkley in turn laid down precise regulations: "Spirituous and intoxicating liquors will not be allowed in camp"; "Natives will be treated with the utmost consideration"; "All work will be suspended on Sunday."

Daily rations were calculated to the ounce. Each man received a basic 12 ounces of bacon, or 20 ounces of fresh or salt beef; 22 ounces of soft bread or flour; 20 ounces of corn meal; and lesser portions of peas, rice, coffee, tea, sugar, potatoes and molasses.

By this time Western Union's telegraph line had reached New Westminster. On April 18, a few weeks ahead of the flotilla, its first incoming message, already three days old, brought many men close to tears: Abraham Lincoln had been assassinated. The first out-going message that day, from B.C. Governor Frederick Seymour to the Colonial Office, reported the key events as he saw them in New Westminster: "Weather beautiful. All well and Indians perfectly quiet." The message flashed to New York, caught a steamer, and reached London in 17 days.

By then the Overland's southern party was forging north. Seymour, on hand for the laying of line beneath the Fraser River, said solemnly, "Your trek will help me to learn my own domain."

It was the literal truth. Virtually nothing was known of the north. Mapmakers still debated whether the Yukon, one of North America's great rivers, flowed to the Arctic or to the Pacific. The B.C.-Russian American boundary had never been surveyed. The Collins Overland was venturing into the unknown.

Its surveyors went first, with axemen blazing the route. Then 80 to 100 choppers hewed a path 20 or 30 feet wide, so falling trees could never break the line. Next marched the stake men, driving markers 70 yards apart. The Chinese hole-diggers followed — patient little men, quietly suffering incessant racial slurs from the whites, keeping to themselves for sheer survival.

The cutters trimmed fine strong cedar poles. The setters nailed on crossbars, installed blue glass insulators and tamped each pole into the earth, 24 to the mile. Finally the wire crews strung good tough annealed copper. The line sped ahead at an average six miles a day. By the end of August it had reached Soda Creek, 350 miles from New Westminster.

But high in Siberia, as winter closed in, life was agony. A letter to Bulkley spelled it out: "Supplies have not come. . . . Temperatures down to 70 below zero. . . . The ground is frozen hard as iron. . . . We must eat seal and walrus. . . . We shiver constantly. . ." One man committed suicide. One black night a small party strayed off the trail, 30 miles from Yamsk, the nearest habitation. With no wood or food and not daring to move for fear of blundering into the Okhotsk Sea, they crept under their sleds, drew heads and arms into the bodies of their fur coats and shivered until morning. In the middle of the night one man shouted down the neckhole of his neighbor's coat, "What would our mothers say if they could see us now?"

Their mothers would have been no more worried than Hiram Sibley, who watched costs mounting and competition looming. In London, that winter of 1865–66, he met millionaire Cyrus Field, whose Atlantic Cable company was preparing its third assault on the ocean. The two Titans of finance and communications sized each other up and shed a few crocodile tears.

"I would give $50,000 to know if you are ever going to succeed," said Sibley. "I hope you will, but I would like to know for certain before we spend any more."

"Sibley, I can get you all the Atlantic stock you will take, for one and a half percent," Field replied glumly.

Given another 18 months, the Overland might have won. On New Year's Day Bulkley supervised the first pole setting in the Yukon, to triumphant volleys of cannon fire that sent startled Indian onlookers running for the bush. By summer, 1866, the wire stretched 850 miles beyond New Westminster, about 25 miles north of today's Hazelton, B.C. Messages were moving at $5 for 10 words, Quesnel to New Westminster. In Siberia, despite the awful weather, 35,000 poles lay ready with crossbars and insulators, and the Russian supervisor, Serge Abasa, proudly reported that St. Petersburg would "all but be linked with Russian America" in six months.

Then the heartbreaking message came down the wire: the

Atlantic cable had been laid successfully on July 27. Sibley immediately wired Bulkley to stop work. It was hardest on the men who had given their sweat and blood. The B.C. crews received the news on July 30, and waited a few days, hoping the cable would snap as it had before. Then most of them glumly trickled back south to find new jobs. Others, well beyond reach of the telegraph's bad news, went doggedly about their work for months after. Surveyor P. J. Leech, far ahead of the line crews, spent New Year's Day, 1867, snowshoeing near the mouth of the Stikine River with two companions. The weather grew steadily worse.

"When we awoke in the morning there was a covering of snow on our blankets about four inches deep, and it still continued," Leech wrote later. "At 8 o'clock we packed up and started back and as long as I live I will never forget that day's journey down the river. It blew a perfect hurricane down stream, and the snow came down so thick that I could scarcely see ten yards ahead. I was thrown down several times by the force of the wind. At one time I was thrown down with such force that I was stunned for a few minutes."

Leech grew too ill to walk, pitched a tent and ordered his companions back. They promised to send help within five days. After 10 days alone Leech gave up on them, philosophically checked his food and rationed himself to survive until spring. Every day he chopped a night's firewood; every night he burrowed into five blankets, folded into a kind of sleeping bag and frozen solid on the outside.

On the 13th day help came. His companions had been close to death on the trail when passing Indians saved them. By spring Leech had plodded to the coast, 600 miles from Victoria, in time to meet a boat with word that his winter ordeal was for naught.

The Yukon crew didn't hear the news until June. They raised black flags of mourning on their abandoned poles, punched into the frozen ground so painfully during the previous winter. About the same time, an American whale boat carried the news to Siberia. Serge Abasa dropped his head in his arms and wept.

Throughout these months, although the Overland's demise seemed irreversible, Western Union had been curiously slow in making a formal announcement. Not until March 6, 1867, did the *Commercial and Financial Chronicle* report that Western Union's directors had decided to abandon the Overland. Not until March 25 was the U.S. government officially notified. Meanwhile Overland stockholders — most of them Western Union directors —

This bridge across Bulkley River at Hagwilget, near Hazelton, B.C., was built by Indians from poles and wire abandoned by the Collins Overland venture. PROVINCIAL ARCHIVES, VICTORIA, B.C.

The New Westminster terminal station of the Collins Overland, as shown in Harper's Magazine. METROPOLITAN TORONTO LIBRARY BOARD.

had been authorized to exchange their shares for Western Union stock any time up until February 1. The upshot was that hundreds of small shareholders had to absorb a loss of $3,170,292.

"Mr. Collins made money and the directors of the enterprise have saved themselves a great loss," said *The Telegrapher*, a trade publication, "but what do the stockholders of the Western Union Company gain?"

The answer was "nothing," but the U.S. government reaped a fringe benefit. U.S. Secretary of State William Seward, inspired by the maps and samples of trees, flowers and rocks in the Overland reports, made a shrewd deal with Russia. That same year, America bought the future state of Alaska for less than two cents an acre.

Thousands of blue glass insulators and tons of glistening copper wire lay abandoned along the way. A salesman to the last, Perry Collins parlayed his ruined dream into a few furs, by persuading the Indians that insulators were superb drinking cups and copper wire would make nets, snares and reinforcements for bridges. For years after, the coastal Indians and Siberian natives used telegraph poles for firewood.

The Chinese labourers went back to their former jobs: storekeeping, trading, farming, working as domestics or eking scraps of gold out of abandoned mines. In one such ghost town the "superior" white man had posted an ominous sign:

NOTICE
TOO JHINERMEN
You are hereby notiefed that iff
you gone into these diggens you
will ketch hell. Sou you better
luk ought or yull smell powder
and brimstone if not hemp.

A few of the unfortunate camels drifted into Kamloops and were used unsuccessfully as mail carriers (mules and horses wouldn't work beside them because of their stink). The Canadian government took over the working portion of the Overland. Charles Bulkley's name still lives on in a northwestern river, canyon and lake. And Perry McDonough Collins? He died in a New York rooming house 44 years later, forgotten by the world that once was almost at his feet.

# Chapter 3

## The Victimization of Fred Gisborne

As Hiram Sibley and Perry Collins vanished into the wings, North America turned its adulation on Cyrus W. Field. He was a prime candidate for Victorian hero worship: a bona fide Christian (son of a Congregationalist minister) who had started young (age 15) and poor (earning $1 a week) and soared to the top of the U.S. paper industry. At 33 Field had made his fortune and *retired*!

Then, as builder of the Atlantic cable he repeatedly staked his riches, and other people's, against crushing odds, and won. It was a classic 19th century success story. When his colleagues at testimonial dinners rang out "Three cheers for Cyrus" and "For He's a Jolly Good Fellow," they cheered and sang from the heart.

Yet there was a meaner side to Cyrus Field that diminished his achievements. He and his colleagues deliberately erased from Atlantic cable history the inventor and telegrapher who triggered the whole thing — a towering figure in Canadian communications. Field would never have dreamed of the cable, had it not been for Frederick Newton Gisborne. Yet in the end, Gisborne was even excluded from an official portrait of the cable's founders.

Gisborne was, of course, out of his league in dealing with New York entrepreneurs. Although he too yearned to be a corporate prince, he was essentially a discoverer, a technician and a doer. For more than 41 years he forged through Canada with accomplishment and controversy in his wake. In that time nearly every Canadian cable and telegraph system felt his touch. Yet cheated as he was of his rightful share of Atlantic cable fame, his other exploits have also been largely ignored by Canadian historians.

He grew up in Lancashire, excelling in the mathematics and civil engineering taught him by a local vicar. Gisborne's family never let him forget that his middle name honoured an illustrious ancestor, Sir Isaac Newton, the inventor of calculus and discoverer of the laws of gravity.

In 1841, only 18, but big, rawboned and insatiably curious, he toured Australia, New Zealand, Mexico, Guatemala. He went home long enough to pack his bags and gather up his brother Hartley, then emigrate to Canada. For two years he farmed near St-Eustache, Que., pushing a plow by day, and at night reading everything he could find on electricity and telegraphy.

In 1847 Orrin Wood, the Samuel Morse protege and Montreal Telegraph's new superintendent, started a school for telegraphers. Gisborne enrolled, passed with top honours and became head of the company's Quebec office. He astonished his employers with his grasp of telegraphy, even to inventing little improvements in the equipment. In a few months he knew everything the job could teach him. He moved on, after carefully collecting a written testimonial (". . .skill, patience, perseverance and integrity. . .") to show his next employer that Gisborne was no idle drifter.

As superintendent of the new British North American Electric Telegraph Association he built a 112-mile pole line from Quebec to Riviere du Loup. Then, with a £75 bonus and letter of appreciation from his directors, he hustled off to New Brunswick, his brain churning with visions of a telegraph right through the Maritimes, with himself in charge.

New Brunswick, more interested in a link with Maine than with Quebec, turned him down flat. Like most impetuous men, Gisborne tended to grate on people's nerves. The New Brunswickers suspected, rightly, that this precocious 24-year-old wanted to control their telegraph system. They sent a warning letter to Nova Scotia saying, in effect, watch out for a hustler from Canada East. But Nova Scotia's influential Joseph Howe, not yet premier but member of a government commission investigating telegraphy, liked Gisborne's style.

Gisborne didn't disappoint him. The young stranger spoke so

winningly in the legislature that he soon was building the Halifax-Amherst line — the same line that ended the pony express. On November 15, 1849, Gisborne spent all evening personally transmitting the first messages to Associated Press in New York.

He took time out to marry and, incongruously, to publish privately a book of his own poetry. It wasn't much worse than other Victorian verse — "Twas dreamy night and the pale moon beam'd calmly bright, From her dark canopy of star-light blue . . . " — but it wasn't Alfred Lord Tennyson, either. It was simply another facet of a complex and restless personality.

In fact, Gisborne was whiling away his boredom. Although manager of Nova Scotia Government Telegraphs now, he wanted to be moving again. He begged leave of absence from Joseph Howe to put a telegraph across Newfoundland and under Cabot Strait to Nova Scotia. As Bishop J. T. Mullock, head of the Roman Catholic church in Newfoundland, had recently pointed out, such a line would speed European news delivery by at least 48 hours.

Newfoundland welcomed Gisborne warmly. Rarely did a mainlander come over to do the island a favour; most of them shunned Newfoundland like the plague. In 1851 he built a line around Conception Bay. Then he dazzled a St. John's crowd with a lecture on telegraphy, followed by an exchange of messages with Harbour Grace.

With a government grant of £500 and a charter for his Newfoundland Electric Telegraph Company, Gisborne now ventured inland. Central Newfoundland was as wild and brutal a bit of real estate as any in North America. Yet on September 4 with winter approaching he blithely led six companions on a 400-mile survey from St. John's to Cape Ray.

For three months he stumbled through forest, bogs, shrouds of mist and deepening snow. Bears and other beasts lurked in the shadows. The food ran out. His six original men soon gave up. Gisborne hired four tough Indian woodsmen. Two of them deserted, a third died and the fourth was ill long after.

Months later Gisborne admitted that it had been an "arduous" adventure, but at the time he dared not alarm his backers. A letter to the newspapers midway through his trip announced "all hands in good health and pretty good spirits." Returning on December 4, he cheerily reported that his fellow travellers were "all in good health" and the telegraph line was "perfectly practicable." The

*Royal Gazette* on December 9 marvelled that Gisborne "appears to have improved by the abundance of air and exercise he experienced." This was not deliberate deception. Gisborne was an incurable optimist, which served him well in the ordeals still to come.

The delighted government fattened his testimonials file with a letter praising ". . .an undertaking of the highest utility to the whole civilized world . . . must result in incalculable benefit to Newfoundland. . .to you is due sole credit for projecting this great enterprise. . . ." Now, with 30-year exclusive rights for telegraph construction in the colony, Gisborne at 28 might have been content. He was not.

Resigning from his Nova Scotia job, he told Joseph Howe of his expanded dream: a telegraph *underwater to England*! How could Canadians truly commune with Europe, hub of the civilized world, repository of everything they revered, with that infernal ocean barrier always between them? There *must* be a way to quickly bridge the Atlantic with words, and Gisborne thought he had it.

But first he would have to settle for cables to Prince Edward Island and the mainland. He needed more money. In what was to become a familiar Canadian tradition, he could get no backing at home but found it easily in New York. Then he went to England to learn about cable from John W. Brett.

In two years Brett and his brother had laid submarine cables from England to France and from Ireland to Scotland and Wales. Their trials and errors had produced a workable line: four separate copper wires sheathed in rubber, tarred hemp and an outer coat of 10 galvanized wires. Gisborne bought enough to stretch 15 miles form Carleton Head, P.E.I. to Cape Tormentine, N.B.

He invented a system of drums to pay out line from a moving ship, a wiring insulation that resisted salt water, a gadget for joining telegraph wires, and a chisel-and-scoop posthole digger. (Before that, telegraph linemen dug each post hole with ordinary spades, going down to the bottom in a series of steps. No amount of fill afterward could prevent the pole from wobbling. Gisborne's digger produced perfect holes.) One bleak November day in 1852, aboard the steamer *Ellen Gisborne*, he laid North America's first cable. It took several tries over 11 hours, with four horses and four oxen to haul ashore that last mile of wire, but it worked.

By now Newfoundland worshipped him. Bunyanesque legends grew up around him (more than a century later, a grandson — who never actually knew him — related that Gisborne once carried an injured man to safety, 100 miles over rough ground in his bare feet). His name appeared in the press as often as the Queen's and — the ultimate compliment — simply as "Mr. Gisborne." Everyone knew who "Mr. Gisborne" was.

As he prepared to lay the Newfoundland line, he and Brett discussed by mail a project called "Brett and Gisborne's Atlantic Telegraph." It would run from Ireland to Newfoundland.

"My impression is, to do it well, and have an odd dollar or two to meet the chances of accident, we must have a capital of £750,000," Brett wrote back. "Can you find £375,000 and good names in America, if I can find £375,000 and good names here?"

But by then Gisborne was in deep trouble. In June, 1853 he put 350 men to work on the overland line. The St. John's *Public Ledger* looked forward to "speedy and efficient accomplishment of this enterprise." Then Gisborne's world fell apart. The earth was hard as flint; frozen, stony, obdurate. Gisborne had hoped to lay wire underground; instead, for 40 miles the crews propped up telegraph posts with rockpiles.

On August 12 the *Public Ledger* noted with alarm, "We regret to learn there has been a sudden and unexpected suspension of operations." The *Ledger* was sure it was only temporary.

In fact, Gisborne's money and backers had run out. His little company owed $50,000. The workmen and suppliers hired a lawyer. The Newfoundland press declared the company "a humbug from the first" and "Mr. Gisborne suffered himself to be imposed upon by being too confiding."

Gisborne's personal property was seized and sold. He mortgaged the company steamer, *Ellen Gisborne*. For a time it appeared he would go to jail. The shame would have crushed most men. Instead Gisborne stubbornly tried to raise more money in England and New York. In January, 1854, sick at heart as never before, he met an engineer and railway builder named Matthew Field, in the lobby of New York's Astor Hotel.

Gisborne's story intrigued the American. That night, in an elegant house on Gramercy Park, Gisborne met Matthew's brother Cyrus. The red-bearded young millionaire was jaded with life. Above the strong shaft of nose, a permanent frown line was settling between his eyes. He had poured all his energies into business, amassed all the money he needed at 33 and found that travel was a poor opiate for boredom. Gisborne's troubles and prospects stirred a spark within him.

The three men talked deep into the night. Gisborne, hurting badly from the Newfoundland debacle, possibly did not mention his Atlantic cable dream. Most of his friends and relatives thought the Newfoundland telegraph was madness enough. Gisborne did not want to scare off a potential saviour by piling one crazy scheme atop another.

Field's biographers maintain that the idea was born later that very night: alone in his library, the visionary Cyrus twirled a world globe from North America to Europe and was inspired. In fact, Samuel Morse had postulated an Atlantic cable 11 years before, but clearly Gisborne had stimulated Field on this occasion.

Field did contribute qualities that Gisborne lacked: a lustrous business reputation, money of his own, and the connections to attract more. First he sought Morse's technical opinion, as everyone did in those days. Morse endorsed the cable. Field found four wealthy partners and at six a.m. one Sunday in May they drafted a company and subscribed $1,500,000 in 15 minutes. Morse was named "chief electrician." With Gisborne's assent they took over his Newfoundland company, with all its rights and debts. Gisborne was publicly cleared of all the shadows hanging over him and the Newfoundland press applauded him again.

He went on the new payroll as chief engineer, but not on the board of directors. It was soon evident that even his engineering title was a farce. When work resumed in Newfoundland, Field sent brother Matthew to run it, with Gisborne as his aide. Six hundred men set out to finish the job in one year. It took nearly three, going around the more accessible coastline. Matthew Field began to sympathize with Gisborne's earlier tribulations.

When Cyrus pressed for progress reports, Matthew wrote testily, "How many *months*? Let's say how many years! Recently in building half a mile of road we had to bridge three ravines. Why didn't we go around the ravines? Because Mr. Gisborne had explored 20 miles in both directions and found more ravines. . . ." By the first winter they had spent $500,000 on this wretched little line alone.

Meanwhile Cyrus began more than 40 ocean voyages to England (made miserable by chronic seasickness), seeking advice and support. To keep spirits alive at home he laid the cable from Newfoundland to Cape Breton. Then he hired a side-wheeler steamer at $750 a day, stocked it with costly food and drink, and triumphantly hosted his directors, their families, politicians, Morse and Gisborne, and a pack of Newfoundland dogs gathered up along the way. Cyrus was seasick but otherwise the trip was a hit.

It seemed a good omen. The U.S. Navy had found a plateau beneath the Atlantic, level and shallow enough for the line. Field's engineers invented a braking system to synchronize the unreeling of a cable with a ship's speed. Morse, with an English electrical expert named Whitehouse, had built 2,000 miles of test cable and pronounced it thoroughly capable of transmitting messages.

## Telegraph Under the Sea

But nothing came easy on this project, even to the gifted Cyrus Field. Money was running out. By the end of 1856 the company had spent more than $1 million, including $250,000 of Field's own — an enormous outlay when the dollar was four or five times today's value. The Newfoundland land line and cable were breaking down. Field hired Alexander M. MacKay, the youthful superintendent of the Nova Scotia telegraph company, to improve Newfoundland's facilities. Meanwhile Cyrus raised more funds in England. In August, 1857, his first line-laying flotilla steamed out of Ireland. Three hundred miles into the Atlantic the cable snapped. Field tried again the next year, this time splicing the cable at midocean and sending two ships in opposite directions. After three tries they laid a line that worked. New York erupted in parades, speeches, bonfires. Queen Victoria cabled congratulations to U.S. President Buchanan. Field was an international idol.

As commercial messages began to move the cable immediately proved its worth. On August 31 the British government signalled its regiments in Halifax and Montreal to stay put. They had been ordered home by mail, to help combat a mutiny in India. Now they weren't needed and the cancellation saved Britain £50,000. The next day the cable went dead.

It was a simple problem of many irreparable flaws in the line, but Field was in disgrace. Some accused him of working a gigantic hoax on the world. Before he could recoup, the American Civil War postponed all further attempts. Yet the Trent Affair of 1861, wherein Britain and the U.S. North almost went to war over two Confederates yanked from an English ship, emphasized the need for cable. Before Lincoln finally relayed peaceable messages by ocean mail, and freed the two men, Britain had poured 10,000 troops into Canada. As the London *Times* put it, "We nearly went to war with America because we had not a telegraph across the Atlantic."

The moment the war ended, Field was at it again. His new cable was a marvel of engineering. The conductor core of seven copper wires, each weighing 300 pounds to the mile, was embedded in a waterproof compound covered with four layers of rubber. The insulation weighed *400* pounds to the mile. Around it, cushioned in tarred hemp, went an armour coat of 10 heavy iron wires, each wound with waterproofed rope. The old cable had weighed a ton per mile; this one totalled $1^3/_4$ tons and was more flexible.

Only the greatest ship afloat could handle such a load. England's *Great Eastern* had been waiting all her 10 years for this assignment. She weighed 22,550 tons, was three city blocks long; developed 6600 hp and a speed of 14 knots — and was simply too big for economical commerce. She was about to be sold at a loss when Field signed her up.

Now the miles of cable poured into her compartments, in three pieces; a single coil of this weight would have set up a fearful roll at sea. Five hundred men and 8,000 tons of coal went aboard. The provisions included a living "farmyard": a milk cow, 12 oxen, 20 pigs, 120 sheep, flocks of ducks, chickens and geese.

Shipwatchers from all over England, including the Prince of Wales, thronged to the landing docks at Sheerness, near Greenwich. Hundreds of them volunteered for the journey. The voyage had captured the fancy of the world.

In July 1865, the mighty ship steamed away, steadily paying out cable with only a few halts. One crew member likened it to "an elephant stretching a cobweb." Once the electricians who constantly made tests detected a flaw in the signal. They hauled in the wire and discovered a needle driven into it. There were dark hints of sabotage, perhaps by agents of the Collins Overland Telegraph. The damage was repaired; guards were stationed, and the *Great Eastern* steamed on.

Less than a day out of Newfoundland, a white-faced Cyrus Field, watching anxiously from the deck, saw the cable suddenly snap. It had been frayed beneath the hull of the ship. All efforts to fish it out were in vain. Surely now Field would give up.

He did not. He reorganized his company, raised another £600,000 (roughly $3 million) and built more cable. In June 1866 the fourth expedition sailed. The weather was kind. There were no breaks. On July 27 the *Great Eastern* steamed into a snug little

F. N. Gisborne, whose pioneering work made possible the Atlantic cable.

Laying the shore end of the Atlantic cable from the "Great Eastern" in Heart's Content Bay, Newfoundland, 1886. PUBLIC ARCHIVES OF CANADA C591.

bay at Heart's Content, Nfld. They hauled the cable ashore where, for almost a century after, messages flowed to and from Europe through a red brick office with slate roof and white gingerbread trim, crammed with intricate mechanical equipment that made Heart's Content the most famous fishing village in the world.

There were cheers, tears, a torrent of congratulations from around the globe. For good measure the *Great Eastern* went back and salvaged the cable of 1865. When that happened, the jubilant Field admitted later, "I went back to my cabin, I locked the door; I could no longer restrain my tears." Now, incredibly, there were *two* links across the ocean. Eleven years before, the cheering crowds of Sherbrooke had waited 12 days for the glad news of Sevastopol. Now Europe was *minutes* away! Messages began to move: £20 for the first 20 words, 20 shillings for each additional word. Even at those outrageous rates the cable carried 2772 messages in two months. Then the rate was halved. Meanwhile, Cyrus Field relaxed for the first time in a dozen years to the acclaim he richly deserved.

## "I Have a Duty to Perform"

What of Frederick Gisborne? His name was not included in the tributes. He was long gone and forgotten. On February 10, 1857, before the first attempted crossing, he had resigned, disheartened at being repeatedly shunted aside. He armed himself with the usual testimonial, from Atlantic Cable's president: ". . .much pleasure in testifying to your scientific ability and great energy as Telegraphic Engineer. . .your perseverance and strict integrity. . .have secured to you our friendship and esteem . . . ."

But from then on the directors pretended that Gisborne didn't exist. Had he alienated them with his impetuous ways? Did they regard him simply as a Canadian bumpkin, unworthy of their company? Whatever the reason, on September 10 that year, an astonishing notice appeared in the New York *Journal of Commerce*. Signed by Cyrus Field, and others, it stated that the Atlantic Cable scheme "originated" with Cyrus and his brother Dudley. The latter, although then active in the hierarchy, was not one of the original incorporating six, named in 1854 by act of the Newfoundland legislature. Gisborne was.

A year later the Boston *Ledger* vehemently took up cudgels on Gisborne's behalf, concluding that he alone was the "projector" of the cable. Joseph Howe agreed, in a letter calling Gisborne "the first pioneer of the enterprise." Yet in 1894 after Cyrus Field's death, his surviving colleagues approved a painting, "The Atlantic Cable Projectors." In the portrait the numbers had mysteriously grown to nine, but Gisborne was not among them.

Gisborne had long since turned his back on these petty men. By 1859 he was in New Zealand, studying its geology. He cropped up next as Nova Scotia's English agent for Mines and Minerals. By the early 1860s he was that province's commissioner at international exhibitions in London and Paris.

He found time to write pamphlets on the theory of telephony and telegraphy. He invented a flag-and-ball semaphore for ships at sea. It won a gold medal, one of seven medals collected in his career.

In the early seventies Gisborne popped up in Nova Scotia as a railroader, building a 12-mile narrow-gauge line, the Glasgow and Cape Breton, for British coal mining interests. He surfaced again in 1879 as superintendent of the Canadian government telegraph service. He was 55 now, bald, with a shaggy beard trailing down his chest, tempered by years of hard travel and disappointment, but with a twinkle still in his eye. He busily compiled maps of all the railway stations, telegraph networks, canals and trails throughout central Canada.

At nearly 60 he trekked south and west from Ottawa, pausing in New York and Chicago to study their postal and telephone systems. In Winnipeg he bought two horses and a buckboard and with son Hartley, now a district superintendent, trotted off to inspect the seven-year-old frontier government telegraph.

No detail escaped his eye. At Fort Qu'Appelle he bought a two-roomed house for a telegraph station for $360. Out on the plains he ordered $125 log huts as winter shelter for linemen and their horses (a 10-by-10-foot space for each, but the humans also got a window and chimney). At Battleford, fretting over the high cost of small logs ($1–1.25 each), he apologetically informed his Ottawa bosses that young Hartley's office would cost $600–800.

Throughout the trip, he was battered and harassed. Thieves stole a horse one night. The buckboard seat fell off one day, taking Gisborne with it "by which I was much cut and bruised." Not until Edmonton, a month after leaving Winnipeg, did he pause for a full day's rest. At Prince Albert, where a branch line was going in from Saskatoon, he stumbled into a hornet's nest of angry pioneers.

Prince Albert had fretfully awaited the telegraph for a year. With 700 people, a flour mill, Presbyterian church, commercial college, post office, a dozen general stores and an Anglican bishop, the town demanded a little respect. "To have to wait three weeks for our letters and newspapers and no telegraph to inform us of the doings of the outside world may have suited the last decade but will not do for this generation," sniffed the Prince Albert *Times* in 1882.

Land speculators had caused the community to grow in three separate clusters: Hudson's Bay store, flour mill and fort, near the two-storey red brick Mounted Police barracks; a commercial and residential section; and a third semiresidential district. Now, Fred Gisborne, crashing ahead in customary fashion, unaware that he was treading on civic toes, began to put the telegraph office in Goshen, the Hudson's Bay post four miles from town.

Prince Albert rose up in fury and tore the line down. Gisborne charged six citizens with "unlawfully and maliciously removing and carrying away telegraph poles." Before the case reached court, he had to be back in Ottawa. "GISBORNE FUNKS AND FAILS TO APPEAR" crowed the *Times*. The federal government slopped oil, in the form of taxpayers' money, on the troubled waters by putting offices in Goshen *and* Prince Albert.

Gisborne brought back a voluminous report on everything, down to a satisfied notation that, having sold his horses and buckboard for $367.50, the entire trip cost the government only $125. Few civil servants, then or after, showed such concern for public funds.

His 16 comments and recommendations included a plea for good galvanized wire, spruce or iron poles, better roads, better telegraphic instruments and better maintenance. The line, Gisborne said bluntly, ranged from "bad" to "on its last legs."

It was his last major report. He died in Ottawa nine years later after an arduous trip to the east coast. His doctor had advised the 70-year-old against it but Gisborne said, "I have a duty to perform and shall make the effort." His western recommendations of 1883 were a fitting finale to a lifetime of knitting his country together — and binding it to Europe — with copper wire.

"In no other manner," concluded this wise old man, "could the Dominion government, at such small comparative cost, so conduce to the welfare of the people, and settlement of the land, as by the establishment of an effective system of telegraphy."

# Chapter 4

## Telegraph West

The western line that Fred Gisborne found "on its last legs" was a creature of government. This automatically accounted for most of its shortcomings. Smirched by scandal, shrivelling from neglect, forever breaking down, it drove its users to fits of rage and frustration. Yet this slim tattered line from Winnipeg to Edmonton, thrummed by the endless winds, singing its cicada song, was for nearly a decade the umbilical cord between east and midwest. It bound the Territories to Canada in peace and war. Without communications, the rebellion of 1885 would have taken a very different course. As forerunner of the Canadian Pacific Railway, the telegraph was the first agent of prairie settlement. It was even a prime medium of entertainment: settlers played checkers and chess up and down the line for evenings on end, telegraphing their moves back and forth while little crowds in smoke-filled shanties hung over the gameboards, cheering the players on.

It had filled the last gap in Canada's cross-country telegraph trail. By the early 1870s, British Columbia had its Collins Overland, from New Westminster to Quesnel, and a landline and cable between Victoria and the mainland via Washington and San Juan and Lopez Islands. The Canadian government had a spur line from Winnipeg to the American border giving Manitoba a roundabout link with eastern Canada.

Why bother bridging that remaining bit of wilderness between Winnipeg and the Fraser Valley? It seemed folly to most easterners. Would the Cree, the Assiniboine, the gophers, the buffalo hunters be needing a telegraph? Would news of great import come forth from those pioneer Winnipeggers in their shapeless coats, baggy pants and funny hats that looked like inverted spittoons? But in fact, the telegraph and railway were imperative, if the newborn nation were to be knit from sea to sea.

Winnipeg was "a muddy disreputable village" without sidewalks, street lights or waterworks, reported western writer George H. Ham in 1873. A drawbridge spanned the Red River, making way for an occasional steamer from the railhead in Minnesota, 222 miles away. In autumn, buffalo hunters rollicked into town, "wild children of the prairie" another writer called them, "drinking, gambling, fighting, dancing, laughing, talking, swearing, horse-racing, trading and singing, they make a perfect babel of the place . . . ."

Buffalo trails, pounded deep into the tall grass, meandered off to the Western horizon. Red River carts followed those trails, their rawhide-bound wheels creaking a shrill symphony to the empty skies. White-topped covered-wagon trains, drawn by plodding oxen, wended among the coulees and sloughs. Traveller F. L. Hunt was trudging behind one in 1874 when his ox took fright "running away — not from me but with me. I braced myself at all impossible angles; he dragged me along like a fly; we dashed down a bad hill and up a worse one. . . ." So he arrived at Lake Qu'Appelle, where everyone asked him for news, "as if a man driving an ox could ever by any possibility have any news."

The Cree and Saulteaux people of Qu'Appelle were anxiously awaiting treaty party number four. All across the plains, Indians were attending these white men's rituals, accepting terms they did not want or understand, going away restless and confused to the new "reservations." Hunt witnessed the signing at Qu'Appelle and wrote: "It may be sentiment. . .but at the final moment my sympathies went strongly out to these people, unknowing what they did — a prayerful thought that these children of our Father, so savage and yet so gentle, so ignorant and yet so wise might not in the hereafter perish utterly away. . . ."

They would not perish; they would merely vegetate. Yet who could believe that the Indians' free life was gone forever! Here in the seventies the west seemed little changed from decades before. There was no Regina, merely a pile of whitening buffalo bones beside Wascana Creek. Near the future site of Saskatoon the sun-bleached stockade poles of Fort Carlton gleamed awkwardly amid the subtle prairie browns and greens. It stood alone, an intruder, the only white man's habitation for endless rolling miles.

Edmonton, metropolis of the northwest, was little more than a fort itself. South of it the prairie rolled off to infinity, where those unkempt renegade hunters, the "wolfers," lived by their own laws, drifting to and fro across the U.S. border. In 1873, 10 of them massacred 36 Assiniboines in the Cypress Hills at the bottom of Alberta Territory. A year later 275 scarlet-clad Northwest Mounted Police rode out across the plains to make the west safe for settler and Indian alike.

The Mounties soon discovered they could not properly patrol their enormous beat without communications. Nor could British Columbia be saved from Yankee hands without a cross-Canada railway. A decade before, Sandford Fleming, the burly Scot whose fertile mind devised everything from Standard Time to the first Canadian postage stamp, had written a careful proposal for a road, then a telegraph, then a railway into the northwest. Now Sir John A. Macdonald had committed the nation to a railway; the telegraph was assured.

Nearly everyone in and out of government assumed the railway would follow the old Carlton Trail, as traders' caravans had for decades: north from Winnipeg between Lakes Manitoba and Winnipeg, across the Manitoba border near the present site of Pelly, Sask., over the South Saskatchewan River a few miles north of Fort Carlton at Clark's Crossing, and on to Edmonton. The telegraph was assigned the same route.

In 1881 the plan was scrapped in favour of the present CPR route. Had the telegraph planners anticipated the change, they could have saved themselves thousands of dollars and years of grief. But Alexander Mackenzie's new Liberal government in 1874 let contracts to build a line west from the Great Lakes. From then on the bright dream of Telegraph West turned into a nightmare.

The first 410-mile leg from Thunder Bay to Winnipeg was assigned to Adam Oliver, Joseph Davidson & Company. Oliver, a stalwart Liberal and former Ontario MPP, had already been involved in some questionable land dealings at Fort William. Now, as a Royal Commission would reveal, the federal Liberals showered Oliver with kindness.

His was not even *among* the original six tenders, but that obviously didn't matter. The lowest bidders, Waddle & Smith of

Kingston, were unceremoniously dumped from contention before they could put up the necessary security. The next two bids, although nominally from separate firms, were tendered by one R. T. Sutton of Brantford. In each company Sutton had a partner — frontmen to lend legitimacy to his ambidextrous act.

Sutton appeared to have the inside track. Suddenly Oliver and Davidson bought him out and went to Ottawa, presenting his lower bid. This dynamic duo emerged with a deal *better* than they had sought, based on the *higher* Sutton bid. In effect, they won a contract $54,000 richer — or poorer, from the taxpayers' standpoint — than the Waddle & Smith bid. Prime Minister Mackenzie, in his secondary role as Minister of Public Works, was intimately involved in the arrangements. When the Royal Commission probed these curious goings-on, Mackenzie and other participants, except the irate Waddle, suffered acute losses of memory.

The job was finished by the end of 1876, shoddy and behind schedule. In some places the builders lopped the tops off trees and draped telegraph wire on them; the trees ultimately died and dragged down the line. The segment from Winnipeg to Livingstone (near the present site of Kamsack, Sask.) wasn't much better. This contract went to Sifton & Glass, another Ontario firm. Their bid on the Thunder Bay portion had been too rich even for the Liberals' blood, but now they received their just reward.

John Wright Sifton, contractor and county politician, and David Glass, lawyer, were staunch Liberals. Again the Mackenzie government — in a bewildering maze of tendering that needed 25 pages of Royal Commission summary to be explained — passed over three other bidders to award the prize to Sifton & Glass. Moreover the pair received a handsome fringe benefit. They had bid on a longer stretch of line, received the contract for a relatively easy stretch, yet were paid as if building the more difficult portion as well. "The contractors got that to which they were not entitled," concluded the Royal Commission.

Sandford Fleming had been involved in these arrangements but, as the Commissioners added, "We cannot learn why these terms were granted. Mr. Fleming has stated that his memory is not a retentive one . . . ." The 295-mile stretch was finished in August 1876, months late and jerrybuilt. In erecting a line over muskeg in winter, for example, the contractors simply cut holes in the ice and shoved poles into the slush. In spring when the ice melted the line collapsed.

In fairness, the western builders faced problems undreamed of in eastern Canada. Forty miles out of Winnipeg a band of Indians rode into the construction camp, demanding provisions in the name of Queen Victoria, the Great Mother. Construction boss George Wright, finding no chapter on hostile savages in the line-builders' manual, stalled them until morning and telegraphed for help. By dawn a hard-riding band of militia reined up in camp. The Indians took to their ponies in haste; a wire that could conjure up armed soldiers overnight was obviously not to be trifled with.

But others blocked the line again at Swan River and at Fort Carlton. Treaty settlements were still pending for many, and this was their only effective means of protest short of war. They could be soothed, Lt. Col. George A. French of the Mounties assured his superiors, with "a slight present to heads of families this fall and an assurance that a regular treaty will be made next year."

Evidently this tactic worked because Richard Fuller of Hamilton finished his 517-mile section from Livingstone to Hay Lakes near Edmonton on schedule, at the bargain price of $213 a mile. Immediately the telegraph worked its magic. A shanty town called Telegraph Flats was renamed Battleford, acquired a Hudson's Bay trading post, the district headquarters of the Mounted Police and the first newspaper between Winnipeg and the Rockies, and became capital of the territory — all before 1882.

Now, with a well-placed telegram, the Mounties could head off escaping criminals. Until doctors arrived, settlers and traders turned to their friendly telegraph office for health services; the Battleford agent dispensed crude first aid over the wire, from a do-it-yourself medical manual in his office.

All of this was made possible by a new breed of western hero, the lineman. Without him, the telegraph would have been a total fiasco. With him, it worked by fits and starts. Where the bare wire touched wet leaves in rainy weather, the electrical current grounded out until messages faded to nothing. Prairie fires raged unchecked each spring and fall, burning the poles to stumps.

Any poles left standing were liable to be rubbed down by buffalo with itchy rumps, who then lumbered away with the wire tangled in their horns. At Buffalo Coulee halfway between Battleford and Edmonton a lineman told his boss, "When I arrived here this afternoon I saw an old bull rub down a pole, put the wire on his horns and start south for Fort McLeod. So I thought the Government had concluded to run a loop in there and had employed buffalo to see if they could make a better job than the Government contractors.''

A sense of humour was as vital to a lineman as a good horse, a gun, bannock and a lump of salt bacon. It was a hard, lonely, dangerous life. John L. Connors, operator and repairman on the Sifton line, once spent 48 days on the trail without seeing another human, and walked up to 56 miles a day. Frequently thieves ransacked a lineman's cabin while he was away. Telegrapher Barney Freeman — a Belgian whose real name, Bernard Tremont, was bastardized in everyday usage — returned from one trip to find his shack robbed of a sack of flour, 50 pounds of bacon, a new $30 suit, his pipe and comb, "everything except the stove and a felt hat.'' It being the second such robbery, Freeman quit and went ranching.

During spring floods, the lineman had to float his buckboard across swollen creeks. In summer mosquitoes rose in clouds from slough bottoms. On the Great Salt Plain west of Humboldt, no grass grew and the water was unfit for drinking. In winter linemen travelled by sleigh or dogsled, going ahead on showshoes to break trail for the team. Every man carried bandages to wrap his horses' legs when they were gouged by crusted snow.

Early one March morning in 1877 lineman Tom Dewan left Battleford with dogs to fetch supplies from Carlton 90 miles away. It was a dazzling day with brilliant sun glancing off a fresh fall of snow. A tough, bony man with a handlebar moustache, an original builder of the telegraph, Dewan pushed off matter-of-factly.

Fifteen miles out, his vision began to fail. At 30 miles he was completely snowblind. He kept calm. He remembered that his lead dog had recently been bought from Carlton. Maybe — it was a gamble but there was no choice — the dog would follow its nose home. Dewan fumbled aboard the sled, wrapped himself in a buffalo robe and gave the dogs their heads.

Hour after hour in total blackness, eyes aflame, Dewan urged the dogs on. At last, chilled through, agonized with pain, and almost ready to give up, he felt the sled stop. Friendly hands helped him up. The dogs had found Carlton. Days later he recovered his sight and went back to work.

For all of this a man earned $60–$70 a month. There was no danger pay, or sympathy. Eccentric John Little, the Battleford telegraph superindendent, once received a frantic wire from his least favourite lineman:

"Indians at door. Going to kill me.''

"Are you sure?" Little telegraphed back.

"Yes, yes."

"Good. Hope they make good job of it."

The lineman kept his scalp, no thanks to Little.

No amount of effort or heroism could salvage a badly built line, especially when the builder also held the maintenance contract. East of Winnipeg, the Royal Commission was told, messages were a month getting through. Of the western portion, Winnipegger Acton Burrows angrily catalogued a list of miseries in a passionate report to the federal government in 1879.

"The route chosen was and is unsuitable, the cost excessive, the annual subsidy for its maintenance is too high; the frequency with which it is out of working order renders it comparatively useless," Burrows wrote. "The line is of the cheapest and most useless description, the poles along the greater portion of the route being miserable attenuated poplar."

In July, he reported, the line was down for three weeks. In late August a militia officer in Winnipeg handed in a telegram for Battleford; nine days later it had not gone through. In October a businessman leaving Battleford telegraphed the news to his Winnipeg home office. He drove 650 miles by cart and arrived two days before the telegram.

The Saskatchewan *Herald* at Battleford added one more horror story: the Northwest Territories did not celebrate Thanksgiving with the rest of Canada that year because an official telegram notifying the Lieutenant-Governor of the holiday didn't arrive in time. For this so-called service westerners were paying $2–$2.50 for 10 words while Sifton and Glass reaped $5,000 a year for maintenance.

The line was most reliable in winter with the poles frozen upright, no wet leaves to bleed away the current, no forest fires, and fewer itchy buffalo on the prowl. On such a day, December 30, 1878, the Saskatchewan *Herald* of Battleford carried a December 21 despatch from Ottawa:

> The carbon-telephone trial took place yesterday between the Governor-General and Princess Louise at Rideau Hall and Sir Hugh Allan at the telegraph office in Montreal. The experiment was completely successful.

The one-paragraph item was buried on a back page. Few in the west had heard of "telephone" and fewer cared. Evidently the east had some new communication gadget that actually *worked*. So what else was new?

# Chapter 5

## "Too Startling for Belief!"

**U**nlike many a 19th century son, who quaked in awe of "The Governor" until his dying day, Alexander Graham Bell could *talk* to *his* father. He and Alexander Melville Bell had worked together since Aleck, as the family called Bell the Younger, was 17. Now 10 years later, Aleck liked to bounce his brainwaves off Bell the Elder at the end of a working day.

In the evening hush of July 26, 1874, they reviewed current events in the family's rambling white home near Brantford, Ont. The handsome dark-moustachioed young man, eyes afire with excitement, poured out a new idea. The older man — his hair taking off in ski jumps over his ears, the lines of his honest Scotch-terrier face drooping into his crinkly square-cut beard — listened proudly. When he answered it was in the precise, modulated tones of the elocutionist.

The electric motor idea was shaping up, Aleck Bell said, but something else was infinitely more interesting. Suppose one could somehow transmit sound vibrations — from a human voice for instance — to an electric current? And suppose those vibrations could be made to travel over wires as fast as electricity? Then suppose, when the vibrations reached the other end, they could be heard as the original sound? That would be electrical speech!

Young Bell didn't really expect encouragement, and he didn't get it. After he'd gone to bed his father jotted in his diary: "Motor (Hopeful). Electrical Speech (?)" Long after, the elder Bell confessed that on that night when the telephone was born, the idea was simply "too startling for belief."

Most others of his time would have shared his disbelief. Even after 28 years the telegraph was sensation enough to ordinary mortals. Only the soaring mind of Aleck Bell, fortified with everything he had crammed into it in 27 years, could grasp the greater miracle.

His entire young life seemed pointed toward that moment. His wise Scottish grandfather — bootmaker, elocution teacher and social commentator (some claimed that a play he wrote had inspired George Bernard Shaw to write *Pygmalion*) — instilled in the boy a taste for discovery. Melville Bell, the father, was a teacher, lecturer, stubborn researcher and an expert on all aspects of speech. His 15 years of research into vocal organs and phonetics had produced "visible speech," a symbolic language for the deaf and dumb. From his gentle mother, a musician before she became deaf, Aleck Bell inherited an ear for music. At 12 he played the piano while she pressed her ear to the sounding board, "listening" through the vibrations.

Three years later the boy was an inventor. When a miller challenged him to do something useful around his mill, Aleck invented a device to get rid of the husks. Talking machines were a current fad. Young Bell made a doll that wailed "Mama" and brought a neighbor woman running to look for the crying baby. By manipulating his dog's throat and vocal cords he induced the tolerant beast to grunt something vaguely like "hello Grand-ma."

Dapper to the top of his slicked-back hair and formal top hat, he looked and acted older than most teenagers of his time. With his brothers, Aleck went on stage helping demonstrate "visible speech." Melville sent them out of earshot while he took requests from the audience. Then, calling the boys back, he relayed each suggestion in his "visible speech." The sons duly sounded out phonetically everything from the moo of a cow and sound of a saw cutting wood to words in Gaelic and Russian.

Within three years both brothers died of tuberculosis — consumption, the doctors called it — the scourge of the century.

Aleck and his mother were prime candidates for the disease. A friend, Baptist minister Thomas Henderson, urged them to join him in the clean, bracing climate of southern Ontario. Melville Bell had fond memories of North America. In 1838 his own doctor had ordered him out of Britain to find "fresh air." The energetic Melville spent four years among family friends in Newfoundland, where the air was, indeed, fresh. He worked as a clerk, rowed often in the harbour, treated speech impediments, directed amateur theatricals and went home in the pink of health.

Now, friend Henderson searched out a home for the Bells on Tutelo Heights near Brantford, a ten-room two-storey white frame house with bath, conservatory, stable and shed on 10$^1/_2$ acres of lawn and orchard. Bell snapped it up for $2,600. Through most of autumn, 1870, the moody Aleck lounged in a hammock overlooking the Grand River, a tall pale invalid with prominent nose, full lips and jet black hair. He expected to die. Instead, his chest condition rapidly improved and, there in his "dreaming place," ideas flowed again.

The next year he went to Boston to teach the deaf children of men who could afford it. Some of them helped him through the difficult financial years ahead. Every summer, Bell went home to dream, plan and sketch ideas.

The puzzle of the telephone was steadily falling into place. Inventors Thomas Edison and Elisha Gray were hot on the scent too. They were technically better schooled than Bell, but this was not a disadvantage. "If I had known more about electricity and less about sound I would never have invented the telephone," he recalled later. He set himself to learning more about electricity, particularly electromagnets. Working with tuning forks, wires and an electromagnet, he produced a kind of electric telegraph based on a musical signal code.

Long before, the brilliant Englishman, Wheatstone, had transmitted musical sounds through solid rods. Bell went a step further. The theory of "hearing," reduced to its bare essentials, was this: a spoken word, or any other sound, sets up waves in the air. If the waves strike something sensitive enough, it vibrates — as does the human ear drum when sound strikes it.

So, Bell reasoned, why not convey these vibrations *and* their variations, by electricity over a wire? Why not create vibrations in the air at the receiving end, exactly like those made by the voice at the sending end? There was even a suitable word for it, "telephone," derived from the Greek. A German named Hutch had coined the word in 1796, while proposing a system of passing shouted messages through trumpets six miles apart.

Bell was grappling with this theory in the historic summer of 1874. He brought home a human ear. If the tiny tissue-thin ear drum could move the bones of the inner ear, why couldn't a stronger membrane move a piece of steel? One day the next year he and 21-year-old Thomas Watson were fiddling with a device to send multiple telegraph messages over the same circuit, using different sound frequencies. The crux of the gadget was a series of vibrating reeds fitted with coils of wire. Suddenly Bell realized that when Watson plucked a reed at his end, Bell's own armature vibrated in unison!

Later, during the long-drawn battles over telephone patents, he explained it. "I called out to Mr. Watson to pluck his reed again. At every pluck I could hear a musical tone of a similar pitch to that produced by the instrument in Mr. Watson's hands. I could even recognize the peculiar quality or timbre of the pluck." He knew now that electric currents, generated by the vibration of an armature in front of an electromagnet would carry sound.

The first crude telephone looked like a hangman's gallows in miniature. When a voice set air waves in motion, its thin tight membrane fluttered accordingly. A strip of iron fastened to the membrane thus vibrated in front of an electromagnet. This sent an undulating current over the wire. At the other end, the reverse process translated the original sounds — more or less. After weeks of work Watson could hear Bell's voice, but couldn't distinguish words.

They were exhausting, frustrating months. Bell worried about his competitors; Gray in particular was close to a working telephone. He kept up his teaching. Watson pulled him out of bed every morning at seven, to sandwich a few experiments between classes.

By now he was in love with a student, Mabel Hubbard, who had been deaf since a childhood bout of scarlet fever. Her father, a strong-willed, wealthy Boston lawyer, was one of Aleck's main financial backers. He urged Bell to forget the silly telephone and concentrate on the harmonic telegraph.

"When will this thing be finished!" the harassed Aleck wrote his family. "I am sick and tired of the multiple nature of my work, and the little profit that arises from it."

Then on the magic day, March 10, 1876, Bell called the words every schoolchild knows: "Mr. Watson, come here, I want you." And Watson, who *heard over the telephone* in a distant room, came running.

It was just the beginning. The words were tinny and faint. But at last Bell's theory was proven. He held "parlor experiments," as he called them, between one room and another in Boston. But as a scientist friend pointed out, "The only way for a satisfactory demonstration is to place the transmitting and receiving instruments apart." Bell went back to the telephone's birthplace, to prove its worth.

Within one week in August, 1876, he performed three critical experiments. To do them he needed the lines of Dominion Telegraph, a vigorous new competitor of Montreal Telegraph, founded in 1870 with strong Ontario representation on its board. Dominion's manager was Thomas Swinyard, an English railwayman who had little enough patience with telegraphs, much less this crazy new proposal.

"Another of those cranks!" he told his assistant, "Consign it to the waste paper basket!" But the assistant was none other than Lewis McFarlane, the peripatetic telegrapher, and the romantic in him warmed to the telephone idea. He coaxed his boss to rent Dominion's lines to Aleck Bell.

On August 3, Bell took a buggy load of equipment to Mount Pleasant, Ont., and put a receiver in Wallace Ellis' general store which doubled as telegraph office. That evening Bell heard his Uncle David's rich Scottish voice intoning "To be or not to be. . ." from Brantford, two miles away.

The next night invited guests filled the Bell homestead for another test. Since the telegraph didn't run to the house, Aleck connected it with stove pipe wire strung along the fences. Again from Brantford — Bell's instruments did not yet permit two-way conversation — came more Shakespeare, a soloist trilling "I Need Thee Every Hour," a vocal trio and tunes from a harmonium.

On August 10 Bell set up his receiver at Paris, in Robert White's Boot and Shoe Store, eight miles from Brantford. At first he heard only "explosive sounds like the discharge of distant artillery." He telegraphed an assistant to change the electromagnet coils on both transmitter and receiver. Now voices came through clearly, including a familiar one that wasn't supposed to be there. Aleck telegraphed for confirmation: was his father really in Brantford? He was, and his voice was recognizable on the world's first long distance call.

For Bell the Younger, the rest was almost anticlimatic. He liked the things that success brought, but only because they enabled more research. And there were harassments. For years he was assailed by other inventors who claimed to have beaten him to the telephone. (In fact, he had filed his first patent just hours ahead of Elisha Gray.) More than 600 attempts to nullify the Bell patent were unsuccessful, but they leached his time away.

He had no head for business and little patience with businessmen, many of whom were astoundingly shortsighted. Once in 1876 he showed a model of his phone to a Bank of Hamilton official and George Stephen, president of the Bank of Montreal. They admired it as "an ingenious toy" but failed to ante up cash. When the Bells asked Sen. George Brown, publisher of the Toronto *Globe*, to file patents for them in England, he was so unimpressed that he never did get around to it.

By 1877 Aleck Bell had had enough. He turned over 75 percent of his Canadian patents to his father and the remainder to Charles Williams, a Boston manufacturer who, in return, was to supply 1,000 telephones for the Canadian market. Then Bell settled down in the U.S. doing what he loved: teaching the deaf and inventing. The telephone had made his name and fame; now he was eager for new explorations.

"When one door closes, another one opens," Bell said once. "But we often look so long and so regretfully upon the closed door that we do not see the one which has opened for us."

## The Other Man from Brantford

One fascinated onlooker at those first Brantford experiments was a solemn youth, clean shaven under a mop of dark hair, a bit baggy of trousers, the sort to go totally unnoticed in the presence of vibrant Aleck Bell. Yet James Cowherd would have become the toast of Canada, too, if life had given him an even break.

The Thomas Cowherd family lived three miles from Tutelo Heights. Cowherd's Brantford hardware store supplied much of the stovepipe wire for the first "telephone line" over fences into the Bell home. Later, with more stovepipe wire and two-way telephones, the two households talked back and forth. Sometimes the Bells dropped in for Mrs. Cowherd's homemade cookies, which Melville liked to dunk into Tom Cowherd's homemade grape wine. The conversations were sprightly. Hardware man Cowherd was also a student of history, and his amateur poetry appeared in local newspapers and in a book, *The Emmigrant Mechanic, and other tales in verse, by Thomas Cowherd, The Brantford Tinsmith Rhymer*.

Sometimes, too, the three Cowherd daughters, Jennie, Amy and Ida, sang three-part harmony to the Bells, through a phone with a triple mouthpiece devised by serious brother James. Their first such rendition over this gadget was during Bell's experiment of August 3, 1876. When Aleck discovered that James, only two years younger, was a mechanic and electrician, he took a second look at the shy man in wrinkled pants.

Cowherd's active hands and mind had already produced small steam engines and a pipe organ. At Bell's instigation he went to Boston to study at the Charles Williams shop on Court Street, where Thomas Watson had apprenticed and where Bell's experimental phones were made. Already Melville and Alex Bell guessed that Williams, swamped with U.S. business, would never be able to meet all of Canada's telephone needs. Also, the duty on imported phones was high and Canadian patent laws specified that failure to manufacture the instruments in Canada within one or two years would nullify Bell's patent. Canada had to make its own telephones.

When James Cowherd came home from Boston in 1878 his father built a three-storey brick factory behind his hardware store, first in Canada and perhaps in the world specifically for telephones. Nineteen phones went to Hamilton in December. In the next two years — in rooms cluttered with strange devices, some like steamship funnels, some resembling human ears — James Cowherd built most of the telephones used in Canada. Around home he had 16 earphones. His wife liked to sing as much as he did, and joined in his constant experiments.

By January, 1881, Cowherd had manufactured 2,398 telephones in 25 months, and was working on a new transmitter and a switchboard. Two months later the Brantford *Expositor* printed his obituary: "of consumption, on the 27th inst., James Cowherd, aged 31 years and 6 months."

"If Mr. Cowherd had lived he would have greatly advanced electrical science," mourned *Scientific American*. Another journal

James H. Cowherd, an electrician and protégé of Alexander Graham Bell, established the first factory for manufacturing telephone equipment in Canada, at Brantford, in 1878. BELL CANADA TELEPHONE HISTORICAL COLLECTION.

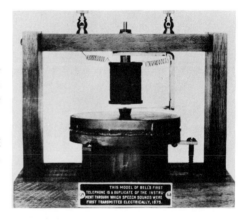

Bell's first telephone, the "gallows frame," through which speech sounds were first transmitted electrically on June 3, 1875, in Boston. BELL CANADA TELEPHONE HISTORICAL COLLECTION.

J. A. D. McCurdy, an associate of Bell and a member of the Aerial Experiment Association, flew the "Silver Dart" in the first heavier-than-air flight in Canada and the British Empire on February 23, 1909, at Baddeck, N.S. COPYRIGHT: ROYAL CANADIAN AIR FORCE.

Alexander Graham Bell at age 29, two years after he invented the telephone. COPYRIGHT: NATIONAL GEOGRAPHIC SOCIETY AND THE BELL FAMILY.

In his later years, Bell spent his summers at Baddeck, N.S., where he continued his prolific research and enjoyed life with his large family. Here he is seen with granddaughters, Gertrude, Lilian and Mabel Grosvenor. COPYRIGHT: NATIONAL GEOGRAPHIC SOCIETY AND THE BELL FAMILY.

Bell, teacher of the deaf, communicating with deaf and blind Charles Crane in 1916. COPYRIGHT: NATIONAL GEOGRAPHIC SOCIETY AND THE BELL FAMILY.

agreed that he was "entering upon an assured brilliant future in scientific work." It was a hard blow for the new Bell company. A year later its secretary wrote to the equally new Victoria and Esquimalt Telephone Company in B.C., "We have been unable to forward you any more transmitters yet, having been unable to get them properly made. Our own manufacturer died rather suddenly and was the only man in Canada who understood the manufacturing. Others have tried and failed. We have now fitted up our own workshop here and hope to be able to send you a supply next week."

So the Bell Shops were born in 1882, managed by an ex-foreman from the Williams shop in Boston. They grew into Northern Electric, now Northern Telcom, the technical and manufacturing arm of Bell Canada today — legacy of the other man from Brantford.

# The After Years

One blue and gold summer day in 1885, Aleck Bell, riding a steamer to Newfoundland with his family, glimpsed the rippling Cape Breton hills. They sang out to him of Scotland. Each year he returned and at last built a summer home and laboratory on a hill near Baddeck. He gave it a lilting Gaelic name, Beinn Breagh, ("Beautiful Mountain"). Here and in his Washington, D.C. home, ideas came in torrents as Bell sought "answers for the unceasing hows and whys about things." He carried five-by-two-inch notebooks, crammed with scrawls and sketches. His mind leaped years ahead of its time.

In 1877 Edison invented a phonograph that recorded on metal foil cylinders. Bell and his associates in 1886 discovered the durable qualities of the wax cylinder and translated an uncommercial idea into the entire modern recording industry. They also experimented with a flat disc.

A year before, Bell suggested that icebergs, terror of the seas, be detected by projecting sound electrically underwater and bouncing back an echo off the berg. Decades later, "sonar" detection became commonplace.

He invented a surgical probe for locating pieces of metal buried deeply in patients' bodies. A version of it was used in medicine until the X ray superseded it. In 1903, shortly after Marie

Curie discovered radium, Bell suggested using it for treating deep-seated cancer. Thirty-nine years before the iron lung was invented he built a vacuum jacket for artificial respiration.

He wrote a voluminous study on genetic development, tracing one family's ancestry through 8,907 members. Flocks of sheep rambled over his fields; Bell was trying to breed ewes that would bear several lambs at a time instead of one. He built a device to turn sea water, fog, or human breath into fresh water. In 1880 he devised the Photophone, forerunner to photoelectric cells. Before 1900 he invented an electrical door lock; by 1911 he had his own air-conditioning system.

Bell was too busy and impractical to pursue and patent such things. His thrill came from creating, then creating anew.

"We should not keep forever on the public road, going only where others have gone," he said. "We should leave the beaten track occasionally and enter the woods."

If he had not lost so much time defending his telephone patents, his friends said, he might have put an aircraft aloft ahead of the Wright brothers. Experimenting with enormous kites in Nova Scotia, he drew together a team of aviation whiz kids. One, Glenn Curtiss, later founded a world-renowned aircraft company. Another, Casey Baldwin, in March 1908 made the team's first public flight. A year later a third protege, J. A. D. McCurdy, made Canada's first powered flight, piloting the Bell group's Silver Dart for eight miles in the Baddeck region.

Bell's team produced the wingtip aileron, a major advance in controlling flight. He personally designed hundreds of experimental propellors. Once, seized with inspiration in the night, he sprang from bed, cut up his wife's new Venetian blinds and glued together yet another laminated propellor model.

As early as 1892, he sketched and described a kind of helicopter. He envisioned the turbine engine. Early in this century, he prophesied that "heavier than air machines of great size and different construction from anything yet conceived will be driven over the earth's surface at enormous velocity by new methods of propulsion, perhaps by the force of high explosives . . . ." He was, of course, visualizing the rocket. In the early 1900s Bell researchers developed a hydrofoil that sped around Baddeck Bay at 70 miles per hour, for years the fastest boat in the world.

With his father-in-law, Gardiner Hubbard, Bell helped found the National Geographic Society in 1888; their descendants still control it. All his life he worked with the deaf. He inspired the education of Helen Keller, who was brought to him as a child, deaf, dumb and blind and later became a famed writer and lecturer. His $200,000 share of income from the gramophone patents went for research into problems of the deaf.

There was always money for him to live comfortably and continue his work. At Beinn Breagh he was surrounded by children, grandchildren, scientists and friends. In his latter years he surged among them with a wild white beard, merry eyes, great beak of a nose and prodigious belly — a Santa Claus in golfer's knickers. The place was always alive with Bell talking, Bell dancing the Highland fling, Bell booming out songs on the grand piano.

He could never stop inventing. He spent an entire afternoon with two researchers, dropping the family tabby from the verandah to a cushion on the ground, trying to find out why cats always land on their feet. When he discovered his driver was climbing four flights of stairs every day to say the coach was ready, Bell gave the man a whistle and a code (two long blasts, three short) — much more efficient, he thought.

He was buried atop his Nova Scotian hill in 1922. On the day of his funeral, every telephone in North America and Mexico was silenced for one minute in his honor. It was the last time Aleck Bell's remarkable invention was stilled.

# New Toy

For civilized ladies and gentlemen of the 1870s there was no morally cleaner nor physically healthier recreation than an evening of song around the piano. What better way, then, to test the telephone than with a jolly good sing into the thing? Accordingly, all over the eastern provinces in the autumn of 1877, small groups in their Sunday best vied for invitations to "socials" like that of September 28 in Quebec City.

As the *Daily Telegraph* described it, "several prominent citizens" — a major, a captain, a Reverend Professor and assorted wives — assembled in the telegraph office around a little oblong wooden box with a spout jutting out one end. Over in Lavigne's music store on St. John Street, to which Mr. Mohr the telegraph operator had thoughtfully attached wires, Miss Wyse and Mrs. Cauldwell tuned their vocal cords around an identical box while Adolphe Hamel crouched at the piano.

Suddenly, incredibly, out of the spout "the singers' voices could be distinctly heard"! Mrs. Cauldwell sang "Comin' Thro' the Rye" and "The Last Rose of Summer." Miss Wyse trilled "Ave Maria." The elated prominent citizens sang back into the spout and were duly and distinctly heard at Lavigne's. Then all went home, "convinced of the wonderful powers of the telephone."

No 20th century Canadian will ever appreciate the sheer wonder of those first trials. Sending signals over wires was amazing enough; a recognizable voice travelling miles between cities simply defied credulity. What later generations came to take entirely for granted was in 1877 first regarded as a scientific trick, then embraced with wild delight. Captains of industry, princes of the church, nobility, the military, the flower of society, all let down their dignity in childlike antics around the telephone.

In October, the Quebec City demonstration was repeated for the Catholic archbishop, 20-odd bishops and priests and the Spanish and French Consuls-General. After listening to the indefatigable Mrs. Cauldwell sing "Thou are so near and yet so far," the reverend gentlemen rose up *themselves* and sang into the box. In Toronto, after a demonstration before the Ontario Legislature, Premier Oliver Mowat ordered phones for his home and the Lesgislative Buildings. The cream of Hamilton's business community, after a hearty lunch at the Hamilton Club, sallied forth to separate homes to witness a three-way hook-up engineered by Melville Bell. The president of the Bank of Montreal, three bank managers, two editors, a lawyer and assorted merchants sat in attentive rows, chuckling like schoolboys, while "Home Sweet Home" issued from the box.

Melville Bell was everywhere now, a burly will-o'-the-wisp with carpet bag in one hand and telephones in the other. As soon as Aleck assigned to him the bulk of Canadian patents, Melville appointed family friend Thomas Henderson as agent-general for Canada. Now the 58-year-old elocution professor and the 61-year-old Baptist minister, mere babes among the telephone poles, were tackling the newest and soon-to-be most cutthroat enterprise in the land. Their knowledge of business and the telephone was minimal but they brimmed with enthusiasm.

Early in August, 1877, Williams, the Boston manufacturer, shipped the first eight box telephones and eight hand models, the latter shaped somewhat like a modern flashlight. Henderson, squinting through his steel-rim spectacles at the flood of enquiries, tried to explain a device that he barely understood.

"The hand telephone is a light instrument that fits the hand," he wrote. "You place it to your mouth when you speak and to the ear when waiting for a response. You may connect them with two wires or a single wire. If the latter is used, a wire connected with the telephone must be partly buried in the earth. I have tried various kinds of wire. The sound seems to travel well with common wire laid along the top of a rail fence."

It wasn't that simple. To signal another party, the user had to tap on the mouthpiece or rattle a box of reeds. James Cowherd later invented a model with a single tapbell at the base, and a button that the user had to hold down throughout the conversation, all the time shuffling the instrument between mouth and ear.

The earliest iron or steel wires were inadequate over long distances. Beyond 60 miles, bad joints and the natural resistance of iron blurred the voice. Where two long lines paralleled one another, the effects of electrical induction produced crisscrossing conversations — "crosstalk", so-called — sometimes ending as an unintelligible jumble.

Alexander Graham Bell in an earlier prospectus had advanced the startling idea that his telephone was not just another telegraph, to be installed and used at central points. He envisaged connections to "private dwellings, country houses, shops, manufactories, etc." Slowly at first, then with a rush, Canadians got the hang of it.

Even at $20 a pair — and they *had* to be sold in pairs at first, else there was no "other end" to talk to — demand outstripped supply. Ordinary mortals had to content themselves with public demonstrations. John Dearness, president of the East Middlesex Teachers Association, held one such show in London's new Mechanics Institute Hall, on September 1, 1877.

Just three weeks old, this sumptuous theatre had stage, footlights, blazing gas-lit chandelier and seating for 900. He charged 25¢ for the few available earphones. Wires ran over the rooftops — a common practice in all cities — to the telegraph office in the Tecumseh House Hotel, where a violinist waited with poised bow. Dearness checked his watch while the lucky few clutched their earphones.

As Dearness described it later: "I said, 'Do you hear anything?' They said, 'No', so I looked at my watch again and said, 'Do you hear anything now?' They still said 'No'. I didn't know what to do! Just then I saw from the rapt expressions that it was coming through. So I said 'What do you hear?' and they answered 'Music!' and they continued to listen with much amazement. I then explained to them that it was coming from the violinist in the Tecumseh House. . . .Of course, there was dumb silence from the rest of the people in the hall who could only watch the proceedings, but when it was explained to them there was great applause!"

In Hamilton a month later 15 telephones were set up in the W.C.T.U. Hall. But instead of 15 people filing through by turns, a disorderly mob of 400 burst into the Hall, tripped over the wires and broke the connections. One woman seized a phone, clapped it to her ear, heard nothing and stalked out shouting "Humbug."

Melville Bell promised no miracles even under the best of conditions. His first advertisement gingerly offered "articulate speech through instruments not more than 20 miles apart. Conversation can be easily carried on after slight practice and with the occasional repetition of a word or sentence. On first listening to the Telephone, though the sound is perfectly audible, the articulation seems to be indistinct; but after a few trials the ear becomes accustomed to the peculiar sound."

One unaccustomed ear belonged to Prime Minister Alexander Mackenzie who in November, 1877, leased phones to connect his office with Rideau Hall, the Governor-General's residence. His phone kept cutting off in midconversation. He ordered Bell to fix it or remove it.

The threat of removal did not rest well with Lady Dufferin, who loved her new toy. Sometimes she sang and played into it. Sometimes a certain mellow-voiced Captain Gourdeau from the marine department sang from the other end at her command, for the titillation of her guests. Lady Dufferin complained to Lord Dufferin.

"D," as his adoring young Irish wife called him in her diary, not only *was* Governor-General but *looked* like one. The haughty eye, the elegantly sculpted profile, the patrician tilt of head, all seemed to have been lifted from a freshly minted coin. Let the telephone stay, said Dufferin icily. Suddenly the Prime Minister discovered that he could hear remarkably well.

In leasing the sets to Mackenzie, Melville Bell displayed a keen sense of history laced with public relations. He backdated the transaction to September and referred to it ever after as the first telephone lease in Canada. It was not. On October 18, 1877, four sets were leased in Hamilton, one of them to Hugh Cossart Baker II, of 13 Herkimer Street.

This banker-cum-broker with the thick stern lips and the

boardroom pallor was about to become Hamilton's Mr. Telephone. He had been the driving force behind the Hamilton Street Railway Company, the Hamilton Real Estate Association and an insurance company, all before he was 30. Communications fascinated him. He and his cronies often played chess by telegraph. Now, at 31, his shrewd hooded eyes instantly recognized the telephone's potential.

Early in 1878 he added the Hamilton District Telegraph Company to his string of enterprises. Its subscribers could rent call boxes to signal for police, firemen, messenger boys, the express office or a cab. Baker realized this network would function far more effectively with telephones.

In July, 1878, he established the world's ninth telephone exchange, and the first outside the United States. Although only six subscribers could be connected at one time, it was an immediate hit. Hamilton users soon could relay all their grocery, fuel, drug, stationery or floral orders to the appropriate merchant via the telephone exchange. Every day precisely at noon, the phone company dinged a time signal into each user's home. Within a year, the subscription list leaped from 40 to 150.

Within 18 months telephone companies across eastern Canada were feverishly trying to outdo one another. One offered three months' free service to new subscribers. Another promised to spy on any company's night watchman: if he fell asleep and failed to phone in, the telephone company would notify his boss. Halifax exchange, for one, provided messengers to answer calls, run errands and deliver packages at 10¢ for 20 minutes or less, 15¢ for 30 minutes or 25¢ an hour.

Church services were "broadcast" over Ottawa phones for shut-ins, until the Dominion Church discovered "members of Parliament and others escaping the collection plate by hearing Rev. Mr. Stafford's sermon by telephone." Doctors were urged to diagnose simple ailments over the wire. To help compensate for lost revenue (the medics were reluctant to charge for telephone advice) the phone companies gave them a cut rate.

Thomas Henderson invited "all sluggards" to get their morning wake-up calls from him. A testimonial described how it had worked for Melville Bell: "Faithful to his trust, Mr. H. sounded the alarm this morning and Mr. Bell was aroused to a sense of duty and wakefulness" and caught his train.

The 1878 award for guile should have gone to a self-styled

"humble book agent" for Rose-Belford Publishing Company. This first-ever telephone salesman cunningly surmised that *one* man in all of Canada could surely not resist a phone call. He rang up Alexander Graham Bell in Brantford.

"I placed my lips to the telephone and told my business, winding up with a brief description of the contents of my book," the huckster told the Chatham *Planet*. "I then listened and the words that always make an industrious book agent happy came floating in my ear like the distant yet distinct voice of a ventriloquist. The words were, 'allow me to congratulate you on the very nice manner you describe your book. I will take a copy in cloth.' The whole time occupied did not require more than one-fourth the time it takes to write it!"

Inevitably, after the first flush of love, users learned that the telephone was fallible. One lawyer, worried about the lack of privacy on his party line, had the phone installed in his vault (which served only to nearly suffocate him). A newspaper, with some prescience, warned that "the invention is entirely untrustworthy in war. . .any traitor could tap the wires at any point and convey to the enemy what he learned."

In London, Ont. the Globe Agricultural Works burned down in the middle of the night because a watchman, turning in the alarm by telephone, could only babble, "There's a fire out here!" By the time someone else had rung a conventional alarm and firemen with galloping horses and pumper discovered the location of "out here," the building was blazing from floor to roof.

The public was tired of demonstrations, such as the one in Pictou, N.S., with ". . .a stout gentleman shouting to an invisible demon, 'Campbell, aloo,' when in a few seconds would come a faint squeak with some shrill sound which the presiding genii would call music and announce to the gaping wonderers as very fine. . . .And all pronounced it wonderful save the inevitable few who grumblingly termed the telephone a humbug and longed for their squandered dime."

Companies and public alike were alarmed by the wild proliferation of phones. There was no coordination of service and, since every line required a separate wire, city landscapes were becoming spider webs of wires, poles and crossbars.

By 1879, exchanges in Montreal, Quebec City, Toronto and seven other Ontario cities were using Bell phones. In the same year models designed by Thomas Edison and Elisha Gray were promoted by the Montreal Telegraph Company. Gray and Edison were professionals but any bright amateur could now "invent" a telephone following the detailed illustrations of Bell's instrument published in *Scientific American* in 1876. The patent laws and penalties were not well known nor much worried about.

In 1879, as an example, Thomas Ahearn, a wavy-haired Irish-Canadian boy, made a telephone "system" from two cigar boxes. Ahearn was already something of a telegraphic prodigy. He had risen from messenger to operator in six months. One day in 1877, as the lone telegrapher on hand for John A. Macdonald's announcement of the "National Policy" that would sweep the Tories back into office, Ahearn filed press copy nonstop from afternoon to midnight.

Now, as chief operator for Montreal Telegraph in the capital, he easily mastered the technical aspects of the telephone. His cigar boxes worked splendidly over the 110 miles of telegraph wire between Ottawa and Pembroke. Eventually Ahearn bartered his "system" to pay a $16 hotel bill.

A Quebec City jeweller and goldsmith, Cyrille Duquet, produced an instrument only slightly different from Bell's (which later caused Duquet to lose a patent suit), ran a line between two of his stores and sold several other phones around the city. The first telephone line in Montreal, between the seminary at St. Sulpice and the cemetery on Cote des Neiges, used a Duquet phone. Duquet also conducted long distance experiments over the telegraph wires between Quebec and Montreal, and Ottawa. The press said Duquet's phone "produces the loudest tones but does not equal Bell's in clearness."

Early in 1880 the Chatham *Planet* summed up a national concern: "Our town in common with other communities all over Canada is agitated just now on the subject of telephone communication between house and house. No less than two telephone exchange companies are engaged in stringing their wires across the streets and over housetops, eager to prove to our businessmen the respective advantages of the Bell and Edison instruments. If the interesting rivalry continues it may be that ere the summer zephyrs blow again, our town will be so thoroughly wired that the spider's occupation will be gone and the unsuspecting house fly will be tripped up at every step."

If the Bell company was to survive, it needed a strong, experienced business hand. Melville Bell knew his limitations. He also wanted to be near his son in Washington. He decided to sell his company to Canadians.

Dominion Telegraph, now general agent for the Bell interests in Canada, was the most logical prospect. Bell wrote to managing director Thomas Swinyard, who proved to be as shortsighted and pigheaded as ever. He didn't bother to answer. Bell wrote again. Still no reply. Bright young Lewis McFarlane was still Swinyard's assistant. Again he pleaded with his disinterested boss. A telephone service would help Dominion compete with its archrival, Montreal Telegraph (which handled Edison phones). Why not invest $5,000, even $12,000 if necessary, McFarlane argued? It was no use. Bell and his minority partner Thomas Williams wanted $100,000.

But for lack of money Canada's largest telephone company today might be known as "Duquet." Hard-luck Cyrille Duquet was invited to buy, but the most he could raise in his home town was $3,000. In Montreal — where he offered to build a line to Quebec City and pay for it himself if it didn't work — he received not a penny and was called a "naive imbecile."

Like countless Canadians after him, Melville Bell could find no moneyed men with faith in their own country. In 1880 he sold to National Bell of the United States. It was the first of two major transactions in two years, that would place control of Canada's biggest communications companies in American hands.

# Chapter 6

## The Rise and Fall of a Boy Wonder

Erastus Wiman was so splendid an example of his species — the Victorian poor boy who made good — that he should by rights have been stuffed and mounted under glass for future generations to admire. He was the quintessential capitalist in an age when "capitalism" was not a dirty word. That he made his fortune in the United States mattered not a whit to his former countrymen.

Indeed, Wiman might have gone down in Canadian history as a sort of national hero-in-exile, had he not committed an unpardonable sin. He delivered the nation's two biggest telegraph companies into Yankee hands. Soon after, he was involved in a bold American bid to take over the newly formed Canadian Pacific Telegraphs. Few Canadians grieved when Wiman's world ultimately fell into ruins, but for a time he was the towering figure in this country's communications industry.

A contemporary of Wiman, the American author Horatio Alger, was famed for his suffocatingly moral books for boys — *Luck and Pluck*, *Strive and Succeed* and some 130 others of similar ilk. In each, an ambitious youth always won out against incredible odds. Alger might have patterned his fictional wonderboys on Erastus Wiman. The lad from Churchville, Ont., near Brampton, even supported a widowed mother, a mandatory requirement for poor-boys-making-good.

Wiman himself once published a collection of essays and observations, oozing with Victorian morals and ethics. He called it *Chances of Success*.

"The past 50 years have been so full of Chances that the wonder is that the rich man is a rarity and that the poor are so plentiful," he marvelled in print.

As Wiman saw it, success waited smiling for any young man who practised industry, thrift and obedience. "To the young loafer whose highest achievement is a good game of tennis, whose chief aim is to dawdle and drivel with a lot of girls, the future is full of uncertainty," he predicted darkly.

There was no dawdling in his life. At 12 he laboured on farms at 50¢ a week. At 13 he was delivering newspapers in Toronto where on New Year's Day, 1846, he waded through driving snow to the Governor-General's residence, Elmslie Villa, amid the wilds of Yonge and College streets.

The butler, seeing him wet and cold on the doorstep invited him in by the fire. At that moment a baby wailed: a daughter was born to Lady Elgin. The Governor-General, beaming with parenthood, gave the newsboy a gold sovereign. Wiman chose to make it an omen: "It may be said to have formed the basis of the fortune which was afterward acquired." It certainly formed a useful friendship in adult life. At a socialites' party in England 45 years later, a certain aristocratic Lady Thurlow remarked that she was Elgin's daughter. Wiman, seizing a Chance, gushed, "Then, Madam, I heard your first cry in this world!"

Still in his teens, he became an apprentice printer at $1.50 a week. In his spare time he organized the Cadets of Temperance, dedicated to resisting booze in all its sinister forms. The evils of drink were an obsession among right-thinking Canadians of his day. Supporting temperance could do a young man's career no harm. (As an adult, Wiman grew pragmatic; although he called saloons "a disaster to good living," he was not averse to a nip of rye whisky to "comfort" him on a cold day.)

The model youth next became a writer on the Toronto *Globe*, then its commercial editor, then founder and editor of *The Grumbler*, a lively journal of satire, verse and opinion. One of its targets was the United States. "Brother Jonathan," the prototype American (forerunner of "Uncle Sam") was a menacing presence.

Plenty of Canadians could remember the war of 1812: how the United States had tried to take Canada and failed; how an American militant had trumpeted, "I would take the whole continent from them!" In pursuit of their "Manifest Destiny" the Yankees had wrested the entire southwest from Mexico and bullied Oregon away from the British. Now, learning that 310 Americans had taken land adjacent to the Ottawa River, *The Grumbler* warned, "Brother Jonathan is buying up Canada!"

But Wiman did not linger long in journalism; there was no money in it. He joined the staff of R. G. Dun and Co., mercantile agents. Business, he discovered, was where he belonged. He was a cool customer, with a round face tending to jowls, close-trimmed no-nonsense hair, and eyes as hard as agates. Behind his ingratiating smile and felicitous phrases lurked a passion for power and the nerve of a burglar. Part of his job was to compile a detailed rating of every businessman of consequence from Halifax to Winnipeg. Useful as this service was to business, it was priceless to Wiman, for it gave him inside information on the entire commercial world.

Six years later he was transferred to the head office in New York at $5,000 a year, "one of a million [Canadians], straying across the border into this glorious nation, and receiving with his fellow countrymen an unstinted welcome." The Yankees were as militant as ever. On the brink of the Civil War their secretary of state had urged Lincoln to attack some foreign nation — British North America would do — and so dispel internal strife. Now, with the Civil War over, the Yankees were clamoring for a corridor to their newest acquisition, Alaska. They indicated that British Columbia, or the entire Northwest, would be acceptable.

Yet none of this seemed to disturb the former editor of *The Grumbler*. He sniffed the air and it smelled like money. He decided Brother Jonathan was not so sinister after all. Soon Wiman was general manager of R. G. Dun.

He had a flair for making things work. With his guidance, a little Niagara Falls company parlayed a new kind of cheque book into annual profits of $250,000. A London, England, promoter tried to interest America in the penny weighing machine and was rebuffed on all sides. Wiman was intrigued. Six years later Americans were happily plunking nickels into seven million public weigh-scales. In the early 1870s Wiman persuaded his firm to pay $5,500 for 100 new instruments called "typewriters." This enabled the inventor to coax a disinterested Remington Company to manufacture them — and the rest is history.

Erastus Wiman, the poor boy from Churchville, Ont., who rose to control the Canadian telegraph industry. METROPOLITAN TORONTO LIBRARY BOARD.

Visions of canals, railroads, telegraph lines and land projects danced through Wiman's head. He moved in high places, trading favour for favour. One incident, "which won the gratitude of a 20-times millionaire, that even the capture of a telegraph system did not equal," vividly illustrated Wiman's connections, and 19th century Canada's social mores.

Montreal's annual Ice Carnival Week with its State Ball was a highlight of the winter season. Even New York's *nouveau riche* came north to brush elbows with the Queen's representative. One year Wiman hosted two wealthy U.S. telegraph families, discreetly unnamed in his narrative, but bitter rivals. As he wrote later, "It required a good deal of finesse to so manipulate things that no preference was shown."

One of the American wives paid her respects to the Governor-General's lady at a levee held for that purpose. Automatically she became a candidate for the coveted "State Quadrille" that opened the Ball. Alas, the 20-times millionaire's daughter-in-law, less skilled in society's guerilla warfare, missed the levee! Her husband then presented Wiman with an ultimatum: she *must* be presented to Lady Lansdowne at the Ball, and get in the quadrille too.

The Governor-General's aide-de-camp was aghast at the request. Was Wiman mad? *No one* was ever presented to representatives of royalty in a public ballroom! Otherwise any riffraff with a $10 ticket might meet Their Excellencies, and then what would the world come to?

The poor boy from Churchville broke into a gentle sweat. If the New York press learned that one wife had been snubbed, Wiman's name would be mud. "The writer, troubled in his mind, cast about. . .," Wiman recounted later (delicately describing himself in the third person). He received "a kindly glance from Lord Lansdowne with whom he had pleasant relations." Wiman candidly told the Governor-General his problem.

"Introduce me to the lady," said Lansdowne, "and I will vouch for her on your recommendation."

He did even better: he danced the quadrille with her himself.

"On the return to New York when the story was told," Wiman concluded, "the millionaire had a warmth of grasp in his hand for the writer that never before or after seemed to linger there!"

Erastus Wiman went on to dine with presidents of the United States, became a coveted guest speaker at banquets, hunted and fished in Canada with wealthy cronies. In 1873 he claimed he shot four wolves in five minutes near Minden, Ont.

Still a Canadian citizen, he became a vigorous proponent of reciprocal trade between the two countries. The mere hint of collaboration with the militant Americans gave many Canadians the shivers. Still, Wiman's approach was the lesser of evils. Once, in a public debate ominously titled "What Shall We Do With Canada?" the editor of the New York *Tribune* cried, "Annex it!" Wiman argued peaceably, "Trade with it!"

To those who did not cross him in business, he was the soul of social consciousness and philanthropy. One year he donated his steamer, Sylvan Dell, "supplied with abundant refreshments," to cruise some Old Timers around New York Harbour. He organized a Buffalo Bill wild west show on Staten Island for 10,000 children, complete with a foolproof antilitter scheme. Each moppet received a paper bag of sandwiches and cake but each bag bore a gaudy picture of Buffalo Bill (printed at Wiman's expense). Not one was left behind.

Wiman pushed through a New York state law, abolishing imprisonment for debt. Then he carried a copy to the nearest jail and personally saw to the release of a dozen prisoners (one of them, he claimed, was A. R. Macdonald, "brother of a great tobacco manufacturer of Montreal").

But on business matters, large or small, Wiman was fiercely single-minded. He went to bed at 9:30 p.m. and rose at 3 or 4 a.m., writing pamphlets and speeches before going to the office. Nothing stood between him and a goal. Once he needed a fence whitewashed overnight. When no workmen could be found, Wiman painted it. During a printers' strike he needed an advertisement set in type, and did it himself. When the strikers screamed "Rat!" Wiman mollified them with sweet talk and $10.

Once he lured all the delegates of the Pan American Congress (heavily laced with Protectionists) across the border to Niagara Falls, Ont. on a slack day during their convention. There he fed them on fine food — and reciprocity speeches. The Protectionists were so angry they wouldn't let Erastus back on the special train to Buffalo, and banned him from a luncheon there the next day. But the New York *Sun* pronounced Wiman's act "A stroke of diplomacy worthy of genius."

In New York he needed permission to build a railway tunnel through federal property, using the cut-and-fill technique. Business rivals tried to defeat him on a technicality: cut-and-fill was not a true tunnel, according to Webster's Dictionary, they argued.

Worcester's Dictionary, the other leading authority, said it was.

The matter went to the U.S. attorney general in Washington. So did Wiman. Arriving early to an empty office, he noticed to his horror Webster's Dictionary on the shelf. He dashed out, bought Worcester's, put it on the attorney general's shelf and hid Webster. Whether or not the ploy helped, Wiman's tunnel went through.

His great coup was in wresting control of the Staten Island Railway and Ferry Company from the fabulous Vanderbilts, a family dynasty built on steamboats, banks and railways, wealthy and powerful beyond belief. One day Wiman showed up at an annual meeting with a majority of the 14,000 shares and was elected president. He then led his directors to a sumptuous lunch, arranged by and for Captain Jake Vanderbilt, the defeated president and "practical dictator of Staten Island for 29 years." Captain Jake did not stay for lunch.

This was the Wiman who in the late 1870s cast an appraising eye at the Canadian telegraph scene, and recognized a Chance. With the oncoming Canadian Pacific Railway, the west was opening up to settlement. The east had narrowed to two telegraph majors, Dominion and Montreal, which, in Wiman's view, were hacking each other to death. Canadian telegraphy was ripe for takeover.

Montreal Telegraph had 20,000 miles of wire, 1,400 offices, 2,000 employees and was sending two million messages a year, not counting press despatches. Its lines ran from Halifax to Windsor, and into Maine, Michigan, New Hampshire, New York and Vermont. It held exclusive telegraph rights along the old Grand Trunk and Intercolonial railways.

Dominion was a strong contender with lines mostly along public highways, from Montreal to Detroit and Buffalo; to Quebec, Ottawa, Saint John, Halifax and Louisburg. The two giants were fighting it out with rates as low as 20¢ per 10 words over 1,000 miles.

"Neither concern had made a dollar of money and indeed both were running badly behind." Wiman wrote later, casting himself in the role of fairy godfather. "It was only a question of time when bankruptcy would be reached. It was left to the good fortune of the writer of these lines to be the means of saving both concerns from this fall and bringing about a consolidation of the two companies. . . ."

First Wiman seized a corporate toehold in Canada. In 1880 several prominent Winnipeggers — the Premier of Manitoba, some of his cabinet, and a few Ontarians (including Thomas Swinyard, who *still* saw no future in the telephone) — incorporated the Great North Western Telegraph Company. They planned to serve Manitoba and the Northwest Territories, and connect with Ontario, but a year later put their charter up for sale. An interested group of Montrealers and New Yorkers made the astonishing error of sending a bid by mail. Wiman knew little about telegraphy, except that it was faster than letters. He wired his bid, followed by a telegraphic deposit of $50,000, and beat the opposition by days. On June 10, 1881, he became president of GNW.

By now American Union Telegraph had leased Dominion's lines for 99 years and Western Union had in turn gobbled up American Union. Western Union, viewing Dominion as a Canadian white elephant, offered it to Montreal Telegraph. Montreal turned it down; why buy a line that ran more or less parallel with its own? The answer soon became painfully clear. Erastus Wiman obtained an option on the Dominion lease and made Montreal Telegraph an offer it couldn't refuse.

In return for a 99-year lease on Montreal Telegraph's lines, he would give eight percent per year on the company's paid-up capital stock of $2 million, this to be guaranteed by Western Union. Wiman described these terms as "a splendid piece of luck for the Canadian shareholders."

The directors of Montreal Telegraph were enraged. But before they could slam the door on him Wiman calmly pointed out the alternative: unless they accepted his offer, his Dominion Telegraph would compete on a scale that would bring them to their knees.

At the annual meeting in June the shareholders stormed — but accepted. On Dominion Day, 1881, Great North Western took over Montreal Telegraph. Erastus Wiman and his American associates controlled all telegraphy of importance in Canada — 44,000 miles of line from Ontario to the Atlantic.

It was too much for James Dakers, the honest Scot who had served Montreal Telegraph from its inception. He resigned, and died in retirement six years later. Wiman swiftly appointed Orrin S. Wood, who never gave up his U.S. citizenship, as vice-president. Harvey P. Dwight, former western superintendent of Montreal Telegraph, an earnest 53-year-old telegrapher with lank strands of hair carefully brushed over his bald spot, became general manager. Wiman acknowledged that Dwight, also an American, "was more or less subject to misapprehension in Canada."

The merger required federal approval. In other circumstances this might have been a mere formality, for it was legal. But John A. Macdonald's Tory government was still smarting from the railway scandal that had dumped it from office not many years before. The current deal, which Wiman called "consolidation," spelled "monopoly" to many Canadians. John A. was in no rush to approve it.

Accordingly, Wiman mounted one of the most formidable lobbies ever to infiltrate Parliament Hill: 60 prominent men including a Catholic priest (Laval University held 1,000 shares in one of the old telegraph companies), a college principal, bank presidents, railway officials, newspaper editors and "a great shipping merchant knighted by the Queen," who surely must have been Sir Hugh Allan.

This all-star team, coached by Wiman, moved straight to the heart of government. One midnight Wiman received a hasty summons to a party. The Prime Minister was there and wanted to ask questions. Wiman flung on a dress coat and was on hand by 12:30. John A. was mellow with champagne, but only enough to oil his wits. The shrewd old eyes in the famous knobbly face appraised the lobbyist. The two began mulling the semantics of "consolidation" and "monopoly."

"Mr. Prime Minister," said Wiman, exuding earnest concern, "the prevention of consolidation is the abolition of competition."

John A. sipped his champagne, savored the tortuous phrase and began to play variations on it.

"The prevention of competition is the abolition of consolidation?" he rumbled.

Wiman smiled obediently at the little joke. (Surely it *was* a little joke?) He pressed on with his description of telegraph economics. Macdonald seemed not to be listening. He reworked the line again.

"The abolition of prevention is the consolidation of competition?"

Wiman, his smile wearing thin, stuck to his guns. . .

"The consolidation of prevention is the competition of abolition!" suggested the Prime Minister.

Like a drowning man Wiman clung to his thesis: if the two companies were not permitted to unite, they would both go under. Then Canada would have no effective telegraph communication.

John A. rose, chuckled into his overcoat and cast an amused eye at the ardent promoter.

"I think we will have to grant that 'Combination for competition and that abolition of prevention,'" he said. "Send your lobby home and your bill shall pass."

And it did.

The rates war ended. Charges were raised to 25¢ for 10 words by day, 25¢ for 25 words by night. About 2500 competing offices closed. Wiman never reported what happened to the employees of those offices. He did have "difficulty dealing with about a thousand hard-headed Scotch shareholders, but victory was achieved over about six months. . . .The result has been eminently satisfactory and highly profitable to all concerned." Certainly it was for Wiman, who soon became a director of Western Union.

Now, in the ultimate power play, Wiman and his American associates reached for the budding Canadian Pacific Railway telegraph system, the only threat to Great North Western's monopoly. By now the czar of Western Union was Jay Gould, a shrewd and ruthless financier who made Erastus Wiman look as pure as a choir boy. Gould's name had been linked with legislative bribes, stock watering and an attempt to corner the gold market in the United States. He had been booted from control of the Erie Railroad but rose again to dominate railroading in the American southwest. By 1882 his worth was reckoned at $73 million.

As Gould's emissary in Canada, Wiman bid for Canadian Pacific's telegraph interests. CP should have been ripe for the picking. The railway, still in construction, was perilously short of money. In late 1883 it formally appealed for $22.5 million to ward off collapse. Some of its officers would cheerfully have sold the telegraph. But Wiman had not reckoned with William Van Horne, the CPR's blunt general manager.

Van Horne stubbornly maintained that railway telegraphy was "not the big tent but the side show" and, at very least, should not be sold hastily or cheaply. In two short meetings the renegade Canadian, representing Western Union, locked horns with American-born Van Horne, now the unyielding protector of Canada's interests. Wiman had met his match.

In a rare tactical error, he then went over Van Horne's head to CPR president George Stephen. Wiman accused the general manager of trying to chase all other telegraph companies from Canada — a ludicrous charge, coming from the choreographer of a massive American takeover.

Van Horne rose up like a wounded buffalo and in March, 1884, penned an angry 6½-page letter to J. J. C. Abbott, MP, the CPR solicitor and a future prime minister. "I am appalled at Mr. Wiman's impudence. . . .Mr. Wiman wanted our telegraph system for next to nothing while I wanted full value for it. . . .Finding that I would be an obstacle in his way he wrote a letter to Mr. Stephen in which he stated that I had presumably a spite against the Western Union Company. . . .Mr. Wiman says that aside from my recent utterance my whole career indicates my desire in the direction of 'disregarding all vested rights or interests of those unable to defend themselves.'"

Van Horne hoped the directors would not be "seduced by Wiman's soft words, deceived by his false words or frightened by his blustering." Western Union would not achieve much, he concluded, "until they set some honorable man at work upon it, which I am free to say Mr. Wiman is far from being. . . ."

Western Union did not give up easily. "In about a month the Canadian Pacific Railway and telegraph service between Montreal and Winnipeg will be thrown open to the public," announced *Electrical Review* in August, 1885. "In telegraph circles it is said that gigantic efforts were made by Jay Gould to get control of the Canadian Pacific lines."

And in November, 1887, *Electrical World* reported from Montreal, "A telegraph deal which, if carried out, will entirely change the face of affairs in that branch of business in Canada, is understood to be underway here." A Western Union vice-president was consulting with CPR officials, but CP refused to sell.

Meanwhile Erastus Wiman was harassed on other fronts. In 1883 a Montreal Telegraph shareholder pleaded for annulment of the 1881 takeover, and very nearly got it. He won his case in Superior Court but lost the appeal. Six years later Great North Western sued Montreal Telegraph for breach of contract, alleging that the subsidiary had not maintained rights-of-way over various railway lines ceded to GNW. As a result the upstart CPR had leased those rights-of-way, put up telegraph lines and was gnawing away at Great North Western's monopoly. Montreal Telegraph retaliated with a charge that GNW was holding back dividend payments to shareholders.

None of this unduly disturbed Wiman, now at the pinnacle of his career. His salary and profits at R. G. Dun ranged from $50,000 to $80,000 a year (probably $200,000–$300,000 measured in today's values). His total worth was estimated at $2–$3 million, although most of it was tied up in property or deals. He kept a magnificent estate on Staten Island, owned a half-dozen race horses and bought vast tracts of land on the Staten Island waterfront, anticipating a railroad terminus there.

Philanthropist Wiman supported his first school mistress and numerous other spinsters, widows, aged men and distant relatives. He was a soft touch for any newsboy or down-and-out telegrapher. Among Western Union's and Great North Western's well-heeled directors, he was deemed the only one that any of "60,000 operators could approach with a certainty of borrowing a ten dollar bill."

Then, as quickly as it came, success deserted Erastus Wiman. The Staten Island railway deal fell flat. Early in 1893 his socialite friends were astounded to hear that his property had been seized; that 63 creditors were claiming $913,000; that Wiman's chief tangible assets, $91,000 worth of bonds, realized only $6900 cash; that his creditors were settling at a half-cent on the dollar.

Worse yet, in February, 1894 he was jailed, charged by R. G. Dun and Company with embezzling more than $200,000. A jury found him guilty but recommended mercy. Higher courts reversed the ruling and Wiman went free, but his fortunes never recovered.

In 1899 two Montreal Telegraph shareholders were *still* chipping away to have the 1881 takeover revoked. But by then Great North Western was a fading nonentity and so was Wiman.

Finally abandoning his secret hope of being knighted by the Queen, he took out American citizenship. In 1904, wracked by a series of strokes, the Canadian who courted success and was a hair's breadth away from being the greatest communications czar in this country's history, died almost penniless. In final ignominy, the week before his death, his household furniture was sold at auction.

# Chapter 7

## "Little Birdie Has Left Us to Join the Angels"

A mere 450 miles west of Winnipeg, where Erastus Wiman's greatest coup began, a little telegraph family was struggling for survival. They knew no presidents or kings. They earned less in a year than Wiman did in a week. Their rough log shanty was a million light-years from his panelled boardrooms, yet they were as vital to Canadian telegraphy as he. From their outpost at Humboldt, in what is now central Saskatchewan, they held together the fragile strand of wire between east and midwest. George Weldon, his wife Catherine, their baby, Birdie, Catherine's sister Margaret and her fiance Alfred Lindeburgh, were that special indomitable breed, the prairie telegraph pioneer.

Weldon was Irish, with a runaway moustache chasing his muttonchop whiskers back to his ears and dreamy eyes that seemed always to be scanning far horizons. He came out from Fintona, County Tyrone, in 1871, and followed the emigrant's standard route: farm labour at $13 a month; jobs in a Montreal wholesale house at $6 a week; clerking in a store, finally owning his own store. Always, the lure of the west tugged at him. Telegraph lines and a railway were building out there. A man, they said, could be rich and free there.

In 1876 he married Catherine Leggett, his hometown sweetheart and an expert telegrapher. Two years later, he hired on at $75 a month with Richard Fuller of Hamilton, who was building part of the government telegraph west of Winnipeg. George would be lineman; Catherine, telegrapher. Sister Maggie would go along for company.

They rattled west by train through the United States and paused in Winnipeg, clamorous with a dozen foreign tongues, bursting with 6,000 traders, hunters, railwaymen, would-be farmers. The CPR was offering land for $2.50 an acre. Real estate men were getting rich. Yet this self-important little city — so strange it was, to the Irish eyes — was only a glorified shack town dwarfed by the soaring dome of sky. And its Main Street, destined to become the widest in Canada, was simply an oversize Red River cart trail, oozing prairie gumbo.

In March the little family gratefully took to the trail again. At the Swan River Mounted Police post, 300 miles northwest by wagon, Catherine, Maggie and six-month-old Birdie stopped to rest. Weldon and a companion drove a horse cart on into the great greening flatland, still called Northwest Territories, to find a homesite. For days they trotted through the sea of grass, dappled with crocuses and buttercups; through littered buffalo bones and beaten-down trails where great herds had passed. At night, curled in his blanket, Weldon listened to coyote howls that sent prickles up his scalp.

Once the cart bogged down and Weldon waded for a mile through icy water over his knees. He tossed restlessly in his bedroll while a party of passing acquaintances kept him awake with bottle and song. He met an Indian medicine man named Picking-Your-Teeth. He read his Bible every day; religion was to be Weldon's bulwark in the ordeals ahead. And he kept a diary — no ordinary catalogue of trivia, but long lilting passages. Weldon was a romantic, which made his prairie odyssey bearable and miserable by turns.

On May 25, after journeying to Prince Albert and back, he staked out his future home beside the trail — Humboldt-to-be. Then, as any proper Irishman would, he planted 1½ bushels of potatoes. Soon Weldon was back with his wife in a wistful mood. "It is June Fair Day in Fintona," he wrote. "Calls up many fond remembrances of the past, of 'Love's young dream' or the spring time of life, or a few hours spent in the hotel in Fintona years ago.

We met then in the 'Isle of Saints.' We meet now many thousands miles away toward the setting sun. We are older but still our thoughts delight to wander back to those sunny boyish days."

Then he wrenched himself back to reality and put Catherine, the baby, and Maggie in the cart. Except for their hairstyles — Maggie's was pulled skintight from her forehead and coiled at the back, while Catherine wore a short curly cut — the sisters could have been twins. Both had the bright defiant Leggett eyes, determined mouths and strong jaws. Their dark serviceable gowns were buttoned up snug around their necks. No *decolletage* for the Leggett girls; bare bosoms on the prairie attracted mosquitoes, caused severe colds and gave the rougher male element wrong ideas.

They pushed off through muskeg swamps and thunder storms. At night bulldog mosquitoes drummed against their tent canvas like heavy rain. By August they were building a log house-cum-telegraph office. A trickle of passing pioneers brightened their days: red-coated Mounties with prisoners; surveyors; a travelling watchmaker; a mixed party from Ontario with oxcarts, "happy as larks" and singing "My Grandmother's Magpies"; a threshing machine, perhaps the first in the west, headed for Prince Albert.

On August 25, 1878, the first telegraph message, carried by hand from Duck Lake, went east over the wire from Humboldt. Two days later a missionary from the northwest sent the second telegram, and offered pemmican as payment because he hadn't seen real money for seven years. The Weldons quickly learned the art of barter. A passing Indian helped raise a heavy corner post. Weldon paid him with a loaf of bread, dried buffalo meat, matches and tobacco, and the Indian "smiled a thousand thanks." Three Sioux came by to trade badger skins for tea and flour.

In a month the logs were up and the Weldons mudded the cracks with water hauled from five miles away. The first snow fell on September 18. With winter at their heels, an English man and wife with guides hurried through after a summer of hunting in the Rockies. They had found the body of Rev. Skinner, a young Methodist missionary who had passed the Weldon home not many days before. Verdict: accidental death by shotgun. "Life is uncertain," Weldon told his diary. "Adieu, Skinner. . . ."

Thank Heaven for the telegraph, the Weldons often said that first year. They chatted over it the way city people gossiped across the back fence. In November Battleford's Saskatchewan *Herald* frivolously reported the latest telegraph "news" from Humboldt: "A badger lost his life yesterday while investigating the contents of Mrs. Weldon's churn. She heroically brained him and then shot him. He is dead."

At eight o'clock on Christmas morning the Battleford superintendent wired a message of good cheer, that same crusty old John Little who had once told a lineman the Indians were welcome to scalp him. On this day Little was wallowing in sentimentality. "To Mrs. Weldon, George, Maggie and Baby I send you the old time greetings with a friendly thrill in my heart," he telegraphed. "I wish you a Merry Christmas and many happy returns with the hope your future may ever be sunny and glad. With the hope that the years as they glide silently by will make up more fully for the Eternal Christmas of a better country. . . ."

The Saskatchewan *Herald* staff followed up with Christmas greetings for "the entire population of Humboldt."

On January 2, Battleford weather station reported 62 degrees below zero. The Weldons went stoically about their chores. A few nights later travellers stopped by on their way to Winnipeg. With the entire population of Humboldt joining in they sang, war-whooped and danced the Red River jig all night until the dogs howled and the baby cried.

Would winter ever end? Through short brilliant days and long nights, through the everlasting wind and cold, Weldon busied himself cutting firewood, improving the house, repairing the line as best he could in waist-deep snowdrifts. Finally after a few false starts — "winter lingers in the lap of spring" he wrote lyrically — the prairie burst into mud, green grass and birdsong. While Catherine manned the telegraph key, Weldon's work began in earnest. During 1879 he "took 1,533 trees from the line, reset 373 poles, set 137 new poles and travelled 2,748 miles. I found five breaks, and grounds and escapes too numerous to keep track of. All this work I have done myself with the exception of help with about 200 poles." It was a poor excuse for a telegraph line, but through no fault of Weldon.

It was lonely for the women while he was gone. Catherine missed church. Maggie missed having fun. Humboldt, she told a visitor, was "four months mosquitoes and eight months winter." To pass the time she became a crack shot, and probably the first white woman hunter in the west.

Suddenly a new interest rode over the flat horizon: Alfred Lindeburgh, a stocky Swedish American with a grand droopy moustache and a face creased with years of smiling and squinting into the sun. The modest Lindeburgh, a graduate of the University of Lund in Sweden, slowly revealed himself as a man of many talents. As a linguist he had served as interpreter on the Allan Line of ships, which carried immigrants from Europe to Quebec. Later he helped build the Union Pacific Railway in the U.S. and the Sifton telegraph line in Manitoba. Now he was assigned to be telegraph agent and meteorologist at Humboldt; the Weldons stayed on to help run the operation. It would be four years before this quiet man won the sparkling Maggie for his wife. In 1880, propriety had to run its full course.

The Marquis of Lorne, Governor-General, called on them in 1881, as he toured Canada with a writer-artist team from the London *Graphic* at his heels. Maggie Leggett blushed with shame when the artist, enchanted with this quaint colonial outpost, began to sketch the log house. "Why do you draw it so true instead of making something nice of it?" she grumbled. The writer waxed equally starry-eyed over these plucky Irish ladies pitted against the wilderness. But, he told his English readers, the savages of Canada were at least friendly: "The Indians in no way molest or bother them — do not even beg — so one may charitably hope that it is only with the government and the official world that the noble red man — in this respect resembling so many noble white men — plays the mendicant so sturdily and shamelessly while in private life, among his friends and neighbours, he is too much of a gentleman to beg. . . ."

Two days before Christmas that year, five-year-old Birdie fell ill. The nearest doctor, 100 miles away at Prince Albert, did his best to diagnose and treat her by telegraph. She had the "quinsy," he concluded, the Victorian term for severe inflammation of the throat, with swelling and fever. In fact the doctor was not sure what she had and anyway the Weldons had no medicine. In a decade when half the children in Canada died before age five, and when rural quacks still "bled" their patients as a cure for puzzling ailments, Birdie was lucky to have lived this long.

For a month the parents nursed her as best they could, and prayed. On Saturday January 28, with the telegraph still ticking off advice from the doctor, the child died. Her shattered father sought comfort in his faith: "Our darling little Birdie has left us to join the angels above the skies."

They wanted to give her a proper burial but the nearest minister was also at Prince Albert. The trail was knee-deep in snow. It seemed they would have to keep her body frozen all winter, a grisly and heartbreaking prospect. Then Alfred Lindeburgh showed what kind of man and friend he was.

He and his lineman, Finlayson, built a hand-sleigh, tied the child's body to it, strapped on snow shoes and trudged 100 miles over open prairie in vicious subzero weather. Taking turns breaking trail and pulling the sleigh, they reached Prince Albert several days later, saw to her funeral and walked home.

If there had been any doubt in Maggie Leggett's mind before, there was none now: Lindeburgh was the man she wanted to marry. But they put it off two years. Decent people didn't rush into marriage. Anyway, they needed time to build up a stake; *surely* their lives would be better from now on; surely the worst was over. The Weldons, Maggie and Lindeburgh could not foresee the terrifying times yet to come.

# Rebellion

The message clattering into Ottawa from his son in Battleford that Wednesday morning in 1885 must have chilled the old man's heart.

To F. N. Gisborne,
Superintendent, Government Telegraph Service.
April 1 — Indians raiding, killing, outlaying settlers.
Barney Freeman, our old repairer, murdered.
Everybody in barracks, expecting attack tonight.
                    Hartley Gisborne, District Superintendent

The Northwest Rebellion was on, and the forces of righteousness were gearing up for it. Few Canadians understood why. Easterners little knew or cared about the years of bungling by Ottawa and its representatives in the west; of the injustices to the Metis as a railway pushed west and speculators gobbled the land; of the dreams and hatreds nursed by Louis Riel. But now it had all welled up into war.

In two weeks Riel and his Metis had raided a store at Batoche, routed a small police party, then shattered a larger force at Duck Lake and sent it home with 12 dead and 7 wounded. Now militia commander General Fred Middleton was in Qu'Appelle awaiting the main force. His flabby plum-colored face, adorned with Colonel Blimp moustache and plumed helmet, bespoke 40 years of putting down fractious colonials around the Empire. Already the vanguard of his force had chugged out of Toronto amid cheers, tears and hoarsely shouted patriotic songs. Already rancher Barney Freeman, the retired telegrapher, had been shot to death by Indians while greasing his wagon, after stubbornly refusing to flee from home.

Now the rebels were besieging Battleford and swooping down on the telegraph lines, sensing how important the words-by-lightning would be in this first Canadian wartime test. Hours after the skirmish at Batoche, where the rebels chopped the line to Prince Albert, a messenger was galloping a circuitous route to Humboldt, 100 miles southeast. Humboldt office was unmanned now. The dreadful old "Sifton" line to Winnipeg was abandoned. In its place a spur line came up from Qu'Appelle, branching off from the new well-kept telegraph paralleling the Canadian Pacific Railway. George Weldon and his family were with the C.P.R. at Grenfell. Alfred Lindeburgh and his bride, Maggie, were at Kutawa, a lonely post halfway up the new spur line. But the Prince Albert horseman knew how to plug into the line at Humboldt and call for help.

His message flashed into Winnipeg, where Middleton was stationed, and on to Ottawa. Within days a contingent was on the trains from Toronto, Montreal, Quebec, the Maritimes and dozens of small places. The news of their coming encouraged the West's Indian agents, missionaries and thin red line of Mounties. The same news, speeding through the Indian nation by word of mouth, kept hundreds on their reservations. Thus the telegraph shaped history.

"The Rebellion proved the incalculable value of the telegraph and abundantly justified its construction," wrote J. S. MacDonald, a Battleford operator attached to Middleton's force during the fighting. "Without it many additional bands of Indians would have joined their kinsmen on the warpath and the trouble could not possibly have been brought to an end during that year. The Rebellion cost the country about $7 million but without the telegraph it would have cost many times that sum while the loss of life would have been infinitely greater."

If the rebels had fully understood the telegraph's power they would have carried off large chunks of line, crippling communications. Instead they merely cut it again and again, and courageous linemen rode out to mend it again and again. Linemen, operators and their families, were front-line troops in this little war.

Members of the Governor-General's Body Guard at the telegraph station at Humboldt, Sask. Colonel Denison is seated. PUBLIC ARCHIVES OF CANADA C753.

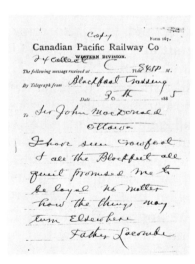

Telegram from Father Lacombe to Sir John A. Macdonald assuring him of the loyalty of the Crowfoot and the Blackfoot Indians. GLENBOW-ALBERTA INSTITUTE, CALGARY.

At Kutawa, Maggie Lindeburgh was pregnant and too weak to be moved to the safety of Moosomin where many settlers took refuge. So the Lindeburghs stayed on together: Alfred beside his telegraph, day and night; Maggie in her bedroom with a coal oil lamp always burning. Sometimes she sprang up in half-sleep, sure that the flickering shadows on the wall were feathered head-dresses. At Clark's Crossing near Saskatoon, 34-year-old Richard Molloy, a former telegrapher and newspaper editor from Nova Scotia, manned the key. Once when a battle raged 14 miles away, Molloy's family hid in a barn while he stuck by his telegraph.

For a while Clark's Crossing was a pivotal point in the Rebellion. Middleton's troops bivouacked there. Supplies trickled in by plodding oxcart and slow-moving river boats running aground repeatedly on the Saskatchewan's sandbars. A torrent of telegrams moved east and west: news of troop movements; orders for food, blankets and saddles; gratuitous advice from retired Northwesterners; anxious relatives pleading for information; wildly exaggerated press despatches. Canadian Pacific's telegraph revenue jumped from $70,000 in 1884 to $145,000 in 1885.

Adolphe Caron, minister of militia and defence, kept a Montreal Telegraph operator in his office. Here alone, hundreds of messages passed in and out during the rebellion. They told the rebellion's official story and they also carried tales of duplicity, bungling, political graft and of a rebellion leader who in the end was a frightened lonely man.

The Women's Christian Temperance Union of Quebec City telegraphed Caron to ban alcoholic beverages among the troops "except in such small quantity as may be required for medicinal purposes. . .lest youths going to their country's defense should contract habits of intemperance which might in the future tend to their own [undoing]. . . ." Political heelers rose up in droves. A Winnipegger demanded that the bread-and-biscuits contract be taken away from a Grit and awarded to one Thomas Chambers, "a good conservative and brother-in-law to Col. Kennedy." In one blatant exchange the Quebec firm of Pelletier and Charlebois wired, "Friends say that you should give here some patronage and get some Medical Boxes filled here for reasons." Caron replied, "All right will do what you want and expect you to do what I wish."

Overlong messages added to the telegraphers' burden. Fred Gisborne personally contributed his share by beginning each despatch with, "I have the honour to report. . ." and concluding

with "I have the honour to be, Sir, your obedient servant. . . ."
There were long silly harangues such as this exchange with Lt. Col.
Alderic Ouimet, commander of the 65th Battalion, Mount Royal
Rifles in Montreal:

> Ouimet: My men turning out splendidly. We only want
> uniforms and equipment.
> Caron: Don't understand what you mean by uniforms. Trou-
> sers have been sent.
> Caron: Why do you delay so long in leaving?
> Ouimet: Things not ready. No winter caps yet. Why don't
> you allow revolvers to officers?
> Caron: We have no revolvers and officers always furnish their
> own arms.

Military messages went by code, thanks to a cipher loaned by
the Bank of Lower Canada. (All banks had telegraph codes for
secrecy in transactions, a circumstance that once caused the Bank
of Nova Scotia some embarrassment: its general manager, vice-
president and two directors accidentally dropped their cipher book
off a bridge into the North Saskatchewan River, necessitating a
hasty rewrite of the entire code.) But there was really no need for
cloak-and-dagger security over the wires. The rebels had no spies
with Morse code training. Anyway, it was easy to detect the
military's secrets and follies.

Telegrapher J. S. MacDonald, travelling with Middleton, was
party to them all. Once a telegram from Swift Current warned him
that the Saskatchewan was in flood, on its way toward Clark's
Crossing, where the banks were piled high with canned beef,
sugar, tea and flour. He warned the officer in charge, who told
MacDonald to mind his own business. Thirty-six hours later the
flood crest swept in and hapless privates of the Midlands Regiment
were set to work moving the cache, too late. One entire barge load
of canned beef sank without a trace. The military, of course,
hushed the whole thing up.

At the final battle of Batoche, MacDonald witnessed another
example of military boneheadedness. By then the officers and men
were restless and ashamed. The government of Canada had some
8,000 troops in the field against a ragtag assortment of 1,000 Metis
and Indians, yet the rebels had made fools of the army, over and
over.

Partly it was the brilliance of Riel's adjutant general, Gabriel
Dumont, with his thrust-and-parry guerilla tactics against the rigid
plodding British-style lines. In late April Dumont had stopped

Middleton cold at Fish Creek near Batoche. On May 2 the Cree chief Poundmaker and 325 men with rifles, bows and arrows soundly defeated Lt. Col. W. D. Otter and 540 soldiers with cannons and automatic Gatling guns at Cut Knife Hill. Poundmaker could have massacred the government troops if he had chosen.

Now, at Batoche in mid-May, the rebels had run out of steam. Middleton's officers wanted to capitalize on the advantage. Their portly commander was an anachronism. He prowled the front lines in full view, once getting a bullet through his plumed helmet and joking about it. Yet he was strangely reluctant to attack.

After three days of careful skirmishing, relations were "strained" between the General and his officers, telegrapher MacDonald observed. That afternoon while Middleton was in his tent, 48-year-old Lt.-Col. Arthur Williams from Port Hope, an MP in civilian life, and Lt.-Col. Van Straubenzie, a grizzled old veteran still hurting from Crimean War wounds, led a charge. With Middleton shrieking "Why in the name of God don't you stop firing!", his army advanced and swept the field.

"The charge having been successful and virtually ending the campaign, the matter, by common consent, was dropped," MacDonald wrote later. Middleton immediately got off a telegraph to Alphonse Caron: "Have just made a general attack and carried the whole settlement. The men behaved splendidly. . . ."

Four days later telegrapher H. P. Dwight sent a play-by-play report to Caron: "Riel was captured at noon. . . .He is expected in half an hour but this is sent off by courier to Clark's Crossing before his arrival. . . .The boys in camp are jubilant over the capture. 3:45 p.m. . . .Riel is now being interviewed by General Middleton, while the men are standing idly round; no demonstration has been made. . . .Riel appears careworn and haggard; he has let his hair and beard grow long; he is dressed in poorer fashion than most of the half-breeds captured. While talking to General Middleton as could be seen from the outside of the tent, his eyes rolled from side to side with the look of a haunted man. . . ."

For 24 hours Middleton clamped a blackout on news despatches. Riel was slated to go to Ottawa for a trial and the cautious General feared angry mobs would attack his train if they knew about it. Then the venue was changed to Regina, Middleton lifted the ban and newsmen sprinted to the nearest telegraph set.

# A Gentleman of the Press

A new breed of Canadian journalist grew out of the rebellion — the war correspondent. Like reporters in any war, some of them were accurate and diligent; others relayed wild rumours as fact; all were hampered by censorship.

They came in several styles. The London *Times*, predictably, provided its man with his own tent, while the penurious Canadians slept wherever they could scrounge shelter. The Montreal *Star* writer affected a flowing black cape — a spectacular target which, fortunately, rebel sharpshooters missed. Two members of the Queen's Own Rifles doubled as correspondents for the Toronto *Globe* and Toronto *Mail*. But the most enterprising and long-lasting in the field was Howard Angus Kennedy, a redheaded Englishman, who had come to Canada to farm five years before and ended up as star reporter for the Montreal *Witness*.

Already at 24 Kennedy had interviewed Mark Twain, Edward Blake and Oscar Wilde. On April 2, the morning when Wandering Spirit and his braves massacred nine white settlers and missionaries at Frog Lake, Kennedy's editor asked, "Would you like to go out as our correspondent?" Kennedy grabbed his hat.

How to prepare for a war? He rushed to a bookstore and bought *Glimpses Through the Cannon Smoke* by a London newspaper veteran of the Crimea. It didn't help. Kennedy devised his own kit: a square black knapsack, two grey army blankets, a waterproof tarpaulin, an English whipcord riding suit and knee-high boots, a Stetson, spare shirt, socks and underwear, copy paper and pencils. A policeman friend gave him a six-shooter with an engraved silver butt. Kennedy had never fired a revolver in his life.

While Canada's troops mucked their way through ice, snow and sub-zero cold in the terrible wilds of northwestern Ontario, where parts of the CPR were not completed, Kennedy, being nonmilitary, was able to take a train through the U.S. to western Canada. At Swift Current he joined Col. Otter's force, moving north to relieve the siege on Battleford. He slapped a new $8 saddle on a bony $75 cayuse, noting sourly that the nag would have cost $7 in normal times. The *Witness* had warned him to go easy on expense money. On the march he lived like the army. He ate hard tack, salt pork and tea, and slept on the ground. Overnight temperatures were still below freezing. The first night he shared a colonel's tent.

"A jug full of water by my head was a solid lump of ice by morning," he wrote the next day. "The next night I chipped in with a dozen of the rank and file. With our 26 feet hobnobbing around the tent pole we kept each other good and warm."

At each rest stop while others napped Kennedy had to finish his despatch (some of which he wrote on horseback), get it cleared by Otter and pass it to a despatch rider who shuttled all messages to the nearest telegraph station. Military news had priority; press news had to wait. Sometimes his scoops were pirated along the way, by unscrupulous operators or rival reporters hanging around telegraph offices.

Even so, Kennedy's long vivid accounts were the best reporting of the war. He attended the relief of Battleford, then rode with Otter in the defeat at Cut Knife Hill. When the Indian chiefs surrendered Kennedy was there, writing verbatim reports in longhand on telegraph forms (he'd run out of copy paper). Then while most other correspondents went home he joined in the pursuit of Big Bear, who held 26 white captives from the Frog Lake Massacre.

Through rain, muskeg and mosquitoes the troops rode north. As the captives were released or escaped, Kennedy interviewed them. Then he sold his horse, took a flat-bottomed steamer along the North Saskatchewan River to Prince Albert and interviewed the captured Big Bear himself, "a stooping, wrinkled, ragged but still proud old Indian, clad in a medley of faded blanket, his bare feet chained together, his only ornament one large blue bead, a charm on a dirty string around his neck. . ."

When Kennedy got back to Montreal the *Witness* rewarded him with the kind of promotion that every roving reporter hates: they made him city editor.

# Endings, Beginnings

On Monday August 3, H. P. Dwight sent Adolphe Caron the message that eastern Canada had been awaiting. The telegraph system that had helped defeat the rebel chief now reported his doom: "Riel found guilty and sentenced to be hanged eighteenth Sept."

So, it was over. Riel was hanged, setting off generations of passion and recrimination. Poundmaker and Big Bear were sen-

A telegraph gang raising a pole in the Rockies. PROVINCIAL ARCHIVES OF ALBERTA.

Inside the first C.P.R. mountain telegraph office, 1880s. PUBLIC ARCHIVES OF CANADA C7632.

tenced to two years in prison. Dumont fled to Montana, returning years later after the amnesty to a West that no longer cared about him one way or the other.

Col. Williams, the hero of Batoche, died of "brain fever" before he got home. General Middleton, left-footed as ever, got into an embarrassing mess by appropriating some furs belonging to one of the rebels. ("Poor Middleton made an awful muck of it," Caron wrote to a friend.) It aroused such a stink in Parliament that Middleton retreated to England. There the grateful motherland made him Keeper of the Crown Jewels in the Tower of London. Howard Angus Kennedy went back to England too, but returned to Canada as a freelance writer and became secretary of the Canadian Authors Association.

Fred Gisborne, never one to hide his feelings, sent a thinly veiled suggestion to Caron: "I assume Mr. Hartley Gisborne will be among the recipients of the North West Medal," adding that his son's "cool courage evinced by his line-repairing trip between Battleford and Clark's Crossing via the Eagle Creek ravine is more commendable than the bravery displayed during Col. Otter's attack upon Poundmaker." Gisborne added that certain telegraph linemen and operators should also get medals "having displayed no ordinary courage standing by their isolated stations during many anxious days of imminent danger."

They should have, but didn't. Alfred and Maggie Lindeburgh stayed on at Kutawa, tending the line and adding a post office to their lonely way-station. It became a favourite oasis for settlers needing a hot cup of tea. Other telegraphers replaced the rotten old government telegraph poles with sturdy iron, which lasted another 40 years. Still others, who had been seconded to the rebellion by Montreal Telegraph and Great North Western, went home to their jobs in the east.

On Sunday November 8, William Van Horne of the CPR sent a telegram from Craigellachie, B.C., to his wife in Montreal: "Last rail laid this Saturday morning at 9:22 a.m. Quite well and very happy." A year later, on a mild rainy December afternoon in 1886, an all-Canadian telegraph system was hooked up between New Westminster and Canso, N.S. The first message vaulted from coast to coast in exactly three minutes. Day by day, the great Canadian distance was dwindling.

# Chapter 8

## Conscientious Fighting Sise

On the very day that Toronto cheered her troops aboard a westbound train for the Rebellion, the dutiful general manager of Bell Telephone did his bit for Queen and country. Charles Fleetford Sise scrawled in his diary on March 30, 1885: "Authorized Baker and Wainwright to continue salaries of employees at the front." Bell's men would have jobs waiting for them when the fighting was over, Sise added.

That he should attend to this detail personally, and before the fighting *began*, was entirely typical of this meticulous man. He also hired the office janitor, and placed all Bell's newspaper advertisements. How else could he be sure these chores were done to his exacting specifications?

Sise ran a shipshape business, as could be expected from one who at 22 was the youngest captain ever to sail out of New England. Even now at 50 he looked like a ship's skipper: a straight-backed, stocky five-foot-nine, with fierce Cossack moustache blooming from his square florid features. One glance from those ice-water blue eyes and recalcitrant employees found themselves looking around for a quarter-deck to swab.

111

For 35 years, most of them as president, C. F. Sise piloted the good ship Mother Bell through one storm after another. Alexander Bell fathered the telephone; Sise fathered the company. Without him, Bell Canada would never have survived its first decade. He trod on employees' toes, locked horns with governments, alienated entire provinces, but kept the Bell afloat while competitors foundered. He build it in his own image: efficient, frugal and abrasive. He once threw a newspaperman from his office by the scruff of the neck. Many people hated the Bell and "Conscientious Fighting" Sise (as employees parodied his name behind his back), but they respected him.

Sise cared so deeply for the Bell that in its darkest hours he loaned it money from his own pocket. Yet unlike most of his contemporaries he did not grow up in love with telephones or telegraphs. It was a marriage of convenience. National Bell in Boston, having been forced to acquire the company when no Canadian could or would buy it, needed a strong man to sort it out. Sise needed a job.

Born to a prominent New Hampshire seafaring family, he had prowled the world in sailing ships in every kind of weather. In the Civil War he fought for the South at Shiloh and later ran shadowy missions through the Yankee sea blockade. After the war he headed an insurance company until it went broke. A Boston bank was then looking for a president, but people in the North were fussy about hiring a former rebel. If Canada had such qualms, National Bell didn't really care; Canada had no choice. The Bell's proposition to Sise was a godsend: $30 a day and expenses, as special agent setting up the new Canadian company.

To a traveller who had lived in England, celebrated New Year's Eve in Paris and sailed around Cape Horn and the Cape of Good Hope, Montreal in 1881 was no thrill. As the evening lamplighters hurried from post to post along St. Catherine Street, the gentle glow of gaslight in their wake shone down on mudholes, ruts and horse manure. The horse cars ran only as far as Guy. Only recently coffins had been removed from the downtown Roman Catholic burial ground, now renamed Dominion Square.

In winter the snow rose up in towering banks along the streets with a narrow trail down the centre for carts and sleighs, and paths, sometimes more like tunnels, along the boardwalks. Montreal winters were so notorious that the Winter Carnival booklet in the 1880s was compelled to explain that local snow was really "like feathers" and that local thermometers did *not* have to be brought indoors to thaw, contrary to a scurrilous report in the London *Times*.

Every spring the St. Lawrence River flooded the lower town, 12 feet deep in places. People rowed to work along St. James and McGill Streets. In 1886 flood waters would reach far up Beaver Hall Hill. In summer the streets of Montreal, like most other cities, were veiled in dust. Hundreds of citizens suffered from inflamed eyes and sore throats.

Not long after his arrival Sise received a tempting job offer from Boston. He turned it down with regret: ". . .You can understand that if I give up my position and the Board were to resign, the stock would go to pot and the Company would be seriously injured. I have never done an unfair thing knowingly, and don't want to in this case. You perhaps know how much it costs me to put aside any scheme which might lead to my return to Boston. . . ."

He tackled his assignment with the stern efficiency that ruled his life. A quick study disclosed 2,165 telephones in eastern Canada: 690 of the Edison variety and 1,475 of Bell's. Sise predicted he would triple Montreal's phone population to 1,000 and raise the eastern Canada total to 5,000 within a year. It took three years, but that was a miracle considering the problems he faced.

It was smooth enough in the beginning. He quickly bought out Dominion Telegraph's telephone interests and got its telephone superintendent Lewis B. McFarlane in the bargain. Private telephone exchanges in Toronto, Windsor and London were happy to sell. Hugh Baker accepted $22,500 for his Hamilton plant.

That master tactician, Sir Hugh Allan, gave Sise a nasty summer. The price for Montreal Telegraph's telephone holdings was $75,000 said Sir Hugh, and by the way, he was leaving for England that night and if Sise didn't buy immediately the deal was off. It was a bluff, of course. Sise didn't buy immediately, but after a sharp scolding from the parent company for excessive spending, he was authorized to pay Montreal Telegraph in Bell stock.

Hamilton's ambitious Hugh C. Baker meanwhile had applied for and received a national charter, at the parent company's behest. Baker evidently expected the head office to be in Toronto, with himself as general manager, but he had to settle for managership of Ontario district. The Bell company was formalized with head office in Montreal. Sise, now learning to like his life in the boondocks, became vice-president and general manager. Then he set out to accomplish his dream: a telephone network across Canada, excluding British Columbia which he considered beyond the bounds of geography and common sense.

All the ingredients were waiting. In 1877 Alexander Graham Bell's father-in-law had brought Nova Scotia its first two telephone sets for use in Cape Breton's Caledonia mines. In 1878 G. & G. Flewwelling Company of Hampton, N.B., installed that province's first two phones. Flewwelling sold wooden matches for one cent a gross.

"They were made from straight grain pine," remembered New Brunswick telephone pioneer Charles Kee, long after. "They made a report like a flintlock musket and the flame often scorched the seat of the homespun pants on which they were struck, while the fumes of burning brimstone made one think a small hell had just broken out. But the Flewwelling match would stand up against a Saxby gale!"

That same year in St. John's, John Delaney the postmaster and John Higgins the meteorologist linked Newfoundland's first two phones, while telegrapher Horace McDougall, the Bell agent in Winnipeg, finally received the pair he'd ordered months before. He paid double customs duty, once on the Boston-to-Brantford shipment, again on the Brantford relay to Winnipeg via Minneapolis.

By 1879 Western Union and Dominion Telegraph had exchanges in Saint John and Halifax. Sise soon bought them out, along with Horace McDougall's Winnipeg exchange. By 1883 Regina had Bell telephones in a hotel, a livery stable, the Mounted Police barracks and the Lieutenant-Governor's residence. Four years later Peter Lamont, the Bell local agent, opened an exchange in a bookstore on South Railway St.

In Newfoundland, where Melville Bell had never applied for patents, Sise momentarily stubbed his toe. The Anglo-American Telegraph claimed exclusive telephone rights, under its 50-year telegraph agreement on the island. Its general manager was still Alexander MacKay, appointed nearly 30 years before by Cyrus Field. This shaggy old veteran, one of the first telegraphers in British North America, was totally unversed in telephony. He thought the telephone would enable him to talk across the ocean. When he found it wouldn't, he lost interest and agreed to use Bell equipment on a royalty basis.

Meanwhile Prince Edward Island, having waited overly long for the telegraph, decided that the fastest way to get a telephone company was to start its own. In 1885 six local businessmen, in cahoots with the local Bell agent, bought out Bell's rights and property, for $2,500 and 40 shares in their own new company. The Charlottetown *Examiner* was pleased: "We will soon be able to sit down in our offices or house and have a quiet chat with friends or others in Tignish, Alberton, Souris, Georgetown. . . ." Earlier that year, Edmonton telegrapher Alex Taylor rang up storekeeper H. W. McKenney in nearby St. Albert, on Alberta's first phones (Bell equipment).

With control or partnership in five provinces, plus Newfoundland and the districts of Saskatchewan and Alberta, Bell seemed to have the makings of a national telephone system. In the end, the embattled Sise was lucky to hang on to Ontario and Quebec. For years the Bell was in perpetual crisis.

Of its initial half-million dollars worth of capital, nearly $200,000 went in the first year to purchase telephone companies. Bell telephone stock went on public sale in December, 1880, at $100 a share. In January, Sise wrote the parent company, "The stock is selling quietly among good people." In fact, the silence was deafening. By September Sise admitted that the Bell was "working solely on money loaned the company by me from personal funds. Of course this will right itself but I would like to sell a little more stock and see the Bank a/c in better shape. . . ."

Customers were slow to sign up. On his first sales trip to the Maritimes Lewis McFarlane pounded Saint John's boardwalks for two weeks and landed one new subscriber. Since it took two to telephone, he had to cast that one loose. Another prospect, upon having the phone explained to him, shrugged, "Why they had those things in China 2000 years ago! Goodbye, young man." Three weeks of canvassing in Ottawa likewise drew a blank. McFarlane stored his equipment until demand picked up.

When the Hamilton-Toronto long distance line was completed late in 1881, reluctant subscribers had to be coaxed with two days of free calling. In 1886, when the Ottawa-Montreal long distance line opened at $1 per call, subscribers balked again. Why phone when you could send a telegram for 25¢? Again, Bell had to offer free service until users got the hang of it.

J. A. Dawson's English Drug Hall in Montreal offered a public telephone (10¢ a call) in 1881. Along with the delights of Extra

Charles Fleetford Sise was the founder of the Bell Telephone
Company of Canada and in 1890 became the Company's second
President. He served in this capacity until 1915. BELL CANADA
TELEPHONE HISTORICAL COLLECTION.

Strong English Peppermints, Pure Norway Cod Liver Oil, Ashton's and Parson's Homeopathic Medicine and Sweet Bye and Bye Bouquet Soap, Dawson's advertisements recounted the advantages of the telephone.

"Instantaneous communication with, and reply from, more than 700 different places in the City and Suburbs!" cried Dawson. "Direct communications at all hours of the night, day and Sundays. . . .To telephone is more satisfactory and more direct than telegraphing as you *talk* direct to each other, without limit to number of words, thus avoiding any possibility of misunderstanding."

The maddening part was that the telephone was already infinitely better than Aleck Bell's original device. An improved transmitter — featuring carbon granules to control the flow of current — made hearing almost easy over short distances. By 1885 most of central Canada was strung with a new hard-drawn copper wire, stronger than annealed copper and a much better conductor. It had only one drawback: linemen had to avoid nicking the wire during installation; otherwise it snapped in cold weather.

Linemen were learning other lessons by trial and error. The 18-man crew building the Hamilton-Toronto long distance line was a typical seat-of-the-pants aggregation.

"Such a gang!" groaned the foreman in his memoirs. "Not one of them had any experience in pole line construction. There were butchers, bakers and candlestick makers, blacksmiths, tinsmiths, old soldiers, with a few honest-to-goodness farmers in the bunch. Our tools consisted of ordinary crowbars and ditching spoons purchased from the local hardware store. The poles ranged from 30 to 50 feet. . . .We literally had to invent tools as we went along. . . ."

At Waterdown they ran into rock and resorted to dynamite for the first time, tamping it into a small hole and covering it with a large rock, according to instructions. The rock catapulted into a pigpen, killing the occupant; the foreman had to pay for it.

The same year in St. Thomas, Ont., lineman Charles Stringer fell 35 feet from a pole. An interested crowd gathered to watch blood pour from Stringer's ears and nose, until a doctor carted him off to his boarding house. Miraculously he broke no bones although when he went home six days later, something of a celebrity, the London *Free Press* noted "it will be some time before he can use one of his legs to advantage."

By middecade the durable Stringers of the business had strung long distance wire from Montreal to Windsor. On good days, telephone users could hear 200 miles. A typical wall phone was a 30-inch slab of polished oak or walnut with three boxes mounted vertically on its gleaming face. At top, the ringer box held a long black receiver cradled on one side, a crank on the other, and two noble steel bells like the goggling eyes of some demented monster. The middle box, with its hole-in-the-wall mouthpiece, housed the transmitter. The bottom "battery box" held a bottle of acid with a zinc rod. Its lid doubled as a message shelf.

To signal Central, as the operator was known, the subscriber briskly twirled the crank (180 revolutions per minute was recommended). It set up a shrill ringing in the house and all along the line, and at the central switchboard caused one of several small metal tabs to drop. The operator pushed it back in place, plugged a cord into the appropriate jack and said, "Yes?"

"Give me Arthur's Grocery," shouted the subscriber. (To the telephone companies' distress, people *always* shouted, and never called by numbers. Directories were appearing — Toronto published the first in 1879, Winnipeg had one with 42 names in 1881 — but why bother looking up a number when the operator knew it by heart?)

"Hoy, Hoy," responded Arthur when his phone rang, using the salutation (from "Ahoy") beloved by Melville Bell. When the conversation ended the caller cranked one short ring, alerting Central to disconnect the line.

The operator was probably a male and probably listening in anyway. Likely he was a refugee from a telegraph office, perhaps one of the men or boys left jobless by Erastus Wiman's Great North Western merger. Very likely he also bad-mouthed the customers.

"We have received several complaints from subscribers about the language used by the boys who relieve regular operators at midday," Lewis McFarlane warned Bell's Montreal chief operator in 1884. "The tone is more or less impatient and the answers are given in a short and surly manner. There is also a tendency to find fault with subscribers."

The boys would have to go. They were one reason that subscribers were resisting the telephone. Another reason was the chaotic rates situation. In one town rates might be $20 a year, in another $40, whatever the local manager felt the traffic would bear. At Canada's first telephone convention in Niagara Falls in 1880, delegates half-heartedly talked of charging per call rather than a flat rate. It might have eased their financial plight but they didn't adopt it. Instead they voted to use "Hello" as a standard response — which most subscribers and operators ignored until the 1890s.

With more money going out than coming in, it took all Sise's pennypinching skill to balance the books. He hired a janitor at $8 a month, noting that the duties included lighting fires and cleaning windows. He placed advertisements in the Montreal *Gazette* and *Herald*, for 4¢ and 3¢ a line respectively. He paid off an inventor for a minor patent with a $240 "Ledoux family sleigh, complete with pole and cover."

When the unfortunate lineman Charles Stringer fell on his head, Sise demanded and received a complete financial accounting:

| | |
|---|---:|
| Doctor's bill | $10.00 |
| Geo. Dutton for nursing Stringer | 5.00 |
| Cab fare | 2.00 |
| Brandy | .60 |
| St. Jacobs Oil | .50 |
| Lent for hotel bill | 6.75 |
| Stringer's railroad fare | .45 |
| | $25.30 |

When the Ontario division's clerical costs ran to $286 a month, compared to $130 in Quebec and the Maritimes, Sise sent manager Hugh Baker a testy query. Later, Baker requisitioned a collection book for daily returns.

"Is it not possible that this book which would take one half a man's time to keep up, is more interesting than valuable?" Sise complained. "I wish you would look into these matters and see if it is not possible to do a little pruning without injury to service."

Yet again Sise rapped Baker's knuckles, over linemen's food bills: "I am surprised to see the extravagance of whoever is in charge. In one bill we pay for pickles $5 in two weeks; cheese, currants, spice, raisins and biscuits; $2 worth of sugar in four days and etc. I have camped out a great deal but never yet found nutmegs to be a necessity."

While harassed by wastrels and nutmeg freaks from within, he fought a continuing holding action with the world at large. The

Toronto *Globe*, assuming its favourite God-like stance, scolded the Bell for making employees work on Sunday. "With all places of business closed, the number of those who would find occasion to use the telephone on Sunday must be very small. . . .In nine cases out of ten all that is needed is for those requiring cabs and other things on Sunday to send their orders on Saturday. The tendency of one or another of our institutions for the public accommodation to encroach on the day of rest is to be deplored. . . .If the citizens do without the street railway for the sake of securing Sabbath quiet, if the telegraph wires are closed, they will hardly approve of the attempt to compel the young women in the telephone office to work seven days a week."

Working on the Sabbath was not actually illegal. Everything else seemed to be. After Bell bought the New Brunswick operations, McFarlane arrived to take over the Fredericton plant. The city marshal arrested him for doing business without a license. McFarlane went to court, where the magistrate ordered him to pay a $2 license fee.

"Do it," whispered his lawyer, "Outsiders don't win court cases around here." So McFarlane, one day to be president of Bell, paid up and grabbed an early train out of town. The marshal, who received a commission on all licenses sold, was distressed at the modest $2 levy. He had hoped for $15.

At St. Jerome, Que., the Bell bought a small exchange. All subscribers supposedly had leases stating that their phone could be removed if not paid for. One subscriber reneged on his rent. A Bell foreman and lineman took out his phone. It turned out he *didn't* have a lease. The Bell men were arrested, handcuffed and condemned to one hour in jail for theft of their own company's property.

Unnerved by this frontier justice, the foreman prepared to resign. The Bell coaxed him to stay. He began building a pole line in Prescott, Ont., and was jailed again. This time he quit and went to the Yukon.

# "People on the Streets will not be Safe!"

Prescott, like most towns, hated telephone poles. They were the air pollution of the eighties. As long as every new subscriber needed a

Effects of a sleet storm in Fergus, Ont., 1908. BELL CANADA TELEPHONE HISTORICAL COLLECTION.

separate line, skies and streets became a jungle of poles, each with as many as 18 crossarms. For 25 years the Bell battled for the right — supposedly assured in its Dominion charter — to place poles on streets.

Letters to editors deplored the "great big unsightly ship's masts." Outraged merchants complained that poles blocked customers' view of their stores. Firemen claimed they hampered firefighting. Some towns flatly banned them, and others had telephone pole vigilantes. One night in Quebec City a dozen Bell workmen slipped out at two a.m. to raise a 40-foot pole bearing 70 wires. "Fortunately," exulted the Quebec *Daily Telegraph*, "the police and a number of citizens were on the grounds to repel any attempt."

The *Telegraph* and its publisher, James Carrell, led the anti-pole crusade. Carrell once took an axe to a pole outside his office. His paper gleefully reported any citizen who refused to let telephone lines run over his rooftop; when one Quebecker threatened to charge the Bell $400 for the privilege, Carrell was ecstatic. When a telephone pole blew down one night, Carrell raged. No one was hurt, but they *might* have been! "People on the streets will not be safe," the *Telegraph* thundered, and seized the opportunity to settle another score. "Montreal has decided to levy a tax on each pole but in Quebec where we have in the magistrate's chair such a poor specimen of humanity to rule over our destinies, is it any wonder that our streets are obstructed?"

Only the Montreal *Star* clung to a semblance of humour: "Boys can't fly kites for these wires; good natured gentlemen slightly at sea can't steer their way home through the poles in early morning. Housewives can't see what's going on in the streets from their windows; tobogganing is fatal; policemen can't catch thieves; runaway horses smash their vehicles; and the poles don't understand the damage they are doing, and therefore it is useless to berate them as we do our equally wooden City Councillors."

It was no laughing matter for the Bell. In Wallaceburg, Ont., a runaway horse dashed its carriage and occupants against a pole with serious injuries. Two courts held the Bell responsible. Quebec City in 1881 banned poles from its streets. When Bell, citing its charter, appealed to the provincial legislature, that august body ruled that the Dominion charter was invalid on provincial matters and, there being no long-distance connection to other provinces, it *was* a Quebec matter. Again, the courts upheld the decision.

Bell then procured "enabling acts" in each province, to reinforce the federal charter, but the battle of the poles raged on. Finally in 1905, when it mattered less (technology had then produced a cable that carried 400 pairs of lines) the Privy Council ruled that the federal charter had been valid all along.

Conscientious Fighting Sise could have used that ruling in 1885. It would have brightened an otherwise miserable year. In January he wrote, "Decisions against us in Ottawa" — grimmer news than his terse note indicated. The Minister of Agriculture, then in charge of communications, had voided Bell's telephone patent.

Canada's Patent Act stipulated that any person should be able to obtain a patented article upon application; also, after a specified time from the date of patent, that article could not be imported into Canada. The Minister interpreted this to require public sale of telephones rather than rental. He also noted that rubber handles for Bell's phones were being imported. Thus, in his view, both aspects of the Act were violated — and his ruling was final.

To some of its friends and all its enemies, this looked like the end of Bell. It opened the field to competition. But Sise knew how hard it was to run a solvent telephone company. He reasoned, correctly, that Bell's head start and superior service would keep it ahead of all competitors.

He had one other major crisis that year. Smallpox, always a lurking terror in pioneer Canada, turned into an epidemic. By mid-August 120 Montrealers were dead and 500 more were ill. Sise ordered every Bell employee vaccinated, under threat of dismissal.

Many Canadians feared and hated vaccination because they didn't understand it. The anti-vaccination forces claimed it put "cow's blood" into human veins. By September 28, with Montrealers dying like flies — 3,000 before the epidemic ended — vaccination was made compulsory for all. The next day and night, men with torches and clubs attacked City Hall and a drugstore, smashed windows and set fires. Then they headed for the telephone exchange because, the rumour went, smallpox was transmitted over telephone wires.

Conscientious Fighting Sise issued axe handles to several sturdy men from his workshop and stationed them outside the door. Just then a militia regiment happened by and the mob fled. The soldiers (led by Col. Van Straubenzie, hero of the North West Rebellion) restored order. After that they travelled from door to door with doctors, until vaccination was completed. Sise paid each workman a $2 bonus for guard duty, and went back to running a phone company.

His job became no easier. The ramshackle wooden frame telephone exchanges were ravaged by fire, once in Montreal, once in Quebec and three times in Toronto during the decade. In 1887–89, to trim his ship, Sise had to sell majority interests in Nova Scotia and New Brunswick. Bell's empire now had dwindled to Quebec, Ontario, Manitoba and the Territories.

## "A Picket Fence Around Himself"

Somehow, Sise found time for voluminous correspondence with his customers. He wrote in strong clear longhand — resisting typewriters for years after their invention — with capitalized nouns cruising through his sentences like brigantines in full sail. To a hospital begging free telephone service, he diplomatically offered a half-price. To a Toronto lawyer complaining that his phone was being used in a "frivolous manner" (his children and servants were always on the line) Sise was courteous:

"We are aware that servants and others abuse the service, using the lines for trivial conversations and also holding them at times for half an hour while others are waiting, but we can have no control over such persons."

To customers afflicted with wrong number calls he was sympathetic: "I can quite understand your annoyance in this matter. At one time a laundry had No. 666 and my own number was 360. Stupid people, wanting the laundry, would ask for 'Three sixes,' whereupon I would be called with the most peremptory demands to know 'Where is my shirt?'. . ." He promised to change the subscriber's number.

Sometimes he even permitted himself a small joke:

"We really do not think that the public has cause to complain of a Corporation whose dividends have averaged five percent, whose stock has never been watered. . .and we fail to see what injury we have inflicted upon the Canadian public, since we charge nothing for the aesthetic manner in which we have decorated the streets with poles and wires."

But any who violated his code felt the sting of his sarcasm.

When a manufacturer demanded that Bell use his cement since he used Bell's phones, President Sise (as now he was) ticked him off: "We do not feel called upon to purchase the goods of everyone who uses our lines, even if to do so would be considered what you term 'British fair play.'"

Every employee knew Conscientious Fighting Sise's tough standards. Once when he toured a regional office, the watchman barred his way.

"Do you know who I am?" said Sise.

"No and it doesn't matter," said the man. "You can't get into the building without a permit."

The local superintendent, tagging at Sise's heels, went ashen. "I can fire him, sir, he's only a temporary employee," he murmured.

"No, give him a permanent job," ordered Sise. "And give him two dollars a week increase. He's a damn good watchman."

But woe to any Bell person who let him down. A businessman once asked for a reference on a former employee. "If the person possessed the qualities upon which you ask information, he would still be in our service," Sise replied. "Persons of 'capacity, ability and integrity' we retain if possible. We made no effort to retain this man."

He expected Bell offices to be as trim as he had once kept his three-masted schooner, the *Annie Sise*. On inspection tours his inquiring finger checked the furniture for dust. Staff men were required to change their celluloid collars and shave daily. He dealt out tongue lashings to office boys and managers alike if he thought they needed it. He was never a buddy to his people. "He kept a picket fence around himself," a contemporary said.

Yet when he could remain incognito, and so not be accused of frivolity, his dry wit emerged. Returning from a fine lunch at the St. James Club one cold day, he met the company messenger labouring up Beaver Hall Hill, blowing on his bare hands.

"You work for the Bell, don't you?" said Sise. "Why doesn't Mr. Sise give you mitts for a day like this?"

"That old bird doesn't give us anything he doesn't have to," growled the messenger.

"He doesn't?" said the president. "I'm glad you told me. Never had much use for him myself. But I'll talk to the old buzzard and there'll be mitts for you boys tomorrow, you'll see." And of course there were.

It was surely a lonely life for Sise. He ran his home as neatly as his offices and ships. His sons, by a second marriage, were 40 to 45 years younger than he. The age gap and Sise's innate reserve bred little intimacy. Sise warned them to drink moderately and in respectable surroundings: "If I catch you in a barroom one of us will get a licking!"

Sometimes he played poker for small stakes and wrote cheques for his losses promptly but with obvious pain. He liked to read biography, history or, best of all, the marine reports in the Boston *Transcript*.

A few friends, mostly outside the telephone company, sometimes dared to chaff him out of his sober self. One such was Father Jolicoeur, parish priest of Ste. Catherine de Port Neuf, who had introduced the telephone to his flock. One chill January day Sise told the priest, "I'm sick to death of this weather. I wish I could get away to a warmer place."

"Yes, yes," nodded Father Jolicoeur, "But. . .you are a Protestant, are you not?"

"Yes, of course."

"Then patience, my friend. Your hope for a warmer climate will not go unrewarded."

Already Sise surely must have wondered if hell were much hotter than the President's chair at Bell.

# Chapter 9

## Over the Hills and Far Away

To the Holy Trinity of telephones — Melville Bell, Thomas Henderson and Charles F. Sise — the new province of British Columbia was a wart on the nose of progress, a Never-Never-Land in an impossible location, inhabited by eccentrics who did not understand their place. These curious pushy creatures, far over the mountains, beyond the ken of civilized men, kept asking for telephones!

The men of Bell ignored or mishandled their requests so assiduously that B.C. finally gave up and went its own way. Eventually its reigning British Columbia Telephone Company became an American subsidiary, and lived happily ever after.

In particular, the Bell trio managed to ruffle the good manners of Robert Burns McMicking. This bright-eyed young man with the dark wavy hair, Fu Manchu moustache and brave attempt at chin whiskers was the king of west coast telegraphy. He was also an amiable soul. Only once before in B.C.'s recollection had he shown a trace of pique. In 1872 when the editor of the New Westminster *Mainland Guardian* accused him of favoritism in handling press despatches, McMicking called him "evil, unscrupulous" and "scurrilous." For him, that was a temper tantrum.

At other times McMicking was the essence of patience, courtesy and rhetoric. He was a letter writer *par excellence*. His voluminous epistles rolled in on his readers like waves. Each sentence, decked out in verbal curlicues, stepped forth to doff its plumed hat, bow deep from the waist and present the compliments of Robert Burns McMicking. Once he composed a sentence 165 words long. He brimmed with Victorian politeness. Only a professional at the art of the snub could crack McMicking's civility. C. F. Sise was that man.

When the telephone reached B.C., McMicking at 35 was already on his third career. Born one of 12 children on a Queenston Heights farm in Ontario's Niagara peninsula, he took up telegraphy at 13 when his father died. After five years with Montreal Telegraph, he joined the Overlanders, an idealistic band of adventures who trekked across Canada to the Cariboo gold fields in the summer of 1862.

The main group, 150 strong, captained by McMicking's older brother Thomas, rallied at Winnipeg and moved west at about 25 miles a day. Each night they pushed their ponies, mules and Red River carts into a tight protective triangle. They reached Edmonton, tired and tattered beyond recognition, rested a while, and scrabbled on through the Rockies. Whirling down the Thompson and Fraser rivers by raft, three of them drowned. At the gold fields, finally, they discovered the only fortunes being made were by purveyors of flour, bacon and sugar at $1 a pound.

McMicking quickly got out of prospecting and into store-keeping. Later he resumed his first profession with the Collins Overland Telegraph. In 1866 as telegrapher in charge of Quesnel office, he had to relay down the line the glum news that the Atlantic cable had succeeded and the Overland was doomed.

In the next dozen years McMicking married and became superintendent of the government telegraph system. He was also appointed a justice of the peace and coroner of Yale, B.C. And he wrote letters. More than one recipient may have fallen asleep over them, but those who hung on to the end always found a hidden nugget. In 1872, for example, McMicking turned the sordid business of asking for a raise into an art form.

"Touching a subject of more interest to myself than the company," he wrote his boss, with a deferential little tug of the forelock, "I beg to ask that my salary be increased to at least $2,400 per annum. The experience of one year has taught me to make this request and I do so with the kindest feeling and purest motives, finding the wear and tear of being pitchforked, as it were, from one extremity of the line to the other, at a moment's notice, in all sorts of weather, and by varied means of transportation, as well as the rate of subsistence when at home, too great for the present remuneration." After all that the telegraph company could hardly refuse a raise.

Behind his candy-coated words McMicking was an accomplished electrician. Inevitably, he was onto the telephone before almost anyone else in British Columbia. William Wall, a young mechanic at the Dunsmuir and Diggle coal mines near Nanaimo, beat McMicking by a few months. After reading about Bell's invention in *Scientific American*, probably in autumn 1877, Wall made two simple box phones using copper bands from empty powder kegs, a borrowed magnet, and photographic tintypes (reportedly of his wife) for the diaphragms. They worked well enough over the few miles between the mine and the loading dock at Departure Bay.

McMicking meanwhile had won the B.C. agency for Bell phones from Thomas Henderson. In March, 1878, two instruments arrived in Victoria over the long tortuous route through the United States and up the Pacific coast. Happy as a child, McMicking held a demonstration for Victoria's bigwigs, with the usual round of whistling, singing and cries of recognition and delight.

He then ran an ad in the *Colonist* offering "Cheap and Quick Communication by DIRECT SPEECH" at $25 per year rental for a pair of phones. A year and a half later, with not one rental to his credit, he had to sell his house and furniture and borrow money from friends. Still, he assured Thomas Henderson, he was "sanguine that quite a trade can be established." Unfortunately, a San Francisco supplier was *selling* telephones $5 cheaper than the Bell annual *rental* fee. Did Bell's charter protect it in British Columbia or not, McMicking wondered? "Am I desiring too much when I ask to be protected in such work?"

He had reason to worry. As he penned his complaint, the proprietor of W. J. Jeffree's Clothing Establishment, at Government and Yates streets, was stringing telephone wires to his cousin W. J. Pendray's soap works, near the mud flats where the Empress Hotel now stands. Jeffree had been in San Francisco to buy "a complete assortment of Gents', Youths', and Boys' clothing" and brought home two phones so he could talk to the soap factory he had secretly financed. By January 1880, silent partner Jeffree was riding herd on cousin Pendray by telephone.

McMicking had now officially retired from telegraphy, with a farewell purse of gold coins from his associates. It sent him into unprecedented flights of prose: "Such genuine magnanimity is seldom thrust upon a retiring officer unprovoked, and it is by no means an easy task, my dear friends, to command language sufficiently expressive to convey my inward sentiments of sincere regard for this unmistakeable tribute for which I thank you most sincerely. . . ." His friends gathered that McMicking was pleased.

Now he threw himself completely into the newly founded Victoria and Esquimalt Telephone Company (R. B. McMicking, general manager). On February 24 he ordered from Henderson 50 telephones at $4 each. On March 4 he repeated the request. A shack behind Victoria's Wells Fargo building became the telephone office, a pole line went up, and wire arrived promptly on order from San Francisco. Still no telephones. On April 2, McMicking wired Brantford. No reply. He telegraphed again four days later. Henderson sent a telephone pamphlet but no phones. McMicking sent a third telegram and a letter stating "the case is urgent."

It became apparent that Henderson, the Baptist minister, and Melville Bell, the elocution professor, either had no interest in serving British Columbia or were incompetent, or both. Only now did Henderson inform his B.C. agent of two years that he would need a license to operate Bell telephones. McMicking was flabbergasted, but generously shouldered the blame "in not making myself acquainted with the formula necessary." He pleaded for phones *and* license. Neither had arrived by mid-May.

Melville Bell now joined in the correspondence. It was evident he hadn't the faintest idea what Henderson had been up to. McMicking told his story again, feverishly, for the restless officers and shareholders of the Victoria and Esquimalt were snapping at his heels. Finally on May 31 came word that the phones were about to be shipped. But Bell had another small surprise: McMicking would have to pay the transportation. "Is it intended that the charges on all shipments are to be paid out of my commission?" McMicking demanded, with a trace of pique. He politely thanked the Brantford bunglers for a recent pamphlet but added "the system here is somewhat different from that treated therein." They had sent the wrong pamphlet.

On June 15 the telephones arrived, three months after the order. McMicking thanked Brantford profusely for the shipment, adding plaintively "I very much regret the absence of transmitters. . . ." The company started up anyway, without transmitters. The 50 sets were rented quickly and McMicking forwarded $171.50 to Bell, retaining his $30.30 commission. He gave his own phone the number "43" — his year of birth.

Robert Burns McMicking, first General Manager of the Victoria and Esquimalt Telephone Company. BRITISH COLUMBIA TELEPHONE COMPANY.

He also ordered more sets but with no more success. By now he was dealing with Sise, who seemed to know little of the earlier arrangements and care less. In September he took the Bell agency away from McMicking (who had held it personally) and awarded it to his employer, the Victoria and Esquimalt Company. McMicking was dumbfounded.

"Where is my reward?" he wrote. "Is it in having the props knocked out from under me without warning?" As recently as April Melville Bell had written that he would be "glad that the Agency remain in your hands." McMicking had been double-crossed. Sise ignored the complaint and worsened his public relations by raising the rates B.C. would have to pay for telephones and transmitters.

In October the long awaited second shipment arrived — without the customs clearance certificate. McMicking put up a $90 bond to get the instruments out of hock and sent Sise the sharpest note of his literary career: "Be kind enough to forward the necessary certificate with all possible dispatch."

The Victoria and Esquimalt Company was now totally disenchanted with the Bell. In November, Secretary-Treasurer Edgar Crow Baker, a leathery ex-naval officer who minced no words, rapped out some terms that Sise would understand: the sudden rental increase was unacceptable; the Bell's treatment of McMicking was a breach of faith. But a December note in Baker's personal diary ("Bad news from Montreal re Telephones") indicated that Sise would not be budged. He won the round but he left a legacy of ill will in B.C.

McMicking got over it. Soon he was planning a cable beneath the Strait of Juan de Fuca; a fire alarm system hooked into the Victoria phone exchange; a little electrical business on the side (before the decade ended he had wired the new Hotel Vancouver). And as general manager of the Victoria and Esquimalt he was hustling new business.

The first telephones on the B.C. mainland went to the Indian village of Metlakatla, near the present site of Prince Rupert. McMicking didn't have to solicit the sale; William Duncan, the unordained and unorthodox Anglican missionary of Metlakatla, came to him. Duncan, who later ran afoul of the church for his views, believed that the quickest way to the hearts of his flock, and possibly to heaven, was with a minimum of doctrine. A sturdy fellow with ruddy Yorkshireman's face and eyes bracketed with wind wrinkles, he stressed sensible secular matters such as teaching the Indians football, setting up a choir and a brass band, celebrating the Queen's birthday with lantern shows, running a sawmill and a store — and connecting the two by telephone.

Another celebrated customer of 1880 was Andrew Onderdonk of Yale, B.C., the contractor building the mountainous portion of the Canadian Pacific Railway — miles of tunnel to be blasted from granite, hundreds of bridges and trestles spanning rivers and gorges. Onderdonk was McMicking's kind of man — impeccably groomed, courteous of manner, a gentleman transplanted to the wilderness. He wanted 15 miles of telephone between his two-storey Yale home, known locally as the "palace," and the main tunnel. McMicking was pleased to oblige.

Upon winning the contract, he took a crash course in building telephone lines. His San Francisco supplier of wire, always more helpful than the Bell representatives in Canada, told him what size wire to use and how many phones to install per circuit. McMicking then hired a contractor even greener than himself and coached him.

"Draw the line up pretty taut and *be sure the poles are solid,*" wrote McMicking. "If you are not posted on making a joint, go to the telegraph office and the young man there will show you. In any case you better borrow a vice and a pair of pliers from him." McMicking apparently didn't question the credentials of a contractor who didn't even own pliers.

The wire shipment was late, with two bales missing. The telephones were late. The contractor wanted more money. McMicking wrote gloomily, "With all these losses, delays and extras I fear my contract, like yours, will go under. I calculated too close for such experiences. I don't get any coin till the whole thing is in working order, but if it should fail to work Eh! What then?"

But somehow these two innocents finished the longest telephone line in B.C. by year's end. McMicking's commission was $29.25.

# The Telephone Boys

As service crept steadily through the province — New Westminster and Port Moody by 1884; a line into Tilley's bookstore in Granville village by 1885; small private systems in the Okanagan later still — British Columbians grew acquainted with a phenomenon already known to Bell subscribers in the east: telephone boys. With Canadian women not yet classified as people (they were still

30 years away from getting the vote), it seemed right and proper in the eyes of God and the Queen for men to be telephone operators.

There were a few exceptions. In Montreal a half-dozen or more women cracked the sex barrier, among them the Lebeau sisters, Maude, Flora and Lillie. In Hamilton, in October, 1880, C. F. Sise of Bell Canada, Hugh Baker of the Ontario division and the president of the American company paused amid weightier deliberations to ponder women operators. Their skepticism is mirrored in the minutes of the meeting: "The President of the American company said he believed that they were employed somewhere, he did not know where, had heard nothing against them and saw no reason why they could not be used." Beulah and Minnie Howell, cousins of the poet Pauline Johnson, thus became Hamilton's first women operators. Two years later, Ida Cates, a pretty little thing with a halo of curls and a tiny rosebud mouth, was handling Winnipeg's switchboard. They called her "the voice with the smile."

But since most telegraph operators had been males, since all men knew that running a switchboard required a brilliant technical mind, and since those same men knew without doubt that males possessed superior intellect, there were few skirts in telephone offices for the first five years. Some male operators were only 13 and 14, but leather lunged, saucy and cocky. Like telegraph operators before them, they revelled in their mystique: they knew something that common people didn't.

This naturally made them popular with women. So long and ardent were some of the personal chats between switchboard boys and female subscribers that the first Halifax director in 1886 admonished, "Operators cannot hold conversations with you. Their duty is to answer calls only." Elsewhere these duties were more complex. In Montreal in 1889, 17-year-old Frank Field worked the switchboard from nine p.m. to seven a.m., seven days a week, for $25 a month, and in slack moments cleaned the carpet and dusted. In one southern Ontario village the operator, also the baker, frequently answered with "Hold the line, I've got my hands in the dough."

In Winnipeg, male subscribers who dared challenge the telephone boys' wisdom or bad manners, were invited to "come up here and fight like a man." Victoria's boys were of gentler persuasion, perhaps because they idolized and were trained by courtly Robert McMicking. He spent hours patiently teaching them to control their voices, which tended to skitter into soprano when

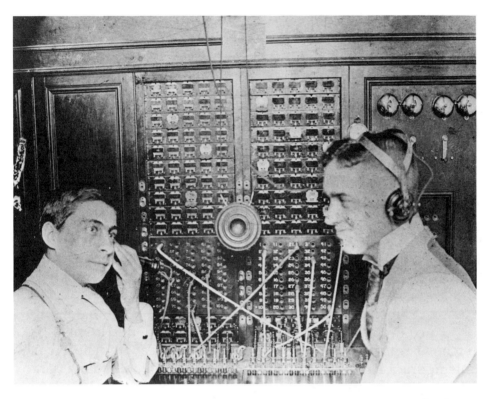

Albert Decelles and J. E. Choquette operating a No. 1 Standard Magneto switchboard in Sherbrooke, Que., 1895. On the upper part of the switchboard can be seen the metal tabs which fell to indicate the number of the caller. BELL CANADA TELEPHONE HISTORICAL COLLECTION.

they handled exciting fire alarm calls. When not working the switchboard, his boys collected money, swept the floor, stoked the furnace and ran any other errands the manager could think up. Secretary-Treasurer Baker examined every coin they collected; phony slugs were deducted from the boys' $20 a month wage.

In 1886, only weeks after Granville became Vancouver, fire tore through its rickety frame buildings and levelled the town in 20 minutes. Telephone boy Charlie Tilley, the bookstore owner's son, fled with the switchboard in his arms. Relief poured in from all over the mainland. Lumber wagons rumbled onto the scene, tents sprang up by the flicker of lanterns and by dawn Vancouver was rebuilding. Tilley put up a new bookstore and the telephone flourished anew. In lieu of a directory, its 100 subscribers could find each others' names and numbers on the back page of the local *News Advertiser*.

Charlie Tilley was office manager by day, operator by night, and a singer and guitarist between times. Most evenings before going on shift he hung around the exchange, singing and strumming with his pals: a banjo player, flautist, and a penny-whistle virtuoso. One night he got on the line and invited subscribers to listen in. They liked his "broadcast" so much it became a fixture. For two or three hours a night Vancouver telephone owners had merely to ring up Central, press receiver to ear and hear such contemporary hits as "Old Folks at Home," "Solomon Levi" and, *of course*, "God Save the Queen."

That year, 1888, the company hired its first woman operator, Ella Lindsay. Visitors streamed in to see what the "voice" looked like. In Regina by then, dark-eyed little Emily Lander in her high-neck ruffled gown had been at the switchboard for a year. All along the nation's lines the telephone boy was on the wane. But young Charlie Tilley had one last moment of glory: in 1889 another fire ripped through Vancouver and again he rescued the switchboard from the flames.

## "What a Wonderful Invention"

Renegade province that it was, B.C. shared one thing with the rest of Canada. It loved the telephone and yet, perversely, hated poles. There were long wrangles with city councils, until civic fathers decided the phone was indispensable. Just then electric street railways came to major cities, laying waste to telephone conversations with their electrical interference. Victoria, being blessed with tall timber, decided to outdistance the crackling trolley wires with 80-foot telephone poles.

These towering masts, painted white with red crossarms, offended the eye of Amor de Cosmos, a local eccentric who wasn't that crazy about electric lights or street railways either. Born William Smith in Windsor, Ont., de Cosmos had composed his new name from a mishmash of Latin, French and Greek. He said it meant "Lover of the Universe."

The Lover of the Universe, a former MP and the second premier of B.C., habitually wore morning dress with patent leather boots, carried a cane and was addicted to strong drink. As the mighty poles rose in front of his property on Government Street, he began a two-year delaying action in council and courts. When asked where he would like to have the poles, he said, "I would prefer to have them taken away and burned." Eventually the controversy petered out, the poles went up and the Lover of the Universe, who spent his latter years in the hands of a guardian, died unfulfilled.

His was a voice in the wilderness. Most British Columbians concurred with the *Colonist*: "What a wonderful invention is the telephone. . . .Social greetings between friends may be interchanged. The butcher, the baker or the grocer may be reminded of forgotten orders or furnished with new ones. The gudewife and man may exchange signals when far apart. . . ."

To accommodate the gudewife and man, the Victoria and Esquimalt Telephone Company in 1896 gave explicit instructions on how to enjoy the telephone together. ". . .Speak fair into it in an ordinary conversational tone, and within about three inches of the cavity in the transmitter. Do not hurry but speak very deliberately in throat or chest tones.

"To Listen: place the telephone fairly against the ear, with an upward motion, so that the lower extremity or lobe of the ear is gathered in, into the cavity of the telephone; in this position it will be found to fit snugly and comfortable — the lobe of the ear acting as a cushion and at the same time closing out all ulterior sounds, thus enabling the voice to be heard with clearness and precision."

It was the kind of detail that a later generation would devote to sex instruction, and appropriately so. At long last, after a slow courtship, the people of Canada were head-over-heels in love with communication — the sheer undeniable pleasure of discourse over the wires.

# The Way It Was

This is a confident Canada — proud, self-assured, a little smug even. On this December Saturday in the twilight of another year, the threat of Brother Jonathan's successor, Uncle Sam, seems to have receded. Today's beloved symbol is Johnny Canuck, a muscular clean-cut chap with jaw of purest granite, whipcord breeches and what later generations will know as a Yogi Bear hat. In the newspaper cartoons of today, Johnny Canuck invariably gives the sleazy unshaven Uncle Sam a very bad time.

The Dominion is secure: five million people, seven provinces from sea to sea, plus the vast sprawling Territories. A surge of nationalistic poems and songs is tugging at Canadian hearts. "Awake, my country, the hour is great with change!" cries Charles G. D. Roberts, the reigning poet. And awakening it is.

A man can phone from Quebec City to Windsor and be heard! A telegraph flies from coast to coast and under the sea. Is it possible that only 50 years ago there was *no* telegraph, or telephone or cable? Yes, the old ones remember it. A strange time it was, they say. Men waited weeks for news, they say. Mind you, they add, it was also a less harassing time. . .but a pox on *that* kind of backward thinking!

Indeed, the hour is "great with change." Where a crude fort stood among towering firs on that other December Saturday 50 years ago, Vancouver's downtown streets now blaze with Edison's electric lights. High in the Yukon a cry of "Gold!" rings out from Bonanza Creek. In two years 25,000 miners, dreamers, prostitutes, adventurers and card sharps will inhabit a Dawson City that today is merely a clutter of tents.

There is gold in the Districts of Alberta, Saskatchewan and Assiniboia, too, reaped by Messrs. Massey and Harris' finest new mechanical "binders" and heaped high in grain elevators. The pile of bones beside Wascana Creek is gone and, presto! there stands Regina, 1,800 people, capital of the Northwest Territories and soon to be centre of the greatest wheat fields on earth.

A new prairie champion is waiting in the wings. Last month Clifford Sifton won a federal by-election — son of the same Sifton whose shoddy telegraph line made life so miserable for the first settlers. But the son is repaying his father's debt to society. A former Manitoba MLA, Sifton is now Minister of the Interior, with *carte blanche* from Prime Minister Laurier. He will glorify "the stalwart peasant in sheepskin coat, born to the soil" and flood the west with immigrants. Tomorrow Brandon holds a by-election to fill Sifton's vacant post. Today the press reports Sifton's farewell speech to his old constituents, viewing "the development of the whole of western Canada as the important problem before the Dominion today."

The east is prospering too, amid electric lights, electric streetcars, phonographs, photographs, typewriters. Lawyer Frederick Fetherstonhaugh has been buzzing around Toronto in an electric car for three years. The gasoline horseless carriage is just around the corner.

Indeed the progress of gadgets and machines is considerably ahead of advances in medicine and human relations. Recently Nicholas Flood Davin, MP, the illustrious Regina editor, urged the House of Commons to give women the vote. His motion lost, of course. As a Quebec MP summed it up: "Let us leave them their moral purity, their bashfulness, their sweetness. . . .It ill becomes the community to change [her] sex and to degrade her by the exercise of the franchise." And so the ladies remain locked in limbo, and in their Dr. Warner's Coraline Corsets ("CANNOT Be Broken").

The nation's panacea for "Sick Headache, Too Hearty Eating, Dizziness, Nausea, Drowsiness, Bad Taste in the Mouth, Coated Tongue, Pain in the Side, Torpid Liver" — *all* those things — is Carter's Little Liver Pills. A new book published in Toronto (dealing gingerly with sex and available only by subscription) advises that "Nothing tears the life out of a man more than lust, vulgar thoughts and immoral conduct."

Smallpox, scarlet fever and diphtheria are still commonplace. A Winnipeg news story today tells of a local epidemic caused because two doctors failed to diagnose a smallpox carrier and sent the unfortunate fellow by streetcar from hospital to hospital instead of directly to "the pest house."

The front-page item in today's Toronto *World* relates a more troubling tale. In Kentucky yesterday a mob pulled father Dink Proctor and son Arch out of jail and lynched them, after murdering son Bill in his cell. The Proctors were on trial for murder and the mob feared they'd get off scot-free. A large crowd viewed the dangling bodies and "the general public approved of the killing of Bill and Arch."

Those barbarous Americans again! But what about the story in today's Victoria *Province* of "the batches of youngsters who within the last week attacked and brutally assaulted Chinamen"? *Well, really, old boy, that's different! Those Chinks are overrunning Canada, what?*

Come, let us all think happy thoughts. In bounteous Canadian shops today, ladies' Russian Calf Lace Boots are only $2, with a box of gumdrops thrown in free. Beaver coats are a mere $12, the best coffee is 45¢ a pound, good Canadian cheddar is 13¢ a pound and a 15-volume set of Dickens' works goes for only $6.25.

In the Bell Telephone office on Toronto's Temperance Street anyone can walk into a "Sound Proof Cabinet" at any hour of the day to "communicate with other cities and towns." The air is full of tinkling new tunes, as shallow and good humoured as their singers: "My Gal's a Corker, She's a New Yorker" and "There'll Be a Hot Time in the Old Town Tonight." Christmas is coming. And in the 59th year of dear Victoria's interminable reign, all's right with the Dominion — for those who do not examine it too closely.

# Chapter 10

## A National Love Affair

Papa I'm so sad and lonely
Sobbed a tearful little child.
Since dear mama's gone to heaven
Papa darling you've not smiled.
I will speak to her and tell her
That we want her to come home.
Just you listen and I'll call her
Through the telephone.

Hello Central, give me Heaven
For my mama's there.
You can find her with the angels
On the golden stair. . .

The idea of ringing up God or His appointed agent on long distance seemed totally charming and almost plausible to those Canadians at the turn of the century. They could phone from Quebec City to Windsor; surely Heaven would be only a small additional toll charge.

So in music halls, saloons and parlours across the land they sang "Hello Central, Give Me Heaven" (in the song, the call does

141

*not* reach Heaven but a kindly operator poses as the late Mama, reaffirming the child's belief in Bell Tel and the hereafter). They also sang "Ring Me Up Heaven, Please Central" and "Hello, Is This Heaven? Is Grandpa There?"

And they sang "Kissing Papa Thro' the Telephone," "Hello Ma Baby," "Love by Telephone," "The Kissaphone," "And the Bell Went Ting-a-ling," and more. Beginning with "Telephone March" and "The Wondrous Telephone" in 1877, Tin Pan Alley poured out some 650 telephone songs over 60 years, and Canadians hummed, crooned and toe-tapped Mr. Bell's invention into their musical mythology.

By the mid-'90s the world's most notorious slow starters had become the world's most ardent telephone users. Canada had 540 sets per 100,000 people compared to 350 in America and 167 in Britain. From a meagre 2,165 subscribers in 1880 Bell's count in Ontario, Quebec and the West had soared to 26,000 by 1892. Montreal's 5,872 subscribers were the nation's top talkers with an average of 12 calls per subscriber per day.

And why not? Conversations were even clearer, over better-insulated wiring and new sensitive transmitters. Compact new cables could carry 100 pairs of wires, steadily putting an end to pole pollution. Big cities were spending up to $200,000 to outfit their exchanges. Yet for users the phone was still a bargain.

Overseas, Paris and London residents paid $100 a year for service. New Yorkers paid $240, Philadelphians paid $100 but Montrealers and Torontonians paid only $50 and $45 respectively. The Canadian average was a mere $31 a year. At these rates telephone service was irresistible, not only for matters of life and death and business, but for the fringe benefits. In New Brunswick, operators gave out information "about trains and steamboats, locality of fires and so forth." The Nova Scotia and P.E.I. companies not only sold wake-up calls but would put a bell right in the bedroom.

The Victoria and Esquimalt Telephone Company in B.C. had its own version of Boy Scouts 20 years before Lord Baden-Powell invented them. Its messengers would perform any "service for which a sprightly intelligent youth can so frequently be used to advantage." From nine a.m. to six p.m., for 15 cents per half hour, they would "commend themselves in the delivery of notes, invitations, circulars, light parcels, etc., in the city; in accompanying small children to or from school or elsewhere in inclement weather;

in escorting ladies through the city after nightfall; in directing strangers to the city to any given point within its limits. . . ."

Elsewhere, the sprightly lads were not above a little blackmail. In Port Hope 13-year-old Frank Moffat canvassed his customers on Christmas Eve with a small printed card:

> Remember the message boy faithful and true
> Who has brought you your messages many or few,
> It's hard on a fellow these holiday times
> To go round with his pocket quite empty of dimes.

He collected $12 in tips.

Was there no end to the virtues of the Wondrous Telephone? An Ontario housewife discovered that the butt end of her telephone receiver, unscrewed, made a superlative cookie cutter. The Bell urged her to desist, upon finally tracking down the source of strange clickings on the line. In Saskatchewan District near Indian Head, Major W. R. Bell (no relation to the telephone family) ran a 5,220-acre farm with his feet up beside his phone. Each night at 8:30 he issued the next day's orders to his foreman and 82 workmen over the farm's private system. He went broke in 1896, but for lack of rain, not communications.

In Alberta the Mounties ran a 70-mile line south from Lethbridge to a hill overlooking the Montana border. There, linked to division headquarters, police patrols kept tabs on cattle rustlers, horse thieves, whiskey peddlers and other undesirables, and literally headed them off at the pass.

The Lacombe, Alta., *Advertiser* went so far as to visualize the telephone as *objet d'art*: "Though it is not yet possible to have the inevitable green tapes [cord from receiver to transmitter] covered with some sort of flowered crepe de chine to match the wallpaper, it is practicable to make the telephone corner in keeping with the rest of the furnishings. The directory can be made an attractive addition to the apparatus and when provided with a pretty removable cover it is transformed into quite an ornament as it hangs at the side of the phone. An instrument should never be shined with any patent preparation or paste. An occasional rubbing with flannel cloth will suffice."

The focal figure of this mass mania was the operator. Her personal interest in her flock was a large reason for the telephone's charm and her bright "Hello" was her trademark.

The "Number Please" response was not adopted until the 1920s, although city companies now insisted on calling-by-number from the skinny new directories. Torontonians and Montrealers even had to specify the exchange — no longer just "243" but "Main — 243". But out on the rural lines everybody's pal, Central, would still call Joe the Blacksmith or Moe the Butcher on request. She knew all the numbers by heart. Her prodigious memory also filed weather reports, sports scores, election returns and other vital news. Montreal operators each handled up to 1,400 daily requests for the correct time. As Sir John A. Macdonald lay dying in 1891, Hello Girls across the country were besieged with questions about the old statesman's health.

Her job was not without hazard. More than one operator, disregarding the universal warning never to use a phone during thunderstorms, was jolted out of her chair when a lightning bolt came down the ungrounded system. When fire was reported in Ridgetown, Ont., Central had to sprint out her side door, labour uphill to the town hall and activate the town fire alarm. Once when fire broke out in a Toronto office an operator extinguished it by sitting on it. In Stratford, a friendly operator stopped to help a man in a phone booth. It turned out he was calling a friend to say he was about to be quarantined for smallpox.

The Hello Girl was expected to be a model of decorum. For some it came easily — they were mere children. Vancouver's Fannie Fowler was still in grade school when she became a part-time operator in 1890. Edmonton's first operator, Jenny Lauder, was only 14. Others, though older, were as innocent as most other products of a Victorian upbringing. Montreal's Mary Warren was known as the "Puritan Maiden" because she refused to speak to a man unless formally introduced.

No girl could apply for a job with the Bell without three character recommendations, including one from her clergyman. Any moral lapse meant instant dismissal. The Bell once fired a shameless hussy who dared to dance the tango at a staff party. Applicants also had to be free of consumptive coughs, tall enough to reach to the top of high switchboards, and have the strength of oxen to bear on their shoulders the ugly $6^1/_2$-pound Gilliland Harness headset. In fact, the headset was not unlike a yoke. Between it and the whalebone corsets that shaped her hourglass figure, the operator was continuously hurting.

Operator's dress and deportment were, of course, among the

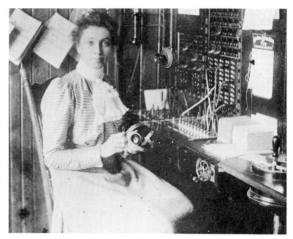

Ida Gardner, the first telephone operator in Winchester, Ont., about 1890. On her right is a calculagraph used for timing long distance calls. BELL CANADA TELEPHONE HISTORICAL COLLECTION.

The Vermilion, Alta., telephone exchange was installed in a corner of Brimacombe's book and music store, about 1908. GLENBOW-ALBERTA INSTITUTE, CALGARY.

Early telephone exchanges were opened in business establishments, stores and residences. This exchange in Bowmanville, Ont., was opened in the 1890s. BELL CANADA TELEPHONE HISTORICAL COLLECTION.

concerns of Bell's diligent C. F. Sise. The girls in Montreal exchange, under Sise's relentless eye, brushed their clothes *and* shoes before starting work. The president once returned from efficient Chicago to find Toronto wallowing in decay.

"I was surprised to see with what a very languid and leisurely manner the operators replied to and made connections for subscribers," Sise wrote the Ontario manager, "a manner which was very graceful but which reminded one of my grandmother playing the harp rather than a lot of women paid to do a certain work." He found fault with Toronto girls' "enormous sleeves" and praised Chicago for making its operators wear "a *short* black dress — not less than two or three inches from the floor."

The Toronto mode of dress nevertheless was typical. In Saint John, N.B., young Charles A. Kee, starting life in 1900 as one of the last male operators, left a vivid picture of his exchange.

"Mr. W. W. McMackin, the local manager, wore a black swallow-tail coat and striped trousers. Across his vest was a heavy gold watch chain which must have been quite a strain on the buttonhole to which it was fastened. He informed me my hours would be from eight p.m. to eight a.m., seven days a week. Sunday night I would come in at nine p.m., giving me time to go to church. My salary would be $25 a month with one week's holidays. After one year's service I would receive $30 a month. In addition to the operating I was to sweep and dust the operating room and look after the furnace during the winter months. Any spare time was to be employed cutting back cords and renewing the hard rubber plungers in the keys on the switchboard. . . ."

His boss sat at a flat-top leather desk while the bookkeeper perched, Bob Cratchit–style, on a stool before a high slant-top desk. In the operating room reigned supervisor Lucy Dunn in standard operator's garb: "white shirtwaist buttoned high on the neck, large balloon sleeves, a long pleated black skirt, black cotton stockings and high laced or buttoned boots. In her hair she wore a rat. She also wore a bustle although nature had amply endowed her. She wore a long black apron on the rear rather than the front, to keep the back of her skirt from becoming shiny with wear. She carried in her hand a long hardwood stick or pointer, for pointing out the numbers and transfer jacks to the new operators. . . ."

Kee was astonished at the noise in the room, but compared to male operators, said one Montreal newspaper, Hello Girls' voices were like "summer streams trickling through a forest glade." In

1898 the Montreal *Watchman* appraised the entire female phenomenon and found it good.

"Why are women chosen as operators instead of men? In the
first place the clear feminine quality of the voice suits best the
delicate instrument. Then girls are usually more alert than boys,
and always more patient. Women are more sensitive, more amen-
able to discipline, far gentler and more forbearing than men.

"Boys and men are less patient. They have always the element
of fight in them. When spoken to roughly and rudely they are not
going to give the soft answer. And every man is a crank when he
gets on a phone. . . .

"The manager insists upon the girls speaking distinctly and
courteously. When a subscriber roars 'Gimme 751 and get a move
on you' instead of the operator dropping the telephone and
running off to hit the gruff-mouthed one with a club, as a man
would feel inclined to do, the girl answers pleasantly with a rising
inflection, and hard words as well as blows are saved."

The Montreal exchange "for pure air, perfect cleanliness and
opportunities for rest could scarcely be excelled." Girls got a
15-minute break every 2½ hours to sip "any amount of hot water
and unlimited tea." In case of fainting fits (a common female
affliction of the time) or getting hit by lightning, the operators had
access to first aid in the form of salt, baking soda, Jamaica ginger,
headache powder, smelling salt, and a very *small* quantity of
whiskey.

For her labours, the sweetheart of the wires received $20 – $25
a month and a torrent of letters, chocolates and flowers from
grateful subscribers. Her mellifluous voice often brought love-
struck admirers around after work. Employers warned their girls to
shun these depraved exchange-door Johnnies. The Montreal
*Watchman*, however, had a warning for *men*, smitten by that
musical "hello":

"For though than a beautiful voice there is no truer indication
of character, oftentimes the face is not so interesting as the voice,
and the beauty lover suffers a violent shock."

# Along the Line

Along the lines and up the nation's telephone poles, it was still
he-man territory. "The lineman was an authentic frontier figure,"

writes Tony Cashman in *Singing Wires*, the definitive history of Alberta Government Telephones, "in the same league as the lumberjack, the cowboy, the prospector, the steamboat captain and the locomotive engineer."

He was called a "boomer" and he boomed his way from town to town, leaving new poles, bruised heads, broken hearts and weary police chiefs in his wake. He carried his own axe, wrench, pliers and climbing spurs. His greased-down hair was parted arrow straight down the middle. He thrived on salt pork and molasses and never tired of posing cockily for photos with his mates, all perched like starlings up the poles and along the crossarms.

The lineman's home away from home was the boarding house or cheap hotel. Bell employee T. R. Woodhouse of Hamilton remembered one of them: "We slept two to a bed, and during sleet storms when the hotel accommodation was inadequate, three to a bed or on a pile of hay on the floor. The meals were hearty because our appetites were enormous. The food was heaped on the table and everyone helped themselves. There were three kinds of soup — pea, bean and vermicelli — but we learned to make other kinds by adding milk, catsup, H.P. sauce, or a combination of them.

"In winter the only heat was two pot-bellied stoves in the bar room and in the hall upstairs, with their stove pipes also radiating some heat as they wandered from room to room on their way to the chimney. Last thing at night they would be filled with knotty chunks of wood and allowed to burn themselves out. By midnight the whole place would be cold, and by morning, really frigid. You did not dare to keep water overnight in your bedroom pitcher, and it was too cold to go out to pump some so we rarely shaved or even washed in the morning. We did these chores at night when hot water was available."

Evening around the boarding house was an endless round of boyish pranks, such as wiring a sleeping companion's toes, cranking the generator and waking him up with a few stiff jolts. At dawn, rain or shine, they whistled and shouted off to work in wagons. Lineman John Henry Martin of London recalled the pecking order: "Only the teamsters, foremen and straw-bosses [sub-foremen] sat on seats. The linemen and grunts [groundmen] sat on the tools, the crossarms, the coils of wire or on the sides or back of the wagon with their feet hanging over.

"The foreman and the straw-bosses wore clean shirts, rubber collars, neckties and Christie hats. You could tell the foreman by the heavy gold watchchain that stretched across his stomach from vest pocket to vest pocket. The men wore slouch hats and overalls over their coats and trousers. During the day they chewed tobacco but at night they smoked cigars. They were strong, hard-living, hard-working, loyal to their company and to each other, and ready to fight at the drop of a hat in defense of either."

Linemen of the '90s scorned safety belts. They shinnied up poles bearing a crossarm on one shoulder and an axe on the belt, clung by their legs, chopped a notch and nailed the crossarm home. Then they slid down in death-defying 10-foot swoops. A favourite pastime in Alberta was to raise a 30-foot pole, anchor it with four guy wires, climb to the top, snip the wires and slide down before the pole fell over.

Accidents were as common as eating, sleeping and getting drunk. A falling tree limb once clipped Bell lineman W. R. Byers square on the top of his tam-o'-shanter (safety helmets were unknown). He plummeted to the ground. A cable splicer named Ross picked him up.

"Let's have a look at your head," said Ross.

"I'm just a little dizzy," mumbled Byers. Ross pulled off the tam-o'-shanter and viewed a bloody mess.

"By God, we better get you to a doctor," he said cheerfully. The doctor shaved Byers' head, put in four stitches, bandaged the wound and sent him back to work. Byers didn't bother mentioning it to the foreman until suppertime.

The durable "boomer" was out in every blizzard and sleet storm, the bane of the telephone industry. In March, 1892, for example, an Ottawa ice storm dragged down $30,000 worth of wire and poles. By that time Ottawa had given the industry another splitting headache — the electric street railway.

For years Canadian streets had echoed to the gentle clop of hooves along the cedar-block paths of horse car routes. Many horse cars were fitted with stoves and a thick floor covering of straw, to keep out winter cold. In January, 1891, North America's third electric streetcar system crackled and sparked down an Ottawa street while its parent, Thomas Ahearn, beamed with pride. It was the same Ahearn of the cigar box telephones.

Young Ahearn, an ebullient optimist ("He never wanted to hear bad news," an associate said. "He could pretend he *didn't*

A telephone line crew, including blacksmith and cook, camping along the route of a long distance line in 1902. The horse drawn steam boiler provided power for pumping and drilling. BELL CANADA TELEPHONE HISTORICAL COLLECTION.

Pike poles, cant hooks and muscle power were the "modern tools" for erecting telephone poles in the late 1890s. BELL CANADA TELEPHONE HISTORICAL COLLECTION.

Modern safety inspectors would be appalled at the bravado of early linemen. Here the crew poses at the finish of the long distance line from Stettler, Alta., to Lacombe, Alta., 1907. PROVINCIAL ARCHIVES OF ALBERTA.

hear it."), had been rollicking from one career to the next. At age 27, after a stint with Bell Telephone in Ottawa, he cofounded a firm of electrical engineers. Ahearn and Soper built several telephone branch lines and won a contract to supply the CPR with telegraph equipment. Now Ahearn had built Canada's first electric railway. Two years later he would win a gold medal at the Ottawa Exhibition for electrical cooking apparatus — forerunner of the electric stove.

All this was gratifying for the handsome Irish-American lad, whom one admirer dubbed "another Edison," but not for the telephone companies. In 1889, C. F. Sise had already sent an emissary to Richmond, Virginia, where the continent's first electric railway was demonstrating that city telephone systems couldn't live with the new city transit.

Most telephone systems used one wire per subscriber from point to point, grounding it to the nearest water pipe or directly into the earth. Now, current from electric streetcars jammed the telephone lines with noise and false signals.

By 1896 Montreal and Toronto had spent thousands of dollars converting grounded systems to double-wire circuits. This vastly improved the range of voice but also doubled aerial clutter and the load on poles. City wiring *had* to go underground, so electric streetcars wiped out pole pollution, something city councils hadn't been able to do in 20 years.

In 1900 Ottawa made history again with Canada's first "common battery" system. It meant no more batteries in the home telephone. Now the phone was a slender candlestick desk set or a small wall box. Callers no long cranked the handle for Central; by merely lifting the receiver they activated signal lights at a new compact central switchboard.

Indeed, Almon B. Strowger, a U.S. undertaker, was out to do away with Central all together. Convinced that his business was dying because unscrupulous operators were routing his calls to competitors, Strowger began mocking up an automatic system, using a circular collar box. By the time he found out the cause of his missing calls (a metal sign outside his door was short-circuiting them) he'd invented the dial telephone.

The Strowger system was introduced to Canada in 1893, in the London, Ont., *Free Press* building, and in the communities of Terrebonne, Que., and Seaforth, Mitchell and Arnprior, Ont.

None of the community systems worked longer than a few weeks. The first successful automatic in Canada was in Whitehorse, Yukon, in 1901.

Meanwhile Romaine Callender, a Brantford electrician known and respected by Alexander Graham Bell, produced his own automatic phone. He demonstrated it in New York in 1895 and newspapers there reported it "triumphantly successful." The Lorimer Brothers, G. W. and J. Hoyt, from St. George, Ont., bought him out, improved on it and organized a company in 1896. Instead of a dial, the Lorimer automatic had four knobs, sliding up and down like throttles, in numbered slots. To get a four-digit number, a subscriber set each lever at the appropriate spot and pulled a handle, setting off a spring that activated electrical impulses. Theoretically, the number rang in 13 seconds.

Delivery took somewhat longer, as Edmonton found out. After waiting nearly two years for an order of Lorimer automatics, the city gave up and installed Strowger phones in 1908. By then Saskatoon had been using western Canada's first dials for a year.

For all of the telephone's charm and utility, telegraphy was still the mainstay of communications. Where later generations would make an appointment, greet a relative or report a birth or death by long distance telephone, late 19th century Canadians did all of this by wire or cable. It was by telegram that British Columbia launched its time-honoured custom of bragging about the weather to miserable countrymen in frigid climes. When the Canadian Pacific line reached Fredericton on February 17, 1889, the mayor of Vancouver immediately sent a gloating telegram to his New Brunswick counterpart: "Wish we had transcontinental telescope as well as telegraph so that you could take a peep at our gardens and fields this morning. Take my word they look glorious." The snowbound Fredericton mayor responded as Easterners have ever since: "On receipt of your telegram several of the audience fainted and the few remaining got up and left for Vancouver."

Telegraphy was faster than ever, because operators were using a sender called the "bug" (officially, the Vibroplex). It had sensitive springs to stress vibration, taking the strain off the operator's finger and relieving the affliction known as "telegraphers' paralysis."

The cable likewise was growing up. By the end of the century, no less than 15 lines had been laid under the North Atlantic.

Schools of telegraphy sprang up to satisfy the railways' need for trained telegraphers. Model trains simulated railway movements at Dier's School of Telegraphy, Ottawa, 1908. PUBLIC ARCHIVES OF CANADA PA42527.

Transmission speed had doubled to 47–50 words per minute. And now, Canada was about to reach beneath the Pacific to her sister members of the Commonwealth "down under."

# Sandford Fleming's Last Coup

On June 11, 1879 — 34 years almost to the day from his arrival in Canada — Sandford Fleming found time in his whirlwind schedule to produce yet another tantalizing idea. His achievement already would have satisfied most men. This astonishing Scot had designed the first Canadian postage stamp, founded the Canadian Institute and recently invented Standard Time. Now he was up to his voluminous beard in plans for the Canadian Pacific Railway.

But Fleming simply had to share this newest thought with fellow inventor and communicator, Fred Gisborne, superintendent of the government telegraph service in Ottawa. The Pacific terminus of the forthcoming CPR would soon be chosen, Fleming pointed out. The railway when completed would escort an overland telegraph from coast to coast.

"It appears to me," he mused, "that as a question of Imperial importance, the British possessions to the west of the Pacific Ocean should be connected by submarine cable with the Canadian line. Great Britain will thus be brought into direct communication with all the greater colonies and dependencies without passing through foreign countries."

Ardent patriot though he was, Fleming was thinking not merely of Britain's interests. A Pacific cable would serve Canada best of all. Canadians at that time could communicate with Australia only by way of England and a telegraph network winding through Europe and Asia, at prohibitive rates.

Fleming envisioned a totally British hookup, the "all-red line" (the UK and its colonies were colored red on standard maps of the world). Although it took 23 years of relentless pressure to achieve his dream, the first Pacific Cable became Sandford Fleming's personal and last great coup.

Gisborne, the longtime cable man, was enthusiastic. So were other Canadians, but Fleming's idea was slow to catch on, partly because building the CPR was an almost overwhelming task. Fleming's proposals to Parliament in 1880, 1881 and 1882 received only lip service; the MPs had the railway on their minds. In 1885 he renewed his case in a letter to John A. Macdonald and managed to achieve a Pacific Cable conference in London in 1887.

There, the atmosphere ranged from boredom to open hostility. British private interests with a financial stake in the eastern telegraph route had lobbied hard and well. Fleming knew that he must raise an issue dearest to British hearts: the security of the Empire.

A meticulous man, a dotter of *i*'s and crosser of *t*'s, Fleming was not the kind of speaker to bring cheering crowds to their feet. He made up for that with carefully marshalled facts and a keen sense of how the British mind worked.

"The telegraphic communication between the home government and every important division of the Empire except Canada is dependent on the friendship — shall I say protection? — of Turkey," he told the delegates. "Is not Turkey continually exposed to imminent danger from within? Is she not in danger of falling prey to covetous neighbours whose friendship with England may be doubted?"

Next, Fleming turned on his rival, the existing Eastern Telegraph Company, and as he spoke invisible choirs seemed to chant "Rule Britannia."

"Are the vital interests of the British Empire to be neglected?" he cried. "Is the permanent policy of England to be thwarted? Is the peace of the world to be endangered at the bidding of a joint stock company?"

He pointed out that the cable could be laid in segments, between connecting islands, and that the route's deepest part was only 3,000 fathoms (about 3$\frac{1}{2}$ miles, *not* the 13 miles his opponents claimed). He ended on a note of solid Scottish thrift: the lowest rate the Eastern Telegraph could offer from London to Australia was four shillings a word. Fleming predicted two shillings a word for messages over the Pacific Cable. With some reluctance, the conference agreed to a survey of the Pacific route.

The Pacific Ocean was still as much a mystery as when Magellan had sailed and named its peaceful waters more than three centuries before. Here was a prime opportunity to learn more of it, yet the British Admiralty dragged its feet. By 1894 nothing had been done. Delegates to a colonial conference in Ottawa passed another resolution, respectfully asking Mother England to stir herself.

More meetings; more delays. The cable's opponents threw up a new alarm. They said transmission over the distance — an estimated 3,500 nautical miles at its longest segment — would be too slow. Fleming was ready for them: he had two existing Atlantic cables joined at Canso, N.S., to form a continuous circuit from Ireland to Canso and back. It carried signals over 4,700 miles with perfect ease and clarity.

The cable opponents did not give up. They spread such horror stories of potential earthquakes, bottomless holes and jagged coral mountains lurking in the Pacific depths that one Australian told a Canadian in London, "The Pacific Cable is as dead as Julius Caesar!"

But the stubborn Fleming would not give up either. Canada was now regarded as the "eldest brother in the British family of kindred nationalities," he told Prime Minister Wilfrid Laurier. "If as Canadians we have faith in our destiny as no inconsiderable element of the great Empire, are we not called upon again to take the initiative?"

He followed up with a long persuasive missive to the Secretary of State for the Colonies in England. He praised England's state-owned inland telegraph (the Pacific Cable would also be state owned). He reviewed the Cable's bargain rates. He mentioned the glorious achievements of Britain's young colonies under the benevolent reign of Victoria. He concluded with a flourish of trumpets and a roll of drums: "Would it not be in the interest of a great commercial people to have all these [colonies] connected by means of a communication so perfect as the electric telegraph. . .?"

The letter was widely printed and enthusiastically read in Canada and the U.K. His case was irresistible. On the last day of 1900, an agreement was signed to connect Canada with Australasia via Pacific Cable.

It would be laid in five sections: Vancouver Island to Fanning Island; Fanning to Fiji; Fiji to Norfolk Island; Norfolk to Australia, and to New Zealand. The Vancouver Island–Fanning section, a thousand miles longer than any span of cable laid to that time, was a challenge. A special ship, the *Colonia*, was built for the job: an elegant vessel trimmed with teak and oak but able to carry about 10,000 tons dead weight. She laid the 3,455 nautical miles of cable in 17 days.

The other sections went down equally well, despite a severe cyclone in the Norfolk-Fiji segment. On October 31, 1902 — two months ahead of deadline — Australia, New Zealand and Canada were bound by nearly 6,000 miles of underwater wire. Fiji — which most Britons still equated with cannibalism — sent out a gracious greeting to King Edward VII. A torrent of messages followed, many of them congratulating Fleming for his perseverance.

That night Fleming delightedly tried a new experiment. He sent messages simultaneously east and west around the world. Fleming noted with satisfaction that a message from London to Australia took 5 hours, 45 minutes, over the eastern telegraph route, but only 18 minutes via Canada and the cable. It was the final proof, if more was needed, that his 23-year crusade was justified.

His old friend, Fred Gisborne, so long ago cheated of his share of the Atlantic Cable glory, did not live to see this triumphant night. It would have pleased but not astonished him. His mind, like Fleming's, was always probing far beyond his time. Shortly before he died in the early '90s a friend, Ellen McNab, caught him in a rare moment of repose.

"A penny for your thoughts, Mr. Gisborne," she said.

"I was just thinking," mused Canada's cable and telegraph pioneer, "that the time will come when messages will be sent across the Atlantic *through the air!*"

Old Gisborne was not in his dotage. He had been reading his electrical journals, just as he had done every night on the farm at St-Eustache so long ago. He knew of the latest theories and discoveries: the proof that electrical current moved in oscillating pulses; the theory — and then proof — that those pulses produced electromagnetic waves travelling at the speed of light. In 1888 a German physicist, Heinrich Rudolph Hertz had actually generated such waves.

Gisborne's instinct told him another breakthrough was near, and he was right. It would be the greatest miracle of all.

# Chapter 11

## How Canada Kept Marconi

The diary of George Kemp told the story, in the sparse wordbursts of a man who dealt in dots and dashes. Coming in off Signal Hill that miserable night of December 12, 1901, soaked, half frozen, but triumphant, he scrawled, "Got sigs 3 dots. Lost first kite with two wires each 500 ft. long, after being up for 2 hours. Then got up another kite with one wire 500 ft. long and kept it up 3 hours which appeared to give sigs good."

It meant that an aerial, riding a kite high over St. John's, Nfld., had pulled in the Morse code signal "S" from a transmitter 2,170 curving miles away in England. Kemp's young associate, Guglielmo Marconi, had invented wireless telegraphy — a feat that most of his contemporaries said was impossible. But then Marconi had a way of soaring over obstacles, as buoyantly as one of his kites.

Life had been kind to the young Italian inventor. He had never known the penury of a Morse, the ill health of an Aleck Bell or the bitter frustration of a Gisborne. He was the sort of man who wore suit, tie and Panama hat in a rowboat. Born into a well-to-do family, he enjoyed the benefits of private tutoring on the parental

159

estate and indulged his bent for science in an excellent home library. He was reading, as usual, on an Alpine vacation in the summer of 1894, when he was seized with the great idea.

It was an obituary of Rudolph Heinrich Hertz who had died in January, and it described his experiments with electromagnetic waves. Marconi was fascinated, then obsessed. If those waves could be magnified and controlled, could they not carry messages through space? If so, why hadn't someone else already thought of it?

Marconi, then only 20, cut his holiday short and rushed home to set up test equipment in his attic. Months later he sent signals three-quarters of a mile across the Marconi acres — without wires! Oddly, they seemed to follow the curvature of a hill, although all scientific wisdom at the time insisted that they ought to fly in a straight line into space.

Marconi patented and improved his device and moved into a vital second phase: the discovery of tuning. It meant that more than one station could share the airwaves, with a minimum of interference and overlapping. Since wireless seemed best suited to communication at sea — after all, telephone and telegraph seemed to monopolize the land — he went to England to practice ship-to-shore communication. There Kemp, a dark and bushy-moustachioed former British Navy man, became his devoted assistant of 30 years.

By March, 1899, Marconi had communicated with ships offshore and had beamed messages across the English Channel. His name was known to scientists everywhere. In September, Alexander Graham Bell urged Canada's minister of marines and fisheries to "make a thorough examination of the Marconi System of wireless telegraphy before deciding to lay a cable to Sable Island." The government did nothing, but Marconi was soon on Canada's doorstep anyway, more or less by default.

He intended in 1901 to beam a signal across the ocean from Cape Cod to his station in Cornwall. In November, weeks before the appointed test, his Cape Cod aerial collapsed. In desperation, fearing that other inventors were breathing down his back, Marconi cast about for a North American point near England. He settled on Newfoundland, which would have been a logical choice from the beginning.

He landed in December to a typically wretched Newfoundland winter. Kemp, with sailor's foresight, laid in quantities of cocoa laced with whiskey. They unpacked their gear on the great bleak hill that stands between St. John's and the open Atlantic. A howling gale tore away their 14-foot aerial-balloon on Wednesday, December 11, just after Marconi thought he detected the faint prearranged signal from Cornwall.

The next morning Signal Hill was shrouded in sleet and rain. The wind snatched their first kite. Kemp lofted another. At 30 minutes past noon Marconi heard the unmistakeable three clicks — dot-dot-dot: "s" — all the way from England. He heard them again at 1:10 p.m. and at 2:20. There was no mistake! Words *could* travel free through the air, and around the curving face of the earth!

The weather now turned so foul that Marconi abandoned further tests. But he was confident enough to cable his directors and hold a press conference. The newsmen met no stereotype down-at-heels inventor. The slim dapper young man, in an elegant suit with harmonious necktie and pocket handkerchief, arrived precisely on time, as was his habit. His voice was soft and calm, but nervous energy seethed behind the dark deepset eyes. Marconi and his achievement made an attractive news package.

By Monday, December 16, he was the talk of the civilized world. Laymen such as the editors of the Toronto *Globe* considered it "the most wonderful scientific discovery of modern times." Old-time telegraphers and cable operators felt the icy chill of competition. Cable stocks slumped. H. P. Dwight, the crusty 73-year-old general manager of Great North Western in Toronto, saw "nothing in sight to make the system available for ordinary messages." Thomas Edison said flatly, "I don't believe it." And that night Marconi received a lawyer's letter from Anglo-American Telegraph Company stating that their firm held a monopoly on all communications in Newfoundland; if Marconi did not stop experiments immediately Anglo-American would take legal action.

To Anglo-American superintendent Alexander MacKay — that same veteran telegrapher who had balked at Bell Telephone, 16 years before — the wireless was a legitimate threat. His tactics, however, backfired. Newfoundland, already chafing under Anglo-American's long-term grasp, was incensed by this high-handed edict to Marconi. Later that week, Governor Sir Cavendish Boyle gave Marconi a lavish luncheon, attended by the premier and his cabinet — "almost a State Affair," said the press. Then Boyle went up Signal Hill to visit the installation, a gesture of

Left to right, George Kemp, Guglielmo Marconi and P. W. Paget, at the Cabot Tower on Signal Hill, December 1901. PUBLIC ARCHIVES OF CANADA C 5941.

Raising the Marconi kite, Signal Hill, St. John's, Newfoundland, to receive the first wireless transmission across the Atlantic. PUBLIC ARCHIVES OF CANADA C5943.

support that reportedly enraged Alexander MacKay. The St. John's municipal council joined in, with a resolution censuring Anglo-American and congratulating Marconi for "the dawn of a new era in trans-oceanic telegraphy."

Marconi was pleased. He still had to take his experiments elsewhere, but the backlash was all in his favour. Support welled up from across Canada. Alexander Graham Bell offered land at Baddeck (too far inland for Marconi's needs). Canada's finance minister, W. S. Fielding, a former premier of Nova Scotia, telegraphed an invitation from Ottawa. On Christmas Eve Marconi gave himself the best possible Yuletide gift: a train ticket out of St. John's. Kemp and he rode across the island's stony face all the next day and crossed Cabot Strait in a blizzard on Christmas night. From then on, Canadian hospitality enveloped them and shut out the chill memories of Newfoundland.

At Sydney, a contingent of businessmen and politicians, led by Premier G. H. Murray, met their boat and whisked them to lunch at the Sydney Hotel. Then they boarded a special train to examine the delights of Nova Scotia as a wireless site. Not far past Glace Bay Marconi remarked, "This looks like a capital place. . . ." The Nova Scotians yanked the bell cord, stopped the train and led the inventor across Table Head, a plateau jutting seaward. Marconi liked it.

They took a steamer back to Sydney, courtesy of the local coal and electric power companies, and dined sumptuously at the Sydney Hotel, with miniature sparking radio towers at either end of the banquet table. Then Marconi and Kemp rollicked off to Ottawa. There, on December 31, the federal finance minister smoothly picked up the rhythm. Fielding hosted a luncheon at the Rideau Club, where the glittering guest list included Wilfrid Laurier, Robert Borden and Sandford Fleming. Marconi — who in his lifetime counted kings, queens and Benito Mussolini as friends — was in his element.

Later, with Cape Breton MP and newspaperman Alex Johnston running interference, Marconi got down to business. Fielding, although known as a man "whose most striking characteristic was not his generosity with public funds," listened attentively to the inventor's proposals. He sent them to the Prime Minister. Laurier too, was intrigued until the talk turned to money.

"Go and see Fielding," he said.

"We just came from him," objected Johnston.

"Well," said Laurier, choosing his words with political caution, "I would interpose no objection to a grant for Signor Marconi." Later, in a private audience with the Governor-General, Marconi said the government "seemed favourably disposed," providing overseas wireless rates would not exceed 10¢ a word for private messages and 5¢ a word for government and press. Two days later the inventor left Ottawa with a draft agreement that would give him the Cape Breton site and $75,000 assistance.

A year after his rude ejection from Newfoundland Marconi sent the first messages abroad from his permanent installation at Glace Bay. He then invited Laurier to send a message to England, providing it "not exceed about thirty words in length." The Marconi Wireless Telegraph Company of Canada, forerunner of Canadian Marconi, was founded in 1902.

Ordinary Canadians were not able to send messages of any kind until 1907. For years after, wireless was most often used at sea. Before, every ocean vessel was as remote as a desert island; now, in calm or storm, it was always in touch with land or other ships. The world stood by in shock when the liner *Titanic* struck an iceberg in 1912 and sank with 1,596 passengers aboard. Nevertheless, 745 others were rescued because the *Titanic* called for help, and all might have lived if every ship in the vicinity had been wireless equipped. Weeping survivors, landing at New York where Marconi happened to be, greeted him like a saviour.

For Canadians, wireless had already flamboyantly proved itself with the first play-by-play capture of a murderer. Early in 1910 Belle Crippen, a former actress, disappeared from her London, England, home. Her husband, Dr. Hawley Crippen, a dentist with some surgical knowledge, said she had died abroad. His neighbours, sniffing for scandal like neighbours immemorial, took up their vigil. They thought it odd when 50-year-old Dr. Crippen's 27-year-old secretary moved in with him. Ethel Le Neve was short, pale and pretty, with light brown hair and the flattering habit of listening intently when men were talking.

Friends of the late Mrs. Crippen thought it even odder when her favourite brooch suddenly showed up on Le Neve's chest at a theatrical ball. Chief Inspector Walter Dew of New Scotland Yard nosed around. Crippen, a short grey-eyed bespectacled man with thick moustache and false teeth, admitted that his wife had not died abroad. She had deserted him, he claimed, and he'd been too ashamed to admit it.

Then Crippen and Le Neve vanished. The case assumed the tones of an Agatha Christie thriller. Inspector Dew sniffed around the Crippen home like a bloodhound. At last, lifting some dusty bricks in the basement floor, he found what appeared to be Mrs. Crippen, cut into small pieces. The manhunt was on, but Crippen seemed to have evaded Scotland Yard.

On board the liner *Montrose*, bound from Antwerp to Canada in early July, Captain H. G. Kendal did a double take when he caught two of his male passengers — "Mr. Robinson and son" — holding hands. Like everyone else in Britain, he had been following the Crippen case. On a hunch, he radioed London and received descriptions of the missing lovers.

Kendal now proved himself no mean detective. He noticed a mark on Robinson's nose, from years of wearing spectacles. He detected a precise use of medical terms in the man's conversation. He made Robinson laugh and noted his false teeth. He saw that Robinson Jr.'s ill-fitting trousers were pinned up at the waistband.

Kendal wirelessed England: he had Crippen. Instantly Chief Inspector Dew hopped a faster boat, the *Laurentic*, to head off his quarry in Canada. Now, as messages leaped from ship to ship and shore to shore, millions of newspaper readers all over the world savored the bizarre chase. On the *Montrose*, Robinson listened to the snap and crackle of the wireless and cried, "What a wonderful invention it is!" Millions of Canadians knew what he did not; that the wonderful invention was spinning a noose around his neck.

As the *Montrose* steamed up the St. Lawrence River near the lighthouse village of Father Point, Inspector Dew and two Quebec policemen came aboard, dressed as ship's pilots. Robinson wondered why *three* pilots were coming to guide the *Montrose*. He was quickly enlightened. With stiffest of upper lips, the first "pilot" said, "Good morning, Dr. Crippen. I am Chief Inspector Dew."

"Good morning, Mr. Dew," stammered the culprit.

"You will be arrested for the murder and mutilation of your wife in London, on or about the 2nd of February last."

A search revealed some of Belle Crippen's jewellery sewn to his undershirt and a note, intended for Le Neve: "I cannot stand the horror I go through every night. . .I have made up my mind to jump overboard tonight. . .I hope you can forgive me."

Inspector Dew next broke the news to Le Neve. She swooned in his arms. Meanwhile an Associated Press man found his way on board. As the *Montrose* steamed on toward Quebec City, he tossed a tobacco tin full of notes over the side by prearrangement to telegraph operator Dave McWilliams. McWilliams sped ashore in a motor boat and soon relayed the story to the world. As the Toronto *Star* piously summed it up, "The great hand of wireless has stretched out across the sea and intercepted the alleged wife murderer and his companion." Le Neve was acquitted but Crippen was hanged in November. In wireless the law had found a new and potent weapon. It gave international criminals something to think about.

# The Forgotten Father of Radio

From the moment Guglielmo Marconi plucked the letter "s" from the swirling clouds over Signal Hill, his name was a household word in Canada. The Toronto *Globe*, among others, recorded his daily movements on pages one and two until he left the country three weeks later. Often a column was simply labelled "Marconi's Movements"; the *Globe* and every other newspaper knew that readers would hang on the inventor's every train ride, current meal or most trivial quote.

Yet, a year before the Signal Hill experiment, Reginald Fessenden, a burly, cranky, red-bearded genius from Quebec, invented radio as the world knows it — and Canadian newspapers ignored him. They likewise ignored the world's first radio broadcast. Fessenden did that, too, on Christmas Eve, 1906 — three years before Marconi won the Nobel Prize for his work.

"Fessenden has been the victim of both the vast progress in science since his death and the almost total neglect of his Canadian compatriots," wrote Canadian author Ormond Raby, whose book, *Radio's First Voice*, in 1970 shed new light on this forgotten inventor.

Fessenden was a poor publicist and a worse businessman, and therein lay the neglect and torment of his career. His probing mind drove him through life at a full trot. While lesser men paused to consolidate their gains, Fessenden forever forged ahead, asking "why?" Born in Bolton, Que., son of an impoverished Anglican minister, he was reading everything he could find at six. At 11 he was academically on a par with students twice his age. At Bishop's College, Lennoxville, he studied by night and taught French, Greek and mathematics by day.

"The great hand of wireless has stretched out across the sea and intercepted the alleged wife murderer and his companion." Dr. Crippen (left) reckoned without the dramatic power of radio when he fled across the Atlantic with his lover Ethel Le Neve (right), who was disguised as a boy. BOTH PICTURES: RADIO TIMES HULTON PICTURE LIBRARY.

Reginald Fessenden made the first voice transmission by radio even before Marconi amazed the world with his transatlantic feat, but this Canadian genius of radio was never recognized. PUBLIC ARCHIVES OF CANADA PA 93160.

After a teaching stint in Bermuda, he joined the Thomas Edison laboratories in New Jersey and committed his life to the U.S. There was no scope nor even an opening for him at home. Canada scarcely knew Fessenden existed.

He was soon chief chemist of Edison labs, and pouring out the first of his 500 lifetime inventions. When Edison went broke Fessenden moved to Westinghouse as chief electrician. He held two successive university jobs, the last as head of electrical engineering at the University of Pittsburgh. McGill University had rejected his application for a similar post.

In Pennsylvania, the university chancellor ticked him off for buying storage batteries and $30 worth of electrical equipment without authorization. Fessenden often yearned for home and frequently holidayed near Peterborough with his Uncle Cortez and their respective families.

"I don't wonder at you wanting to leave the United States," wrote a friend from Trinity College at Port Hope, Ont. "Nothing would induce me to live there. . . ."

Nevertheless, there was enormous distinction to being a "professor" in the Victorian era. Fessenden, like Melville Bell and Samuel Morse before him, bore the title proudly before his name, like a feudal banner. Moreover, the U.S. academic/scientific community stirred his juices. Sweeping along in a flowing black cape like some 19th-century Batman, chomping a cigar, arguing with anyone about anything, Fessenden was a colourful, inquisitive soul. While Uncle Cortez pleaded for an occasional letter, his nephew kept up a voluminous correspondence with inventors, soldiers, scientists and academics. Once or twice, he sent suggestions to the President of the United States.

His roving mind kept returning to one persistent idea: a telephone without wires. By 1899 it was close to reality but Marconi was ahead of him. Fessenden hastily quit his university job and set up an experimental station, aided by a weather-reporting contract from the U.S. Weather Bureau. As usual he was on the verge of poverty. He was constantly dickering with railway lines, camera suppliers and manufacturers of all kinds for cut rates on goods or services.

Marconi and most of his contemporaries believed that radio transmisson was a whiplash effect — an impulse created by the violence of an electrical spark shot into the air. Fessenden disagreed. Riding a train between Toronto and Peterborough one day, he theorized that sound was transmitted as a continuous wave, like the light from a flame. As such, it could be made to carry speech. Pursuing this theory back in his lab, he invented a way of interrupting a radio wave many thousands of times per second, theoretically making voice broadcast possible.

In 1900, two days before Christmas, he rigged crude equipment between 500-foot towers, a mile apart, and called to his assistant, Alfred Thiessen. The muddled sound, Thiessen telegraphed back, sounded like "the flapping wings of a flock of birds." Fessenden made adjustments and spoke slowly and distinctly: "Is it snowing where you are, Mr. Thiessen?" Thiessen *heard*, through the air — words without wires!

Yet still Marconi dominated the headlines. Fessenden's own scrapbooks contained more news of his rival than himself, including Marconi's smug remark to one reporter: "I don't think Prof. Fessenden will interfere with my plans."

Fessenden set up the National Electric Signalling Company with help from two Pittsburgh millionaires. The crux of his inventions at the time was a "frequency alternator" that transmitted power at 70,000 cycles per second. Radio waves travel in the air, ripple fashion, like a series of expanding domes. They move at approximately 186,000 miles per second, the speed of light. To create them, a transmitter must send electrical pulses at a very rapid rate: many thousands or millions of waves per second. These various "frequencies" — which do not alter the speed-of-light rate of travel — are commonly stated as kilohertz and megahertz. One kilohertz is 1,000 waves or "cycles" per second; one megahertz is a million waves per second. Fessenden had achieved a 70 kilohertz frequency — "low" by today's standards but adequate for his purposes.

In 1906 he piled one achievement atop another. He sent the first two-way broadcast across the Atlantic in code; to that point Marconi had only managed one-way transmissions. In November while making voice tests in New England Fessenden received an astonishing message from his man in Scotland: the latter in early dawn had heard fragments of the tests. By sheer chance, the first voice transmission had crossed the Atlantic!

Fessenden was elated. He planned a demonstration to satisfy all doubters. On Christmas Eve, from his station near Boston, he stepped before a crude little microphone to broadcast a Christmas program to specially equipped ships a thousand miles away in the

Caribbean. The assistant who was supposed to help stood frozen in the world's first recorded instance of mike fright. It became a Fessenden one-man show. He played "O Holy Night" on the violin, sang, read "Glory to God in the highest and on earth peace and goodwill to all men" and signed off with a "Merry Christmas" to all his listeners. For good measure, he did another broadcast on New Year's Eve.

Yet even this remarkable feat won him no particular attention. For years after, he enjoyed neither peace nor goodwill. Shrewd Marconi had tied up all rights for radio transmission throughout the British Empire. In the United States, Fessenden fought continuous court actions against corporations that were using his radio patents. All the time, a torrent of inventions spilled out of his labs, including a sonic depth finder for ships, a turbo-electric drive for battleships, a wireless compass, and various submarine signalling devices. At one point he dabbled in experiments with solar energy.

In 1928, with his life and health almost gone, he won a settlement for close to a million dollars. It was too late for the pleasures and honours he deserved. After he died in 1932, the New York *Herald Tribune* editorialized, "It sometimes happens that one man can be right against the world. Professor Fessenden was that man. . . .It is ironic that among the hundreds of thousands of radio engineers whose commonplaces of theory rest on what Fessenden fought for bitterly and alone, only a handful realize that the battle ever happened."

# Chapter 12

## The Independents

Reginald Boss was that luckiest of men, a Canadian exactly right for his time. He had no scientific education. Indeed, he didn't get to grade school until he was eight years old, and his formal learning ended with a commercial course at Kerr's Business College in Saint John, N.B.

Nor was he any matinee idol. His warm but protuberant puppydog eyes peered out from an otherwise unremarkable face and his severe haircut left his large ears alone and out-thrust like semaphores. But in the Golden Age of Tinkerers, Boss could tinker with the best of them.

About 1883, as a Bathurst, N.B. teenager, he launched his telephone career with two five-by-three-inch tin drums, two pieces of sheepskin and a quarter mile of bare copper wire. He covered the drums with sheepskins, attached the wire with buttons and connected his home to his father's general store. "Transmission was real good and the calling was done by tapping on the centre button," Boss recalled later.

He made a similar set for an admiring neighbour and "painted them walnut colour so they would look nice." When other customers rapped on his door Boss never refused them, through sheer good nature and because he revelled in tinkering. He went to Boston, buying and begging parts for proper telephones. He began building pole lines. He incorporated the Gloucester County Telephone Company, installed Bathurst's first exchange, and in 1897 bought the Miscou and Shippegan Telephone Line from the federal government. Some years later Boss ended up as district superintendent of the New Brunswick Telephone Company.

All over Canada young men like him were fussing with homemade equipment and starting their own telephone companies. None had the genius of a Fessenden or the financial resources of a Bell Canada. But they gave telephones to villages, hamlets and farms when no major company could or would.

After Bell's patents were voided in 1885 anyone could make or deal in telephone equipment. So many contenders sprang up that the Bell Company began signing individual community contracts (more than 70 in Ontario and Quebec between 1891 and 1910) to meet local competition. Toronto closed a sweet deal in 1891, getting lower rates for its subscribers *and* $8,000 a year cash for the city.

One way or another Bell stayed on top of the heap. The Federal Telephone Company and Merchants Telephone Company of Montreal rose to challenge the big company in its heartland. The Canadian Machine Telephone Company in Peterborough, proudly touting its new Lorimer Automatic, vowed to charge no rental until it had as many local subscribers as Bell. All three were eventually swallowed up. They simply could not match Bell's service. The latter argued (with such slogans as "Two Bells Means Two Bills") that competition in the telephone industry offered a choice of evils rather than benefits: half the service or double the cost. City subscribers seemed to agree.

Smaller communities were sometimes hard pressed to get *one* Bell. In Sudbury in 1902 the Bell Company demanded 25 subscribers before opening an exchange. Only 23 Sudbury residents applied for service, but they got it by adding to their ranks the well-known Canadians, John Doe and his brother Richard. The exchange, in Herbert Young's drugstore at Cedar and Durham streets, gave day and night service. The night operator slept between calls on an old four-poster bed with sawed-down legs. By day druggist Young hoisted the bed to the ceiling with a pulley so he could use the floor space.

Beyond the sweeping skirts of Mother Bell, scores of other small companies made it on their own. Their members were often ignorant of the principles of telephony, and their subscribers even more so. Some housewives refused to answer the phone until they had donned a clean apron. The Burgessville, Ont., system was slow to start in 1904 because the locals believed "if a kink is left in the wire the call will not get through, it will come right back again." The service was slapdash. Sometimes the exchange was in a farmer's kitchen. In at least one town it was run by the blacksmith. But subscribers loved the independent companies, for they drew hundreds of byways and backwaters into the communications revolution.

"When sickness is in the home and moments stand between the life of the sufferer and medical aid, the value of the rural telephone can not be computed in dollars and cents," glowed an Ontario Municipal Board report in 1910. "When fire threatens destruction a moment or two will suffice to summon the prompt assistance of neighbours and in this way many valuable buildings are saved every year. Thieves and tramps no longer prowl through districts terrorizing the women and children and stealing whatever they can lay hands upon, for the telephone pursues them with relentless speed and renders escape impossible."

Independent companies were started by whoever felt the need. In Aylmer, Ont., it was four farmers, who strung wire along their fence lines. In Dryden, Ont., it was the storekeeper. (Earlier, one leather-lunged resident used to call the store by megaphone from a half-mile away.)

Northern Telephone — eventually extending across northwestern Ontario from the Manitoba boundary to the shores of Hudson Bay and into northern Quebec — began with two innocents from southern Ontario. In 1895 Durham schoolteacher Angus McKelvie, taking a boat to Lake Temiskaming to see what "New Ontario" was all about, met Bobcaygeon druggist Tom McCamus who didn't even know enough to bring a tent. They quickly wised up to the ways of the north, went into the sawmill business, dabbled in mining and discovered the fabulous silver deposit that is now Cobalt.

In 1904, tired of shouting back and forth from sawmill to office, they started Temiskaming Telephone Company, based in New Liskeard. They immediately demonstrated their prospectors' flair. To establish rights in Cobalt ahead of a rival, Temiskaming Tel's representatives simply raced in and nailed a pay phone to a tree in the middle of town.

In 1905, 73 small companies in Ontario and Quebec came

together in the Canadian Independent Telephone Association. Their object was survival and the enemy, as they saw it, was the likes of Bell Telephone. Their membership did not include Central Telephone of New Brunswick, which was a pity. Howard Perley Robinson of Central could have taught them his David and Goliath act.

# The Battle of Central Tel

If the directors of New Brunswick Telephone had owned a crystal ball in 1905 they would have never sparred with Howard Robinson. They would have gazed into the future and seen in him a director of a dozen companies including the CPR, International Paper and the Royal Bank; the chairman of their very own New Brunswick Tel; a director of the Canadian Press; associate owner of the Saint John *Telegraph Journal* and *Evening Times Globe*; an organizer of New Brunswick Broadcasting and owner of a 130-acre island. In short: a man who got what he wanted.

But in 1905 anyone who did not take note of the steely gunfighter's eyes in the pugnacious face assumed Robinson was a harmless young fellow who should have been running a spool factory. For years his father had manufactured wooden spools for British thread manufacturers. When the British began making their own, Robinson Sr.'s Sussex, N.B., factory closed down with a last keening wail of its siren. With that Howard Robinson dropped out of university.

Robinson Sr. bought a weekly newspaper and printing press. His son learned the trade. They started a mail order business, supplying dairies with the parchment to wrap around pounds of butter. When the father died in 1901 Robinson, then 27, planned to publish farm magazines across Canada. But in 1904 he agreed to be treasurer of the new Central Telephone company, started by a Kings County merchant and his son. This simple civic-minded act brought Robinson to a crossroads in his life.

By 1905 the company had several lines between Sussex and Saint John but the merchant's son, as general manager, had made an unholy mess of the books. Robinson trustingly covered Central's $50,000 overdraft from his personal savings — and placed himself on the verge of bankruptcy. The merchant's son resigned. Robinson unwittingly became general manager, secretary-

Howard P. Robinson challenged New Brunswick Telephone and ultimately took it over. NEW BRUNSWICK TELEPHONE.

treasurer and director of a company that was "beginning nowhere and ending nowhere."

He offered Central Telephone to Senator F. P. Thomson, head of New Brunswick Tel. "Not interested,"said the Senator.

"Can I at least meet with your board of directors?" Robinson asked.

"It would be a waste of time," said Thompson.

"Then go to hell!" snapped Robinson, whose red hair went with a short temper. "The next time I make you an offer, you'll be interested!"

He stomped the streets of Fredericton, cooling off, and went back to his hotel room, ashamed and discouraged. All night he racked his brain for a way out. At dawn Robinson grimly decided to make Central Telephone succeed.

He tracked down seven influential New Brunswickers, induced them to put up $10,000 apiece and paid off Central's debts. Then he built up a work-force (including one Reginald Boss), declared war on New Brunswick Tel, and won the opening rounds.

In Sackville, the older company's wires were strung on electric light poles. An obscure clause in the charter stated that the municipal council must approve any third line of poles to be erected on any town or city street. Accordingly, Central put up a second line in Sackville. It meant New Brunswick Tel could not build a *proper* line of its own — namely, the third in town — without the nuisance and delay of going to council.

New Brunswick Tel was building a line around the coast toward Bathurst. Central, with permission from the federal Minister of Railways and Canals, took a short cut along the Intercolonial Railway and got there first. New Brunswick Tel complained bitterly to Sir Wilfrid Laurier, but too late.

To this point Central, being short of toll lines between larger communities, was sometimes permitted to share its rival's. In July 1906, New Brunswick Tel cut off that privilege. The telephone war turned nasty. With lawyers standing ready for court and linemen swarming in the field, Robinson started building parallel lines in enemy territory. It was clear within a month that this cutthroat competition would kill both companies. New Brunswick Tel was ready to deal. So was Robinson, but on his own terms.

As the merger took shape, each participant was to have equal financial footing and could appoint seven directors to a 15-man board. Shareholders of both sides would elect the 15th; the side controlling the most votes would therefore elect the president.

Robinson knew his future hinged on that vote. He poked and probed for angles and learned with delight that Mother Bell, owner of a third of New Brunswick Tel's voting stock, was unhappy with her offspring. The New Brunswick company had broken a cardinal rule: instead of buying equipment from the Bell subsidiary, Northern Electric, it was dealing with a Chicago supply company.

Off to Montreal went Robinson, to capitalize on the family quarrel. He won an audience with C. F. Sise. Would Bell abstain from the vote? Sise appraised the young man from the east and liked the cut of his jib. All right, he told Robinson; Bell Telephone would stay out of it.

At the stockholders meeting in June, 1907, New Brunswick Tel's establishment was smug, but Robinson could scarcely suppress his glee. When the proxies were counted Central had a clear majority and so named its designate, S. H. White, as president. Robinson became managing director and chief executive officer, a job he held until his death. In five years he had come a long way from making butter paper.

# Dr. Demers' Little Empire

Of all the occupations and professions, none was so addicted to telephones as the medical one. Dozens of small exchanges began because of it. A telephone from home to office, drugstore or the next town saved the MD countless hours and miles. More than that, the scientific mysteries of telephony tickled every medic's curiosity. Dr. Alexander Carruthers Beatty of Garden Hill near Port Hope, Ont., didn't even charge the first people who shared his line. This entitled him to listen in (and join in) on other conversations when he felt like it (which was often) and to answer trouble complaints with a brusque "Get a ladder and fix it yourself!"

The king of them all, who parlayed one line into a modest telephone empire, was J.-Ferdinand Demers, M.D., of Saint-Octave-de-Métis, east of Rimouski on the St. Lawrence River. In 1897, 26 years old, not long out of Laval University medical school but an entrepreneur at heart, he put up the first line from his house to the railway station. Soon he extended it to the neighboring village of Sainte-Flavie. His main rival was, of all people, his medical competitor in Saint-Octave-de-Métis. Dr. François-Xavier Bossé had just opened the first telephone office in the region. The two locked horns in town council that autumn and the following spring, to see who should get local tax exemptions. Demers won.

Spending more time with his ear to a receiver than to a stethoscope, he founded the Métis Telephone Company with $2,500. His little firm scrambled along the railway line from Ste.-Flavie to Matane on the east and toward Rimouski on the west. With the Great North Western telegraph line on the opposite side of the track, train passengers rode between columns of "sentinels," as a contemporary put it.

Since 1890 Bell Telephone had held Rimouski firmly in its grip. Dr. Demers now sent the mighty Bell a brisk letter. As he explained it later for a Parliamentary committee, "We told them they would have to sell the plant or we would ruin their company. We would build a parallel line taking all the subscribers away from their plant. They decided to sell it for $2,000."

Why did the Bell bow to such a rank amateur? Perhaps because already Métis Telephone was "family" to all the little villages on the South Shore, generating a loyalty and affection that the Montreal monolith could never match. Certainly, Demers ran a charmingly informal business. When asked how many employees he had, he admitted cheerfully, "I never counted them." His "65 or 70" operators — he wasn't sure how many — were paid on a percentage basis: 10 percent of subscription revenues and 20 percent of long distance tolls. His four linemen tended 1,200 miles of line for $9 a week. Certain farmers on a four-party line could get local service for $12 a year. Town people, with local and long-distance service day and night, paid $20. Large companies, such as saw mills, paid $25.

By 1904 Demers had quit medicine; there was more money in telephones. A dapper young man with oval face, prim bow of a moustache and a sleek dark cap of hair, he moved easily in the business milieu. His brother, a lawyer, and his father Georges, a Quebec broker, joined with him. Company profit that year was $12,000 after expenses, maintenance, interest on capital and a seven percent dividend. Demers' success intrigued the Select Committee of 1905, a Parliamentary probe into the Canadian telephone industry. He was a willing and entertaining witness at the Ottawa hearing.

"Tell us about your toll rates as compared with the Bell's," he was asked.

"From Levis to Riviere du Loup we give them five minutes for 25 cents," Demers said proudly. "The Bell rate is 60 cents for three minutes, so that our price is more than one-half lower for nearly double the time. . . .And we give a perfect service, we can hear talking plainly without pronouncing words."

The committee members exchanged startled glances.

"What do you mean by that?"

"Just in a whisper," whispered Dr. Demers.

Joker though he was, Demers was no country bumpkin. Joseph H. G. Bergeron, MP for Beauharnois, tried to back the doctor into a corner and came up with handfuls of air. Demers' rate calculations included a charge for something defined as "$10 incidental." Bergeron asked, "What was that $10 incidental?"

"I wanted to raise as much as possible the cost price of building that line, I wanted to set the cost, the price, as high as possible and to show the revenue as little as possible in order to demonstrate to this committee that it is still a paying business proposition."

Bergeron reeled before the tortuous reply but pressed on.

"Could you not give service to the farmers at less than $12 and still make money?"

Demers did not like the question. "It might be done, we have not tried it."

"As a matter of information, doctor, you could rent your phones cheaper than $12?"

"I am not interested in replying to you any more on that subject. You ask me to demonstrate to you that this was a paying proposition at a $12 rate and I have done so."

"Yes, but can you not supply them cheaper?"

"You asked me how I calculated it and I have shown you."

"There is a little dark spot there, that little allowance of $10?"

"There is a little dark spot in most places," said Dr. Demers.

# Chapter 13

## The Bell at Bay

The atmosphere in the House of Commons committee room was charged with excitement that morning of May 19, 1905. On this day, Charles Fleetford Sise would appear before the Select Committee of the House of Commons on Telephone Service in Canada. Today the Bell would grapple with its enemies.

The old man's unseen presence had hovered ghostlike over the Committee for nearly two months. To everyone familiar with the telephone business — as some Committee members now thought they were — the mighty Bell was at bay, and Sise *was* the Bell. Would he fight? Would he win? Was he too old? He was a mystery to most of them. Few had even laid eyes on him.

When he entered the packed room every eye turned. At nearly 71, his hair was grey and his hearing was failing. But the piercing blue eyes were as chilly as the raw winds sweeping Parliament Hill that morning, and he stood sturdy as a mast. He had lived through hurricanes in the south Atlantic. He had been dashed to his deck with smashed ribs off the coast of Australia. In the logbook of Conscientious Fighting Sise, the Select Committee qualified as a minor gale.

He sat aloof through the cross-examination of a previous

witness. He was sworn in, and fielded a series of routine questions in monosyllables. The Committee members, like politicians since time began, never used one word when ten would do. Sise answered in the same way he managed his business — with absolute economy: "Yes," "No," "It was," "That is correct." For the first half hour his longest answer did not exceed six words. The Committee appeared to have a tame witness on its hands.

Then he saw an opening, on the matter of Bell acquisition of patents, and his sarcasm flashed.

"There has been stated, I see in the report of the Committee, by some one who could not have known much about it," Sise said acidly, "that the company gave $1,928,000 for these patents, making a burden of $3.60 per subscriber. To show how absolutely incorrect this is, at the time these patents were purchased the company's capital was $1 million, of which $600,000 was in live assets, and I can hardly see how anyone could expect us to give away $2,000,000 out of $1,000,000 capital!"

The Bell supporters grinned; it was going to be a virtuoso performance. The Committee men soberly reappraised their witness. Obviously, they had better have the facts straight or he would eat them alive.

Nevertheless, Sise did not take the Committee lightly. He knew that his company's future, perhaps its very existence, depended upon the men in this room. So far, all the omens had been bad. Government regulation was in the air. In 1892 Parliament had ruled that telephone rates could not be raised without government permission. Ten years later it made telephone service obligatory wherever technically possible, regardless of economics.

The same year, 1902, Fort William and Port Arthur started cooperative municipal telephone systems in competition with the Bell. A civic committee in Saint John, N.B. recommended the same. Peterborough granted a franchise to an independent company. Ottawa and London renewed the Bell franchise only after bitter controversy. Even immortal Brantford refused to renew the exclusive franchise, after all that Alec Bell had done to put it on the map. Competition was so vicious in some areas that rival linemen actually sawed down the opposition's poles. By 1905 the Dominion Grange, a farm organization, and the Union of Canadian Municipalities had both called for federal operation of long distance telephone lines. All three prairie provinces were fretting under the Bell's yoke.

The Select Committee was convened to examine and sort out the chaos, but clearly not for the benefit of Bell. Its chairman was Postmaster-General Sir William Mulock, a revered elder statesman heaped with honours. His strong square face with the ever-popular King Edward VII beard beamed down from the walls of Toronto University — space reserved for portraits of the movers and shakers of his time. When Sir William confessed to a bias, as he now did, right-thinking people everywhere tended to side with him.

"I can not see why it is not as much the duty of the state to take charge of the telephone as it is to conduct the postal service," he told the Commons in 1905.

The Bell was therefore wary when Mulock's motion for a Select Committee passed the Commons on March 17, 1906. Subordinates cabled the news to Italy where Sise was holidaying with his wife. On March 28, a week after the Commons convened, they cabled again: "While nothing especially alarming, the Board, and Boston, advises your return."

Sise took the next ship home, conferred with officials of the parent company on April 18, and was in Montreal the next night. For the next three weeks he closeted himself with his troops, marshalling facts and rebuttals against the accusations pouring out of Ottawa. In the end, Sise's personal touch, his voluminous memory, his intimate knowledge of every detail, would serve his company best.

The charges against the Bell were clear enough: its service was inadequate, its American parentage was detrimental to Canada (the Committee did not know, or care, that the American parents had never wanted Bell Canada in the first place), its rates were discriminatory and it used its long-established position to thwart efforts at competition.

The hearings opened with a distinctly anti-Bell tone. The first major witness, Francis Dagger, was a state telephone man. At 40, he already had 24 years' experience, mostly in England. Two years before, Mulock had hired him to compile a telephone report. Now he was special advisor to the Committee. As he rose in his crisp wing collar, eyes shining with missionary zeal behind heavy-rimmed glasses, it bespoke trouble for the Bell.

Dagger was the kind of man who once advised a meeting of independent telephonists, "If you sup with the Devil you will need a long spoon. In other words, keep clear of entangling alliances with your competitor, the Bell. There are only two sides in the battle you are engaged in, Bell and the Independent, and he that is not with you is against you. . . ." Now Dagger came out flatly in favour of public ownership. It would, he claimed, "give service, at much lower rates and earn satisfactory profits." He cited the British state telephone system as a model.

Another Committee member, early in the hearings, said, "I want the Bell to be treated in the best possible way when it comes but the idea I want to get out is that it is a monopoly and that it is pursuing a policy of queering every attempt of the public to improve the situation."

And when doughty Dr. Demers regaled the Committee with the tale of the Bell's retreat from Rimouski, MP Joseph-Gédéon-Horace Bergeron chortled, "What do you think of that, Mr. Chairman!"

"I suppose the Bell Telephone Company had to surrender before its powerful competitor," Mulock said mockingly.

On his return to Canada, Sise wrote Hugh Baker: "Instead of enquiring into the pros and cons of Governmental and Municipal Ownership they are simply sending out a dragnet for evidence with which to injure the Bell." Yet he was cool and in complete control in his five appearances between May 9 and May 20. He had rates, mileages, contracts, the weight of telephone wire, all at his fingertips. His evidence amounted to 243 pages of printed text. Yet often, after Committee men had laboured for minutes through the highways and byways of a longwinded question, Sise gave them a laconic "Yes" or "No."

Sometimes, though, when the situation seemed to call for it, the old man laid on his lash of scorn.

"Have you any agreement for exchange of business with the New Brunswick Company?" a Committee man asked.

"Well, as we don't go within 500 miles of them," said Sise dryly, "it is rather difficult to exchange."

"The public are not getting the best possible service under the Bell system?" suggested another.

"I beg your pardon," snapped Sise. "I take issue with that. We give a better service than anybody else."

"In England the government controls the long distance lines," remarked Mulock.

"Yes," Sise shot back, "and gives conspicuously the worst service in the world."

"You say you have paid in the history of the company a fair dividend to your shareholders?" demanded another member.

"*They* don't think so!"

Sise's fiercest antagonist by far was Toronto MP William Findlay Maclean. Of him, a contemporary writer said, "He is the voice of one crying in the wilderness, self-isolated, persistent, oftentimes petulant, always picturesque. . . .If you oppose him, you are an enemy to 'the people'. . .Mr. Maclean is perhaps as little loved as any man in public life. . . ."

Maclean did not want to be loved. For all his 52 years he had resisted the Establishment in all its forms. His bold handsome profile was devoid of whiskers, in an era when nearly every man wore a beard or, at least, a moustache. He deplored the Parliamentary liquor bar. He opposed free railway passes for MPs and MLAs. He voted against pensions for ex-ministers of the Crown and against increased pay for MPs. When a raise came through anyway, he gave his own to charity.

Maclean wanted the name "Hudson Bay" changed to "Canada Sea" and, at a time when Canada was bound heart and soul to England, proposed that his country "should make her own constitution, should negotiate her own treaties, and should elect her own chief magistrate." As editor-in-chief of the *World*, liveliest and most opinionated of the Toronto dailies, Maclean had attacked the Bell for years. Now, bristling with the joy of battle, he faced the resprepresentative of everything he hated.

For hours he and Sise stood verbally toe-to-toe, hammering away. As Maclean's newspaper reported peevishly, "important testimony was wormed out of Mr. Sise" but he was "not by any terms what might be termed a willing witness." Indeed, when the editor-MP spoke, Sise was as obstinate as only he could be.

Once Maclean cried accusingly, "That is in your charter, to give telephone service!"

"No, it is not to give it," said Sise.

"Well, what?"

"To furnish it under rental."

Maclean tackled him on a recurrent sore point: Bell's refusal to hook long-distance lines into small companies.

"We do not wish and the public do not wish that a man building a 15-mile iron line should occupy our copper line from Toronto to Quebec," Sise retorted, "in a vain effort to talk to a man in Quebec so that the man in Quebec will throw down his telephone and curse the Bell and refuse to pay the toll because he can not hear."

Maclean took another tack.

"In some cities there is discrimination in some shape or another. If it is not in the rental it is in the use of the phone and in some others almost free phones."

"We have had no complaints from those having free phones," said Sise, deadpan.

"Who takes the responsibility for interrupted telephone service?" demanded Maclean.

"Who compensates us if lightning burns down an exchange, as has happened?" countered the Bell president.

"We are going to pass a law that will compensate you, perhaps."

"Perhaps," sniffed Sise, "but we are not working on perhaps."

In the end — although his logbook once termed the questioning "venomous" — Sise yielded not an inch, and immeasurably strengthened the Bell's case. A few days later it received another assist from Herbert Webb, an English telephonist of 25 years. Webb shot holes in Francis Dagger's testimony, which he found "rather vague. . .a good many of the figures are really inaccurate." Webb went on to deplore the British long-distance service, adding, "The other day I spent a whole morning trying to get a call through from Brighton to London, 50 miles." Finally, he sent a telegram.

After hearing 50 witnesses in 43 sittings the Committee went away to deliberate. On July 15 it released an astonishing statement: "Owing to the voluminous nature of the evidence submitted and to the late period of the session, your Committee feel that it is impossible for them, during the present session, to come to any conclusions, or to make any recommendations to the House upon the subject referred to them."

And that was the last Canada heard from the Select Committee.

There were loud cries of "Foul!" from the anti-Bell forces. Maclean tried to amend the Committee resolution but lost. In October, Mulock retired as Postmaster-General to become Chief Justice of the Ontario Exchequer Court. The *World*, supported by the Toronto *News* and Opposition leader Robert Borden, claimed Prime Minister Laurier had offered up Mulock as a sacrifice to the telephone and telegraph corporations. Certainly Laurier's choice for new Postmaster-General seemed to bear out the accusations. He was A. B. Aylesworth, Bell telephone's legal counsel at the Select Committee, the man least likely to rock Mother Bell's boat.

A year later the House passed a bill bringing all federally chartered telephone companies under the Board of Railway Commissioners. In the debate, Bell's efficiency was praised but its refusal to allow some competing companies to connect to its lines was criticized.

Under the bill all telephone tolls, contracts and agreements between companies would be subject to the Commissioners' approval. It was an effort to prevent telephone monopoly and get uniformity of regulations. The legislation reaffirmed Bell's charter and status, thus tacitly endorsing most of its procedures. In effect: the Bell wasn't perfect but it was the best Canada had.

Sise and his troops quickly learned to let well enough alone. As the bill neared its final stage, the Bell was planning to increase its capital stock. This would have required an amendment to the new legislation currently before the Senate. Laurier himself called Sise in for a benevolent chat. The government couldn't accept the amendment, warned the Prime Minister, and if the bill found its way back into the Commons there might be a nasty backlash. Sise got the message and backed off.

The bill passed. Winner and still the heavyweight champion of Canadian telephony, Sise climbed on the *Empress of Britain* to resume his holiday, only 16 months late.

# Dwindling Empire

The Bell's reprieve was brief. A groundswell of resentment was rising in the West against telephone giants, railways, grain companies, anything that bespoke eastern power and monopoly. Cooperative movements were in the air. Grain farmers wanted telephone connections to the Canada they were helping to feed. In rapid succession, the three prairie provinces founded North America's first state-owned telephone systems.

Although Alberta was first to build a government line, in 1907, Manitoba began planning one in 1905. It hired Francis Dagger as "expert advisor," at $6,000 a year, to sponsor a vigorous public ownership campaign. Dr. Demers, the saviour of Saint-Octave-de-Métis, was invited from Quebec to tell Manitoba's French-Canadian population of the glories of a non-Bell system.

The Bell sent its own speakers stumping across the province. In a 1906 referendum only 54 of 123 municipalities backed public ownership — far short of the necessary three fifths — but more than half of the popular vote was in favour. The government interpreted that as a victory.

When the Tories were reelected in 1907, Premier Rodmond Roblin (grandfather of latter-day Premier Duff Roblin) notified Sise that Manitoba was going into the business. If Bell wanted to sell, Manitoba might buy.

"Manitoba is not the entire Northwest," Sise replied crustily. "The Company has large interests in the Provinces beyond Manitoba which must be protected."

When Roblin went ahead anyway, Sise had a change of heart. In December he agreed to deal. Manitoba bought out Bell for $3,300,000, which Francis Dagger screamed was "a present of $1 million over and above the actual value." On January 15, 1908, Manitoba had its own telephone company.

Saskatchewan accepted public ownership without fuss. It had only 3,250 phones. In 1907 hired-gun Dagger rode into the province and recommended provincial control of long distance lines, and local ownership in cities, towns and municipalities. (After his western triumphs, Dagger moved to Ontario to be telephone superintendent of the Railway and Municipal Board for 25 years.)

Most of his Saskatchewan recommendations were embodied in three separate acts. One of them permitted five or more persons to organize and operate their own system, under the new Department of Railways, Telephones and Telegraphs. In 1909 Saskatchewan took over the Bell operations for $358,000. By the end of the year, with new construction and other acquisitions, it had 5,710 subscribers.

Over in cow country the Bell had been warring with the people since 1883 when its Winnipeg manager, Frank Walsh, remarked patronizingly, "When Edmonton is large enough and desires an exchange I will appoint an agent for that purpose, but I think it will be a long time before that will be necessary." Edmonton thought its population of 500 *was* large enough. Two years later the *Bulletin* was "pleased to hear that the Minister of Agriculture has voided the Bell Company's patent in Canada."

Bell's problem was really the eternal eastern Canadian problem: it simply didn't understand the West. This was not entirely the East's fault. Westerners *were* erratic and unpredictable. At one point — mercifully, not during the reign of C. F. Sise — Alberta had a gunslinging telephone technician named Fred Daniels, a tall boy with an angel's face and wild curly hair. He used switchboards for target practice.

Nor did Bell executives ever learn to relate to their first Calgary manager, Jack Innes. He wore fringed buckskins, cowboy boots and a coonskin cap, spent most of his time drawing cartoons and was fired within a year. The second manager at least had tradition going for him. As a Mountie in Battleford in 1877, Major James Walker had received the first telegraph message sent out of Alberta territory. Later he quit the force, started a lumber mill in Calgary, was the town's first mayor, and installed its first telephone. He *looked* like a manager, with his lean face and gimlet eyes carried proudly on a frame that seemed always to be standing at attention. The Major's big flaw was his easygoing western attitude toward collecting debts.

"I do not think our auditor will accept your explanations of why outstandings are unpaid," the Bell treasurer wrote sorrowfully, in 1889. "Out of 30, the first on the list has 'skipped out' and the other 29 are 'away from home.' You do not appear to understand our system. . . ."

That autumn Sise himself went west to trim the sails. His logbook from Calgary noted glumly, "40 subscribers, no revenue. . . .Service, lines, instruments and accounts in wretched condition. Exchange in an old shanty in charge of a boy." He hired another manager (who held him up for a 35 percent commission) and went away believing that Calgary "has a good future."

Calgary had but Bell did not. In 1892 the company sought to transfer its western holdings to the North American Telegraph Company. Sise was president of North American and its directors were also Bell directors. This clumsy attempt at subterfuge was rebuffed, and simply made Alberta angrier.

A staunch advocate of public ownership, Calgary's Charles Walter Peterson, former deputy minister of agriculture for the Northwest Territories, now conducted a one-man crusade. Eyes blazing beneath the neat archways of his centre-parted hair, he said that telephones were imperative for farms and ranch evolution but "in every instance we have been blocked by the Bell people." When the CPR in 1904 gave Bell exclusive rights to put telephones in railway stations, it sealed the telephone company's doom. If there was anything Alberta hated more than the Bell it was the CPR.

The tide of ill will rose higher. Bob Edwards, editor of the irreverent Calgary *Eye Opener*, wrote, "Great God, the Bell telephone service in Calgary is a disgrace!" When Sise visited the city, a *Herald* headline greeted him with "KILLING COMPETITION OBJECT OF BELL OFFICIALS." Edmonton went its own way. Its telephones belonged to Alex Taylor, who had made Alberta's first phone call in 1885. He wanted to sell his system for $25,000. Sise offered half that. Edmonton city bid $17,000 and, on January 1, 1905, found itself with a telephone system, which it has operated ever since.

A full-fledged province now, Alberta budgeted funds for long-distance lines in areas not served by Bell — Calgary-Banff, Edmonton-Lloydminster, Lethbridge-Crowsnest Pass. Construction began in the winter of 1906–7, one of the worst in prairie history. Trains from the East were three weeks late. South of Calgary, two-thirds of the range cattle died. Telephone crews around Banff slept in tents at 50 below zero F. Yet by spring, North America's first government telephone line was finished.

Now, backed against the wall, Sise sent an emissary west, offering to share the province's telephone systems. Alberta refused. Bell threatened to build an exchange in Edmonton. "DECLARATION OF WAR" chortled Alberta headlines.

On February 14 the Alberta legislature met to offer Sise a valentine. W. H. Cushing, minister of public works, denounced the Bell charter as "the most pernicious and iniquitous piece of legislation that has ever been perpetrated upon people claiming to be free." For once the Conservative opposition agreed. An MLA from Gleichen termed the Bell "A bloodsucking corporation," winning for himself a hearty round of applause. Then pioneer telephone man John T. Moore of Red Deer rose up like an avenging prophet of old. Gone was his customary twinkle of eye and his grandfatherly smile couched in the immaculate Van Dyke beard.

"This is Emancipation Day in the very broad sense," he thundered. "Alberta kindles today a beacon light of wise legislation that will illumine the pages of Canadian history for many years to come. . . .The Bell Telephone Company should have been hewn down long ago. . . .Yonder in Montreal there is a man named Sise, the Napoleon of the Bell Telephone Company. . .and today the Bell Telephone Company meets its Waterloo."

The Irish brogue of John T. Moore rose and fell like a shillelagh around the head and shoulders of the absent C. F. Sise. He likened

Sise to Belshazzar, last king of Babylon, whose doom was forecast by handwriting on the wall.

"Thou art weighed in the balance and found wanting," John T. Moore warned the wretched Sise. "Thy Kingdom in Alberta is to be taken away and the People will come into their own."

Applause billowed around the Member for Red Deer as he envisioned thousands of Albertans "bound together by cords of copper and steel. . . .Commerce will be stimulated, time and money will be saved, friendship will be promoted; sociability will be encouraged and these ever extending wires will not only bring pecuniary profit to the people and the province but will also carry into hundreds and thousands of hearts and homes throughout this broad land cheering messages of hope, encouragement, grace and good will."

Rhetoric did not automatically put telephones into Alberta hands. More letters flowed between East and West. The government offered to buy out Bell. Sise said he'd sell to any company in which the province could be controlling stockholder, if the Bell could also hold stock. Alberta laughed in his face. Sise read Alberta a little lecture about the Canadian penchant for shunning risks but claiming the spoils: "In the 27 years in which this Company's stock has been offered for sale I am not aware that one Citizen of Alberta has ever taken or offered to take one share of stock. . . ."

But he was beaten. The government's new line worked. Alberta cared little about the cruel economics of telephony and for a few years it wouldn't matter. In 1908 Alberta bought the Bell holdings for $675,000. Significantly (or so the Bell men thought), the deal was closed on April Fool's Day.

# Chapter 14

## The Turbulent Years

Like a giant aroused from a long deep sleep, the nation rose and shook itself. Dynasties toppled. Heroes fell and died. For 20 strange unsettling years, 1900–1920, Canada was convulsed by amalgamation, tragedy and technical change.

Silent movies flickered from the silver screens of five-cent theatres called nickelodeons. Flying machines soared crazily into the air at Baddeck. Horseless carriages snorted down every city street. Sam McLaughlin of Oshawa made the momentous change from carriages to automobiles, thereby founding General Motors of Canada. Bell Canada bought its first auto in 1909.

Queen Victoria was dead, incredibly, after 64 years of reign. Dr. Demers, after a term as president of the Canadian Independent Telephone Association, left his beloved Quebec telephones in 1909 to found and manage La Traverse de Lévis Limitée (the Quebec-Lévis Ferry). A year later he died of typhoid. Robert McMicking, Sir William Van Horne and Sandford Fleming died in 1915; Charles Sise, three years later.

In British Columbia, the Victoria and Esquimalt, New Westminster, Nanaimo and Kootenay companies came together into

British Columbia Telephone Company Limited. Maritime Telegraph and Telephone bought the down-at-heels P.E.I. company for $117,000. In Newfoundland a half-century of Anglo-American domination ended when Western Union bought the company. Having no interest in telephones, the American telegraph giant resold to J. J. Murphy, whose United Towns Electric already owned telephone exchanges on the island. Murphy, a martinet who filled his employees with terror and punctuality, formed Avalon Telephone Company in 1919.

Telegraphy was winnowing down to two all-Canadian giants, one of them tracing its bloodlines back to the first message of 1846. Canadian Northern, a railway extending through northern Ontario and the western provinces, started a telegraph division in 1902. The Grand Trunk Pacific followed suit in 1906. Nine years later Canadian Northern embraced Great North Western Telegraph — the Erastus Wiman company that had scooped up Montreal Telegraph nearly 35 years before, after *it* had swallowed that smaller fish, the Toronto, Hamilton and Niagara Electro-Magnetic Telegraph.

The Canadian government then acquired Canadian Northern, plus the telegraph operations of Grand Trunk Pacific and the National Transcontinental Railway (running from Quebec through Ontario to Winnipeg). In 1920 all of these came together in the name of Canadian National. Now, in telegraphy as in railroads, it was CN versus CP.

The poet Robert W. Service, saluting the Yukon telegrapher in 1909, had written, "Faintly as from a star,/Voices come o'er the line;/Voices of ghosts afar. . . ." But the "voices" on telegraph and telephone were no longer faint. The new teleprinter made it possible to take a message off the wire, printed and ready to deliver. In the 1870s Edison had produced "quadruplex" — the technique of transmitting two telegraph messages simultaneously in each direction over one wire. Now in the early 1900s, one wire could carry *six* messages in each direction at one time.

In 1910 metallic doughnuts appeared on the Bell wires out of Montreal. These "loading coils" — magnetic material wound with insulated wire — reduced transmission loss. A phenomenon called the "phantom circuit" was giving telephone companies three channels for the price of two: on any two-wire circuit they could install coils at either end and induce a third voice circuit between them *without wires*!

Improvements in wireless telegraphy were sending ripples through the entire telecommunications industry. Early wireless experimenters had been hampered by two serious deficiencies: the methods of detecting waves were insensitive and cumbersome, and there was no way of amplifying the signals when they were received.

The first breakthrough, in 1904, was the diode valve which allowed signals to pass in one direction but not the other. It turned the rapidly varying radio waves into audible signals, but could not amplify them. Then in 1907 an American, Lee DeForest, fed the faint radio impulses to a wire mesh grid placed inside the diode. His was the first amplifying vacuum tube, an epoch-making invention that ushered in the electronic age. It brought wireless radio pell-mell into the 20th century, and was a boon to telephone repeater systems. Bell introduced Canada's first at Kingston in 1917. The human voice was reaching ever farther through the distance.

# The Canadian Press

For newspapermen there was a new "voice" on the telegraph wires. For half a century, telegraph operators — Robert McMicking among them — had been the original newspaper "stringers." As part-time correspondents they filed reports of local murders, fires, robberies and deaths of prominent citizens. It was mutually profitable: newspapers needed news; telegraph companies needed revenue. Press despatches travelled in the 1880s at the preferred rate of 40¢ for the first 100 words, 25¢ for each additional hundred. The telegraphers' sign-off — "30" — became standard on newspaper copy.

Through the last 25 years of the century, every editor from Quebec City to London knew the name "Easson," slugged on thin hand-written tissue sheets with news from home and abroad. Robert F. Easson, who'd started as a messenger with Montreal Telegraph in 1847, was Great North Western's superintendent of press and commercial news. In effect he ran Canada's first newspaper wire service, and editors revered him.

But when the CPR completed its cross-country network, Great North Western tumbled to second place. Tradition be damned: GNW had no wires west of Winnipeg; CPR reached from coast to coast. By 1889 CPR telegraph coverage was so coveted that the mayor of Vancouver sent a plaintive note to CPR president William Van Horne. Why was Vancouver alone and unloved, telegraphically speaking?

"While the other cities like New Westminster and Victoria, are constantly mentioned in the press despatches forwarded for the benefit of the continental papers and other journals," complained the mayor, "the City of Vancouver hardly ever finds reference abroad. I beg that you will be good enough in our mutual interest to bring about a change and remedy of this apparent neglect and make arrangements so that Vancouver gets her proper dues."

When Canadian Pacific in 1894 won the exclusive right to carry Associated Press despatches across Canada, Great North Western's ultimate doom was sealed. CP Telegraphs might have monopolized the field forever, had it not pulled a colossal boner. In 1907 it curtly informed the three Winnipeg dailies that their previous composite summary of Canadian and foreign despatches, direct from Montreal, would be cancelled. Thereafter, they would have to buy AP news via leased wire from Minnesota and bring Canadian news from the east at their own expense. All together, the edict tripled their wire-service costs.

To that point the Winnipeg newspaper owners rarely exchanged anything but insults. *The Free Press*, edited by the legendary John Dafoe, was owned by Clifford Sifton, he of the sheepskin-coat pioneers. The *Telegram* belonged to the Tories, including Manitoba Premier Sir Rodmond Roblin. The *Tribune's* owner, R. L. Richardson, a former Independent Liberal MP, had once opposed Sifton in a general election. Sifton, a Liberal MP and former cabinet minister, hated Roblin (a former Liberal) and was not exactly enamoured of Richardson. The feelings were mutual. But now, in uneasy truce, the three banded against the common enemy and formed their own Western Press Association.

The CPR retaliated, hitting the new association with a whopping 50 percent surcharge on all its news despatches. The Winnipeg dailies sidestepped the blow by using Great North Western and Canadian Northern telegraph services at normal press rates, and running up hefty long distance telephone bills. In print, they opened fire on the CPR.

Stung by these prairie upstarts, the mighty railway on a day's notice increased the press rate for *every* newspaper in western Canada. The extra costs ranged from 66 to 233 percent. While every editorial writer in the West rose up in wrath, the CPR — having not yet heard the phrase "public relations" — compounded its errors. The small but feisty Nelson, B.C. *News* had slung more than its quota of stones at the Goliath. Now the CPR cut off the *News'* AP service completely. The little paper stayed alive with a daily news digest, sent at commercial rates by Western Associated Press.

The newsmen, being not without political clout, took their case to Wilfrid Laurier. He stopped the feud and the CPR's bone-headedness reverberated among all telegraph companies. In 1910 they were stripped of news-gathering rights. Henceforth they would only transmit press news. In 1911, the Canadian Press cooperative news gathering agency was founded. Out of the telegraph wars rose a respected institution, a Canadian household word, the "CP" of a million datelines. And when the dust settled CP and the CPR had kissed and made up, with the former transmitting news along the latter's telegraph wires.

# Trial by Fire

In the welter of emergencies and disasters that cluttered those first 20 years, communications proved their worth again and again. How had the country managed before telegraph, telephone, and radio came to sound the alarm and help pick up the pieces? A sense of pride and *esprit de corps* surged through the industry. It was understood, without ever being said, that telephone, tele-graph and wireless men and women would stay at their posts, even at risk of death, until the job was done.

On July 11, 1911, fire raged into the mining community of South Porcupine in northern Ontario. Telephone operator Marie Gibbons stayed at her switchboard, calling the warning, until flames licked at the doorstep. A neighbour burst in shouting, "What the hell are you doing here?" As she seized her shoes and the company cash box and followed him out the door, the blazing stairway collapsed.

One day later a hot midafternoon gale from the northwest whipped a fire through Campbellton, N.B. In four hours churches, hospitals, three mills, opera house, two banks and dwellings for 4,000 people were reduced to cinders. Reginald Boss, 45 years old and as much in love with telephones as ever, rigged up an emergency set and worked all night. At four a.m., Boss had a cup of tea and one slice of bread, his first meal since noon.

World War I carried off every able-bodied man with puttees round his shins, dishpan helmet on his head and a patriotic song on his lips. As the men marched away to save the world for democracy, Canadian women astonished themselves and the opposite sex by doing "men's work," and doing it exceedingly well. The men who ran the country rewarded them by finally allowing women to vote.

"We were busy all the time; we took on anybody who could operate at all. We even had a society dame who came to help out," remembered Hamilton telephone operator, Ethel Hannaford. "We would roll Red Cross bandages in our rest periods. . . .When the armistice was signed the place went wild. It was mad excitement, girls crying, laughing and nearly every [switchboard] signal in Hamilton burning.

"When we finally got off duty we went out on the streets where pandemonium reigned. Fellows with feather ticklers, horns and others throwing talcum powder on you. We got 'roped in' with a gang and were taken away down King Street East before we made a breakaway. Over in the Court House square the bands were playing old hymns, 'Unto the Hills,' 'Oh God Our Help,' 'O Canada' and 'God Save the King,' and people were crying."

In Victoria, the words of peace put such a load on the telephone lines that the main switchboard blew out.

Impossible as it seemed, more tragedy was already on the way. Although no accurate count was ever made, the influenza epidemic of 1918–19 killed 30,000 to 45,000 Canadians. In Montreal, 3,028 died in one month; in Toronto 68 succumbed on a single October day. Entire families were buried in one week.

Telephone and telegraph employees were sick along with everyone else — Bell at one point had 80 percent absenteeism — yet traffic was up 10 to 20 percent. In British Columbia, where 28 percent of the telephone operators were laid low by November 1, a typical message came into headquarters from the Rossland office: "Town quarantined. Impossible to get help. Linemen all ill. Will work as long as possible."

Fire, war, epidemic — these terrors were as old as mankind. The Halifax explosion of 1917 and the Regina tornado of 1912 were different. They struck so swiftly, so unexpectedly, that only wild freaks of chance separated the living from the dead. In both incidents telephone and telegraph people, like other rescuers, reached deep into resources they never knew they had.

Regina was simmering in a heat wave that Sunday afternoon of June 30, 1912. At four p.m. two black clouds massed in either corner of the southern sky. At 4:50 they collided, building a funnel of wind that slammed into the city like a fist. Its ground speed was estimated at 50 miles an hour; its swirling vortex may have been 500 miles an hour.

In three minutes it levelled an area three blocks wide by 12 blocks long, killed at least 28 people (estimates went as high as 65), injured 200 and left 2,500 homeless. The property loss was at least four million dollars, and Regina was nearly 47 years paying it off.

People were tossed in the air like dolls. A waterspout erupted from Wascana Lake beside the Legislative Buildings. The Methodist Church was torn to rubble. The telephone exchange at Lorne St. and 11th Avenue, directly in the tornado's path, shuddered under the impact. Its roof came loose and a wall collapsed. The nine operators and two maintenance men on duty had no time to escape. A 15-ton switchboard crashed from second floor to basement, carrying three screaming operators with it, headphones still at their ears. The other occupants were buried.

Incredibly, none was killed. A janitor helped the three out of the rubble and they stumbled to the Regina *Leader*, which was untouched by the wind and unaware of the disaster. At first the editors thought the girls' story was a stunt to get their names in the paper.

With radio still unknown, and all the telephones out, some Reginans were hours learning exactly what happened. But within an hour Canadian Pacific telegraph repairmen patched together a wire and a terse message reached the outside world: "Cyclone hit Regina, 16:50. City in ruins." Telephone and telegraph linemen worked through the night. By Monday afternoon the telephone line was open to Moose Jaw and a replacement switchboard was on its way from Montreal. By Tuesday, long distance lines were working.

The telegraph office meanwhile was deluged with incoming and outgoing messages — 5,000 on the night of the tornado; 8,000 the next day. Rumours ran wild across Canada: that Moose Jaw had been wiped out, that 40 telephone girls had been killed, that a train and all its passengers had been swept off a track. By July 5, the *Leader* was publishing long lists of telegrams awaiting recipients at railway telegraph offices. The CPR boosted its normal complement

The Regina Cyclone
of 1912 tore a swath
through the city,
demolishing
numerous buildings
including the
telephone exchange
shown here.
SASKATCHEWAN
ARCHIVES.

Telephone lines across the Prairies. ALBERTA GOVERNMENT TELEPHONES.

John T. Moore, who led the
movement for the takeover of Bell's
operations in Alberta by the
province. ALBERTA GOVERNMENT
TELEPHONES.

of 8 operators to 20. Their chief went 48 hours without sleep, and with only 2 meals.

The telephone service was a month returning to normal but the tornado had one salutary effect. Since Regina had to rebuild most of its system, it went to modern automatic telephones.

The Halifax explosion struck with even less warning. On the morning of December 6, 1917, the French freighter *Mont Blanc* was steaming along the waterfront toward Bedford Basin. She was a floating bomb: loaded with 35 tons of benzole, a highly inflammable petrochemical, 200 tons of trinitrotoluene (TNT) and 2,300 tons of picric acid, even more destructive than TNT.

A little before nine, directly in front of the docks, with the *Mont Blanc* whistling frantic warnings, the Norwegian ship *Imo* — in broad daylight, travelling down the wrong side of the channel — rammed into the starboard side of the munitions ship.

The *Mont Blanc* did not immediately explode but the benzole caught fire. The crew abandoned ship. At first, the watchers on shore were unperturbed. Among them, railway despatcher Vincent Coleman, a handsome young man with a strong cleft chin and a plume of dark hair, curiously eyed the blaze. He did not dream it would touch him.

Suddenly a sailor burst in with the awful facts of the *Mont Blanc's* cargo. Coleman and his chief clerk sprang for the door. Then Coleman turned back. Trains were due soon. He must warn them. His clerk begged him to flee; Coleman had a family. But he went to his key and began telegraphing the message ". . .munition ship on fire in the harbour. . .Goodbye. . . ."

At 9:06 the *Mont Blanc* blew up.

The harbour churned. Piers, ships, buildings vanished. The blast uprooted trees, swept away bridges, tossed railway tracks and freight cars. In seconds, a square mile of Halifax was obliterated. Then the air forced out by the blast rushed back to fill the vacuum, sucking lethal debris with it. Hundreds of fires flashed up from scattered coals and live wires. A tidal wave surged from the harbour. A mushroom cloud of smoke and gases towered three miles in the sky.

Aboard HMCS *Niobe*, seaman Dave McWilliams — the former telegrapher who relayed the news of Dr. Crippen's capture seven years before — heard steel fragments falling like peas on the deck overhead. Yellow fumes from TNT billowed through the *Niobe's* portholes. "Abandon Ship!" came the cry.

"I went down the sea ladder into a life boat which was running with blood," McWilliams remembered afterward. "Soon afterward I was crawling up a slime-covered wharf, wondering how I got there."

Later he tried to telegraph his family. Since the wires were down he had to send a cable via Halifax, Bermuda, New York and Montreal to reach Quebec City.

At the CPR telegraph office in Saint John, N.B., 150 miles away, a fellow operator said to 21-year-old Dan Hanneberry, "The building's shaking!" They wondered idly if it was a mild earthquake.

By evening Hanneberry was on a train to Halifax. The crippled city needed all the operators it could get, as lines went back into service and relief messages and casualty lists poured through. He arrived at four a.m. and 58 years later still remembered the eerie quiet that hung over the city: "I never heard such a deep silence. It was a feeling of terror."

Many of the dead (estimated from 1,600 to 1,960) and injured (9,000 to 10,000) had been taken to temporary hospitals and morgues but the city was still a ruin. Hanneberry and others worked and slept in the telegraph office for six days.

Maritime Tel and Tel had already staggered back into service although 582 phones were knocked out. A section of pole line along Barrington, the waterfront street, was obliterated; even the wires were torn to shreds. The four city exchanges were damaged in varying degrees. In one, an 18-pound piece of iron plummeted through the roof and sank into the floor of the operators' room. No one there or in any other telephone office was killed, although some were badly cut by flying glass. Operators Mary and Nellie Elliott died in their downtown home. Mary would have reported for duty at 11:30 a.m.; Nellie should already have been at work but had phoned in sick.

By afternoon part of the telephone system was working. For three days, the volume of traffic was 120 percent above normal. Haligonians queued up in the streets to phone friends and relatives until MT&T pleaded through the newspapers to limit nonessential calls. While every available operator worked at the switchboards — some in bloodstained bandages — headquarters clerks and managers began boarding up scores of broken windows. Female clerks organized emergency kitchens on the spot. "Meals at all hours!" read a sign in one exchange.

Telecommunications were vital to the war effort at home and at the front. Personnel of the Canadian Signal Corps laying cable during the major Allied offensive east of Arras, France, September 1918. PUBLIC ARCHIVES OF CANADA PA 3080.

Operators at the switchboard in the operations room, Canadian Corps Headquarters, France, 1917. PUBLIC ARCHIVES OF CANADA C 64009.

Newspaper advertisements urged conservation of telephone use and materials. BELL CANADA TELEPHONE HISTORICAL COLLECTION.

The day after the explosion a blizzard and bitter cold compounded Halifax's misery. With windows still gaping, some operators worked at their boards in whirling snow. With streets impassable, MT&T found blankets and made beds in the exchanges out of tables and chairs. Many employees had no homes to go to anyway.

Intercompany rivalries were forgotten. New Brunswick Tel's general superintendent was on the first train into Halifax, offering help. Northern Electric sent a repair team from Sackville. New England Tel shipped an expert from Boston and Lewis McFarlane, president of Bell Canada, telegraphed promises of assistance. Together, with hundreds of other volunteers, they lifted Halifax back to its feet.

When the crisis passed reaction set in. Of MT&T's original 165 operators in Halifax, 82 were gone within a few months. Many had been left homeless and moved away to join relatives. Others had lost families but kept working on sheer adrenalin. Now, with the job done, they broke down and put Halifax behind them. MT&T canvassed the province for retirees as temporary replacements, put its training school on double shift and by 1918 had 107 new women on the job.

Several navy men were decorated for their gallantry during rescue operations. Evidently no one thought of a medal for telegrapher Vincent Coleman, who gave up his life to send the warning.

# Chapter 15

## The Agonies of Government Ownership

The October 1920 issue of *The Transmitter*, Alberta Government Telephones' company magazine, mirrored the private dream of every country cousin in the land. "Signs of a Prosperous District" cried the cover line. There, in the background, a perfect tiny farmhouse nestled beside a hiproof barn, friendly windmill and tall silo. In the middle distance Father and the hired man were cutting golden grain, with the newest tractor and reapers. Regiments of stooks marched eyes-front through the foreground. A Model T spluttered over a road smoother than any prairie trail ever was. And high in the sky, binding Prosperous District to the world, stretched the lines of AGT.

There it was, enshrined forever in picture postcard art, the Good Life every farmer wanted and expected, now that the war-to-end-all-wars was over. But not one farm in a thousand looked like that. The prevailing style was rusty machinery, tired horses, fields ravaged by drought, and buildings buffed silver-grey by wind, sun and rain.

As for Alberta Government Telephones — it hadn't seen prosperity for 12 years. The prairie governments were learning in a hurry the hard lesson that Bell and other private companies had acquired over a quarter century: running a telephone company was more complex than hanging wire on tall poles. Always they were haunted by the additional hazards of any state-controlled system: potential corruption, bad management and political meddling.

Saskatchewan came out best, with twice as many phones per rural person as its neighbours. Its farmer companies were a happy compromise: the government kept the lucrative long-distance revenue itself; rural people ran their own show, which they liked. Their inexperience sometimes cost them dearly in construction errors, and their phone bill — $18 a year or less — did not reflect additional hidden costs. It covered only operation and maintenance; debenture payments came out of land taxes.

Those disadvantages aside, Saskatchewan by 1918 had 337 rural companies with 8,024 subscribers. By 1920, this latecomer to telephony was in the forefront. Its 90,506 phones were exceeded only in Ontario and Quebec. Its 54,000 miles of lines topped all provinces. There had been shaky moments. In 1916 corruption charges rocked the government and several MLAs were expelled and convicted of criminal offences. A Royal Commission was assigned to examine telephones, but after 21 inconclusive months and $50,000 expenses it fizzled out.

Alberta Government Telephones, with the other prairie systems, suffered from what Dr. James Mavor, a University of Toronto professor of political economy, called "a total lack of the elementary principles of commercial accounting." U. of T. historian George Britnell in an M.A. thesis pointed to Alberta's ". . .lavish use of public money to bolster up the waning political fortunes of the administration."

Alberta went on a building spree with its public funds while holding to unrealistically low rates. For nearly 20 years, residence phones cost $24 a year in cities and $15–$20 in the country. Throughout this time AGT made little attempt to set up a depreciation reserve. While service expanded the books retrogressed.

In 1917 Edward R. Michener, the darkly handsome leader of the Conservative opposition (whose 17-year-old son Roland was destined to be Canada's Governor-General) charged "mismanagement and waste in construction" and losses of $2 million. He claimed the government had destroyed documents pertinent to the losses and demanded an independent audit. The Liberals voted him down but by 1920 could no longer ignore the facts. Allowing even a minimal four percent depreciation, AGT lost $160,000 that year.

One of its more celebrated boners was in buying a million dollars worth of telephone poles. By 1920 the yards were brimming with trimmed cedars, tamaracks and jackpine. For years Saskatchewan bought most of its poles there. The CPR took some for telegraph lines. Drumheller propped up coal mines with them. Others were cut up for railway ties and still others went into buffalo compounds in national parks.

Manitoba Government Telephones showed a similar passion for poles. A Royal Commission exploring MGT's vagaries discovered nearly 163,000 poles on hand and 20,000 on order by the end of 1911. That was enough to build 4,000 miles of line, roughly the total mileage of the previous four years. The reason for this embarrassment of tall timber, said James Mavor, in an exhaustive study of the Manitoba system: "The Telephone Commission had practically been obliged by a member of the government to purchase an excessive number of poles from a client of his who was in financial difficulties."

As a revered professor of political economy for 27 years, Mavor wielded enormous influence. He numbered George Bernard Shaw and Leo Tolstoy among his friends. Through the latter, and through his clout with the Canadian government, Mavor brought the Doukhobors to Canada from Russia at the turn of the century. For 25 years he headed the exhibition committee of the Art Gallery of Toronto, and he helped found the Royal Ontario Museum. A lean patriarch of 60, with a domed forehead and wild flowing beard, Mavor looked, one writer said, "as though he might have taught Noah how to re-establish civilization after the ark stranded on Mount Ararat."

In 1914 this "Aristotle of Toronto" had just published a massive 400,000-word *Economic History of Russia*, a classic in its time. It took 17 years to write. Mavor then whipped off *Government Telephones — The Experience of Manitoba, Canada* — a lucid, crushing indictment of the system.

Mavor admitted his candid distaste for state ownership of any kind. "Where, from a mistaken view of the public interest, the State establishes a monopoly in its own favour, the inevitable result is the suppression of individual initiative and the absence of reserves of technical skill and efficient labour," he wrote. "The cost to the nation of any service rendered by the Government is *always* greater than the cost of the same service rendered by competent persons other than those in the Government service."

He deemed Manitoba a classic example. The government had plunged into telephone expansion "without regard to the cost of it. . . .The public interest was wholly disregarded. . . .The Government from the beginning assiduously used the telephone business for political ends. . . .Manitoba Government Telephones have up till the present time involved the province in a loss of upwards of a million dollars."

On taking over from the Bell, Manitoba had promised to cut rates in half. Premier Rodmond Roblin also pledged that the system would be self-supporting and "must be kept clean and clear of all party politics or influence." A three-man telephone commission was appointed. Four years later, one member reported, "The whole running of the system has been permeated with politics."

Plunging feverishly into construction, the government lashed its commissioners on to greater and greater excess. It forced them to build unprofitable and unnecessary rural lines and to give night service where none was needed, all to pacify government critics or please government heelers. Employees were imposed upon the commission — "recommended" was the euphemism — by cabinet ministers. Late in 1911 the commission chairman told the Manitoba *Free Press* that "every mile of rural telephone line which was estimated would cost us $150 four years ago we have found by actual experience now costs us $200."

Meanwhile the government announced large annual profits, by including large amounts of unearned rentals as income and by setting aside no reserve for depreciation. After three years' operation, Mavor found deficits conservatively estimated at $300,000.

One tawdry side effect was the growing cynicism of Manitobans. A commission memorandum noted, "not only have we had to contend with the fact that politics came into the question so much, but apparently a large percentage of hotel-keepers, storekeepers, and liverymen have been hand in glove with our men — foremen and others — in cheating the government." The commissioners added that the same corruption probably would have prevailed under a Liberal administration.

Roblin's Tories now proposed rate revisions on numbers of calls for business phones in Winnipeg, and a higher flat rate for residence use almost everywhere. Winnipegers, for instance, would pay $48 a year instead of $25. The public was outraged.

In the historic Canadian manner, the whole mess fell into the laps of a Royal Commission. It produced, in Mavor's view, a "whitewash" of the government. It found that the system had "been administered extravagantly and that very large savings could be made by economical management; that there has not been a proper system of accounting. . . ." The province's telephone commissioners, having been made the goats, resigned.

"The Government deliberately sacrificed their loyal servants that their sins might go unpunished," declared Mavor. "After four years of public ownership a prosperous business was well on the road to ruin."

Although reorganized under a single commissioner, the telephone system ran up more deficits. The Winnipeg *Telegram* denounced MGT as "one of the most iron-clad monopolies imposed on any people." It said rates ought to be "cut in two" — the very phrase Premier Roblin had used in castigating the Bell nine years before.

Nonetheless the prairie systems lurched into the '20s. By the end of the decade, George Britnell found that prairie people were getting reasonable and even superior service, even if paying through the nose via provincial deficits and higher taxes. Although devoting less attention to economy than a C. F. Sise, the systems were "extended far beyond what they would have been, probably, under private ownership."

To rural people that most precious commodity, human contact, was worth some financial penalties. In farming, where time meant money, parts could be ordered and grain or livestock sold or purchased in minutes instead of days. Friends or the doctor were only a call away. The cooperative movement blossomed under the new communications. There was even frail hope that the telephone would lessen a new and alarming trend — the retreat of youth from the land.

"The day is near at hand," said the Calgary *Albertan* "when thanks to the Alberta government, every successful farmer in the province will be able to possess a telephone that will help to keep the boy on the farm. He won't need to be jealous of his city friends."

# Legends of the Party Line

Early each morning during World War I, the telegraph-telephone operator at Dunvegan, Alta., a man named Vaillancourt, rang "nine shorts" along the party line. Every subscriber instantly reached for the receiver and heard Vaillancourt read the latest war news off the telegraph wire. That was how Dunvegan heard about armistice on November 11, 1918. Indeed, it was how Dunvegan heard about everything.

From the first "Great War" to the second, the party line was the soul of rural Canada. Sometimes a single copper strand, rarely more than four, it ran on spindly poles down all the back roads of the nation. In winter the wire turned into white ropes of ice and hoar frost. Then, louder than other times, it hummed like hives of bees. Winter or summer, a country boy could press his ear to a wooden pole, hear the wires' eternal song and know, in ways he couldn't truly understand, that it tied him to the far-off world.

The party line was everyman's line, in every sense. Whether it rang nine shorts, six shorts, or three longs–two shorts, every subscriber heard the signal, identifed it, weighed its possible gossip value and indulged in the God-given right of rubbering (from "rubber-neck": one who listens in). Lifting the receiver with minimum noise became a delicate art, perfected by the hand that rocked the cradle. Sometimes rubberers betrayed their perfidy with heavy breathing, a telltale cough, the background cry of a cuckoo clock or the gabble of the only parrot for 30 miles around. Companies such as the Baird Secret Service System of Chicago stood ready with gadgets to foil these eavesdroppers ("Let Us Stop Your Rubbernecks"), but made few rural sales. Tuning in on other people's private lives was exquisite entertainment. It was daytime soap opera, for real. It nurtured a sense of community. Sometimes a rubberneck even felt obliged to participate.

A Kirkland Lake cattle buyer, dickering with an Englehart farmer over a Northern Telephone party line, finally declared, "Twenty-six cents a pound, that's my final offer." The farmer said he'd think about it. A third voice spoke up, "Take his offer, you damn fool, you can't beat 26 cents!" A Newfoundland woman on an Avalon line was about to order $2 worth of stewing meat from her butcher when a third party shrilled, "Mr. Lawlor, don't you dare send meat to that woman! She's tried every butcher in town and hasn't paid one of them yet!"

That rural lines were the lifeblood of Canada was evident from the statistics for 1921. Of 2,365 telephone systems, 1,544 were rural cooperatives. Saskatchewan, predominantly rural, had 1,215 companies, more than twice those of the runnerup, Ontario. Northern Electric, the nation's leading telephone supplier, catered to the rural market with a booklet, "How to Build Rural Telephone Lines." The sixth edition in 1923 was a wealth of information: history of the telephone; how to set up a constitution and bylaws; how to sink poles, splice wires, attach crossarms — even what size holes to drill and the kinds of bolts and nails to use. It told rural folks how to hang the wall phone (there was no other kind, in the country): never in a damp place, never near an open window, never near grounded metallic objects. The mouthpiece would please all users if located precisely 56½ inches above the floor. Tall men or small children could swivel it up or down.

Northern Electric told the uninitiated how to "Ring Up": "First turn the generator crank briskly in a clockwise direction. This causes a current to be sent through the line which rings the bell of the party wanted. After 'ringing up', remove the receiver from the hook and apply it to the ear. The hook, relieved of the weight of the receiver, immediately springs up. As soon as the called party responds, you begin the conversation. . . " On completing the conversation subscribers were expected to "ring off by a rapid turn of the crank in a clockwise direction, thus informing the other parties on the line that you are through. . . ."

In Northern Electric's suggested numbering code, the first party's number was two short rings; the second, three shorts; the third, one long and one short; and so on, through 20 variations, until at three longs–four shorts it grew cumbersome. The suggested general signal for fire alarms, weather forecasts or market reports was two shorts and one long.

To call Central the subscriber had to "ring once by turning the crank with the right hand at the same time pressing the button on the lower left hand side of the telephone with the left hand. . . ." Central was still catalyst of the party line; friend of all the people; fount of all wisdom. Subscribers regarded her as personal property. A New Liskeard woman, leaving home for a month's vacation, called Northern Telephone to say they might as well lay off her operator and save the company some money.

Central knew everyone's number, address and habits. More than one country doctor was tracked down at a poker game, curling rink or the bootlegger's by his telephone watchdog. Dorothy Smith of Ferintosh, Alta., won a $100 reward in 1928 for phoning farmers on all the appropriate roads and coordinating a posse that trapped bank robbers before they could get out of the neighborhood. The operator at Mannville, Alta., served briefly as a go-between for a warring husband and wife who had moved to

Bell Canada's employees demonstrating the new dial system to Toronto firemen, policemen and streetcar conductors in preparation for the cutover of Bell Canada's first dial exchange, "GRover", Toronto, in July 1924. BELL CANADA TELEPHONE HISTORICAL COLLECTION.

adjacent houses and would speak only through a third party.

In 1928, the Regina *Star* summed it up: "Ting-a-ling called a bell, or to be accurate 68,638 bells, for every blessed one of the rural telephone systems in Saskatchewan has been working overtime during the past few weeks. If it wasn't a call to town for harvest help or a spare part for the binder or thresher, it was a telephone conversation with the neighbours as to weather prospects and whether to tackle the crop next morning or leave it for another day. . . .It has robbed farm life of its isolation and helped link up the life and work of the province."

## "Welcome to the Yukon"

And still the North lay silent. That, in fact, was why some Northerners chose to live there, but progress was never one for letting people alone.

The Yukon goldseekers of 1898 had insisted on a telegraph tie-up with the transcontinental system. It made little sense because, as the federal government had suspected, the boom was short-lived. At first a line crept from Dawson City to the place later known as Whitehorse; then on to Skagway, where steamers docked off the Pacific.

Messages by slow boat did not fit with the grandiose dreams of '98. The Canadian government reluctantly extended a line to central British Columbia, picking up the old Collins Overland. It was a mistake. Maintenance was impossible over the hundreds of miles of wilderness. The telegraph was out for weeks on end, and never functioned properly.

With the advent of radio, the government asked the Army to take a different tack. In 1923 eight officers and men of the Royal Canadian Corps of Signals trekked north from Edmonton to see if wireless would work in the Great Unknown. Some went to Dawson, the others to Mayo, 125 miles southeast. Among the latter was pink-cheeked Bill Lockhart, a 20-year-old signalman who had learned Morse code from his Scoutmaster 12 years before.

They squeezed themselves and a 120-watt transmitter into a small frame shack. "There was a little gas engine in the kitchen, filling the place with fumes," Lockhart recalled, long after. "It's a wonder we weren't all asphyxiated."

Both parties began "calling and listening, calling and listening." They were not surprised when nothing happened. Most technicians feared that the northern atmosphere, particularly the

Aurora Borealis, would ruin transmission. On October 20 Sgt. Lockhart was playing a hand of bridge, after interminable tests, when his set whined "wee-oo, wee-oo" — a sign of contact. He sprang to the transmitter and shouted, "Welcome to the Yukon!" No reply. Sick at heart, he called again. This time Sgt. Frank Heath, the Dawson signalman, came through.

"Why didn't you answer my first call?" demanded Lockhart.

"Because we were all dancing an Indian war dance around here," shouted Heath.

Soon the radio shacks were jammed with well wishers. Banks, mining companies, steamship companies, government, trappers and storekeepers fired off messages. Now they could do business "outside" in hours instead of months. Wireless had unlocked the North.

The federal government now planned a Northwest Territories network, with stations at Fort Smith, just over the Alberta boundary, at Fort Simpson where the Mackenzie and Liard Rivers meet, and at Herschel Island, a natural harbour on the brink of the Beaufort Sea. Messages would go to an Edmonton terminal and on to the CN and CP telegraph systems.

The Signal Corps assigned Lt. Hugh Young and three men to the tricky job of setting up at Herschel Island. Although only 26, Young was a good choice. He had been through an entire war, was wounded at 18, and had earned a postwar engineering degree from the University of Manitoba. The Army had lured him away from a tempting job offer in the U.S., where he would have worked on the crazy premise that silent pictures could be turned into "talkies." At the personal instigation of chief of staff Gen. Andrew McNaughton, Young did an about-face from Hollywood to the Arctic Ocean.

"Maybe it was because I was an ex-farm boy from Manitoba and McNaughton thought I could handle the difficulties of the north," Young recalled, 50 years later. "Or maybe he thought he'd never make an officer and a gentleman of me." (In fact, Young retired as a major-general.)

His party went north the way everyone did it in 1924: slow train from Edmonton to Waterways, then aboard a wood-burning steamer, *HBC Distributor*, across treacherous Great Slave Lake, and down the magnificent Mackenzie. There were tedious stops at tiny settlements — Providence, Simpson, Wrigley, Norman, Good Hope — oases in the aching emptiness of 1,100 miles of sky, water and timber. Finally, picking their way through the jigsaw puzzle of islands and channels that make up the Mackenzie Delta, they anchored at the Eskimo village, Aklavik. They sailed the last 180 miles to Herschel on an Eskimo schooner.

Their equipment and food were due to join them in early August, aboard the Bay steamer *Lady Kindersley* sailing around Alaska. By late August she hadn't arrived. An American whaler put into Herschel for repairs.

"The *Kindersley* will never make it now," the skipper told Young. "You better come out with us." Young was tempted, but there was a slim chance their boat would arrive. He chose to wait, and bought a little flour, salt pork and sugar from the whaler at outrageous prices. The bill totalled $4,000.

By September the short Arctic summer was over. Ice formed in the harbour. The *Kindersley* was obviously lost. (She had been crushed between ice floes at the northern tip of Alaska. Before she sank the crew radioed for help and sprang nimbly to solid ice carrying their rum ration.)

Young and party resigned themselves to a winter of living off the land. They shared Herschel Island with five Mounties, two Hudson's Bay traders, an old Australian beachcomber and five Eskimo families. The Signals men took over an abandoned missionary hut, covered it with snow blocks and converted two 50-gallon oil drums into a heater. There was unlimited coal. Through a small clerical error, a Bay ship had dumped 140 tons in Herschel the year before (the local man had ordered 40 tons).

With Eskimo women helping, Young and his men each made a suit of reindeer skin, worn fur in, and a suit of deerskin, worn fur out. They made sleeping bags in similar fashion. Although the temperature was often 35 below zero Fahrenheit with 35 mph gales, they were warm.

They built a sled with timbers from a wrecked ship in the harbour, bought a dogteam and learned to handle it. The farm boy from Manitoba and his most resourceful man, Cpl. Frank Riddell, were soon hunting caribou, trapping fox and living like natives, eating Herschel Island's version of the TV dinner: beans and bacon cooked, frozen in lumps and reheated on the trail.

On Christmas Day they splurged with one can of peaches to relieve the monotony of caribou and bannock. Through the evenings they improvised a radio: two glass plates and cigarette foil for tuner and condenser, metal armbands for rheostats, rabbit-snaring wire for coils, and some discarded batteries recharged with vinegar. Fumbling through the air waves, they hoped to reach

Dawson or Mayo. Instead they picked up dance music from a San Francisco hotel.

In midwinter Eskimo travellers brought news of the sunken *Kindersley.* Young and Riddell hitched up their dogs and made the 180-mile trip to Aklavik in five days, dining on rabbits and ptarmigan along the way. They learned that a food barge sent to them from Fort Smith in August had also gone down on Great Slave Lake. Young had had enough of Herschel. He sent a letter to Ottawa recommending Aklavik as the permanent station.

It opened in October, 1925. A year later the Northwest Territories and Yukon Radio System was functioning. By taking much of the risk out of aviation, radio opened wide the door to Canada's North. It would take more than that, however, to acquaint Ottawa with life north of the Arctic Circle.

As soon as Aklavik station was operating the military bureaucracy sent Hugh Young a stiff message: "Why and on what authority did you purchase dog team?" Young radioed his explanation. The Army ponderously granted authority to buy the dogs, 14 months after the fact, but drew his attention to a paragraph in King's Regulations, Canadian Army. Young looked it up. It pertained to horses. It advised all troops, "When animals are purchased numbers must be printed on hoof of animals."

Young had the last word. "Appreciate authority for purchase of dog team" he radioed back. "Regret unable to locate hoof on paw on which to print number."

# Radio on the Rails

By the '20s, Canada was primed for a radio explosion. It came in two forms. Prior to 1923 only long waves were considered capable of carrying signals over long distance. Short waves, deemed useful only at short range, were given over to ham operators who grumbled at this second-rate treatment. Then in 1923 they discovered they had the world at their fingertips. Short waves did, indeed, fade out a few score miles from a transmitter but they bounced off the ionosphere and came in again, strong and clear although erratic, thousands of miles away.

While the ham operators jubilantly searched out one another around the world, Guglielmo Marconi resolved to harness and exploit the phenomenon with beam systems. By the late '20s, with short wave beam stations, telegraph signals at 300 words per minute flashed across the longest distances on earth. Canada became part of a British Empire beam network, with a transmitter at Drummondville and a receiver at Yamachiche, both in Quebec and operated by Canadian Marconi.

Meanwhile Reginald Fessenden's brand of radio — broadcasting — had lain dormant since his historic Christmas and New Year's Eve broadcasts of 1906. Not until December 1919 did Canadian Marconi's Montreal transmitter, XWA, begin the first regular Canadian broadcasts, mostly code practice and phonograph records from a bare factory room. The company also advertised wireless receiving sets for $15: "Just the Christmas Gift for Your Boy."

The following May, XWA — later CFCF, Montreal — broadcast music to a select Chateau Laurier audience, including Sir Wilfrid Laurier, Sir Robert Borden and William Lyon Mackenzie King. But radio for the next couple of years was regarded as a boy's toy — odd noises coaxed to life with a crystal, a few batteries, a pair of headphones, a wire-wrapped cardboard box for an aerial and a wire probe called a "cat's whisker."

In 1922 Canada suddenly embraced the new medium with wild delight. The ugly war was almost forgotten. The country rollicked with loud music, bold women and bad booze. Good times were just around the corner, and radio's time had come.

On the night of March 28, 1,100 Torontonians queued up in a downpour for the privilege of crowding into the Masonic Temple around a square black box and a flaring speaker-horn. It was Toronto's first major demonstration, courtesy of experimental station 9AH.

At 8:30 a soprano sang "Annie Laurie" out of the horn and Luigi Romanelli's orchestra played "Wabash Blues." The people applauded madly. It was like 1877 and the telephone all over again, but this time, no wires. The miracle came out of thin air.

In May the first commercial broadcasting license went to CJGC, the Manitoba Free Press station. By 1923 Canada had 34 stations and Sir Henry Thornton, the new president of CNR, was hatching one of the brightest ideas in Canadian communications.

Thornton was already rather an oddity. He was an American with a British knighthood. He had won the hearts of union men, after assuming the general managership of a British railway, by insisting that a workmen's delegation be seated at a directors' meeting and by addressing them as "gentlemen." In World War I Major-General Thornton stood out again, in his uncommon courtesy toward all ranks.

On taking over Canadian National he habitually mingled with his workers, shaking every greasy hand within reach, his round, well-barbered face radiating good cheer. Now Thornton was putting radio on board moving trains, before most Canadians had it at home.

It began with transmission from CHYC, Northern Electric's Montreal station, to a special radio car with earphones at each seat. A group of Brooklyn tourists were the guinea pigs. Heading west, they heard music and a sales pitch about the scenic wonders they would view from CNR. The same year on New Year's Eve Sir Henry and his directors lined up before a microphone in Montreal to wish Ottawa a happy New Year — the first "network" broadcast — and to announce the new CN radio department.

Then CN took the plunge. It built CNRO Ottawa, and CNRA (for "Atlantic"), Moncton, and leased "phantom" stations in Edmonton, Calgary, Regina, Saskatoon, Winnipeg, Toronto and Montreal. Existing stations in those cities rented their facilities and substituted CN's call letters (CKAC, Montreal, for example, doubled as CNRM) during the two or three hours a day they transmitted railway programs. Broadcasts were interlocked with the schedules of passing CN trains. With additional phantoms in Quebec City, Halifax, London, Yorkton and Red Deer and the railway's own CNRV in Vancouver, Canada had a transcontinental network. Although it was primarily for CN travellers, any local listener within range of the phantom station could tune in.

There were gripes — members of Parliament deplored "this radio craze" and expenditure of "fabulous sums on radios and other frills and fads" — but passengers were entranced. Many heard their first broadcast on a train. Some bought tickets expressly to hear championship boxing, drama, news, music or market reports. The railway carried the first network coverage of an NHL playoff game — Montreal Canadiens against Ottawa Senators. Travellers heard Gordon Olive, a technician belatedly drafted as announcer, blurt "Dirty Ottawa!" in the heat of the game. Nobody had told him to be impartial because nobody knew. In 1924 there were less than a half dozen "sportscasters" in Canada, including a slim boyish-looking Toronto reporter named Foster Hewitt.

When CNRO celebrated its first birthday, listeners showered it with 6,000 telegrams and 20,000 letters. By 1925 CN had 37 radio-equipped cars staffed with uniformed operators. Broadcasts began with the distinctive clang of a locomotive bell. One Sunday, travellers were so moved by a silver-tongued prairie parson that they passed the hat on his behalf. On New Year's Eve, a train passing through Alberta picked up festivities from four different time zones and the passengers celebrated them all.

The biggest event in CN radio's short life was the July 1, 1927, Diamond Jubilee broadcast. Over a 21-station network 1,000 children chanted patriotic songs, the Peace Tower carillon chimed, bands played and Mackenzie King orated. A million Canadians listened at home or around speakers in public squares. It was a cooperative effort: Bell Canada was responsible for engineering, Northern Electric manufactured and assembled much of the equipment, and Canadian Marconi beamed the broadcast to Britain. It required 400 people and 10,000 miles of telephone and telegraph lines, including duplicate standby circuits. And the impresario-in-charge was Thomas Ahearn, 72, long since graduated from cigar box telephones, a grizzled handsome millionaire and a Bell Canada director.

"Such quickening of national feeling, such impulses of brotherhood has never been known at any one moment before in the history of Canada," glowed one report of the broadcast. In truth, this partnership of telephone, telegraph and radio stirred something in the Canadian psyche. As CN rolled to the end of the decade with 80 radio cars, it became a showcase for Canadian talent.

In 1929, radio manager Austin Weir produced Sunday concerts with the superb Toronto symphony (the musicians were reluctant to perform at first, lest radio not do justice to their music). A year later Weir hired young Merrill Denison (later a noted writer of Canadian corporate histories) and English producer Tyrone Guthrie (years later of Stratford Festival fame) to create "Romance of Canada," a quality dramatic series. A regional French-Canadian network produced its own music and drama. Between October, 1929, and May, 1931, CN averaged 20 hours of broadcasting a week from autumn to spring, strong on Canadian content.

But the listeners of October, 1929 also heard the ugly news of the Wall Street crash. Their world and CN radio's crumbled. On November 5, 1931, a terse announcement from Montreal said, "Radio reception on trains this month will be discontinued as a further move in the rigid economy campaign being carried on throughout the National system. . . ."

The Depression had killed radio on the rails, as it was killing so much else across the land.

# Chapter 16

## Bad Years

Officially it was the Great Depression, but many who lived through the '30s referred to them, with eloquent understatement, as the "Bad Years." The phrase was apt. Between 1929 and 1932, Canadian National's Telegraph revenues slumped from $6,122,152 a year to $3,676,338. For the first time in telephone history, "takeouts" exceeded installations. Bell, with about half the nation's phones, had a net loss of 113,657 during 1931–33.

The first three years were the worst, because they caught companies off guard. Between 1931 and 1933 Maritime Tel and Tel lost nearly 3,000 subscribers. New Brunswick was 10 years regaining its 1930 losses. British Columbia in those early years lost more than 12,000 phones. In one awful month, July 1932, an average of 40 B.C. subscribers a day dropped out.

The prairies reeled under a multiple blow — the general economic collapse coupled with crippling drought, insect plague and crop failure. The wind blew and blew, as always, but now it filled the air with drifting topsoil. The telephone systems, so predominantly rural, wilted along with the withering grain. Manitoba lost 16,000 customers between 1929 and 1932; Saskatchewan, 28,000; Alberta, 19,000.

Adding insult to injury, one of the worst sleet storms in Alberta history laid tons of ice on every span of telephone and telegraph lines in 1933. An Alberta Government Telephones man rode a pony out of Calgary the next morning into total desolation. More than 2,000 poles were down. Crossarms were shattered. The best copper wire, one-sixth of an inch thick, was broken or stretched thin as thread. The telephone man and his weary horse took a train back to Calgary; there was no other way to carry the bad news.

Ironically, telephone and telegraph service had never been better. Canadian National had just introduced a "carrier current" system — fast transmission of messages by waves similar to those of radio broadcasting but different in two respects: the waves were controlled and they did not leave the physical wires. Carrier current permitted the simultaneous exchange of 96 messages over frequencies guided by one pair of wires. Canadian Pacific soon provided the same service.

By 1933, a long-distance telephone connection could be made in 78 seconds, compared to 3.4 minutes in 1929. It spread over the one-year-old Trans-Canada Telephone System — 4,260 miles of #8 copper wire, cedar poles and steel pins fitted with pyrex insulators. It was built to a standard never before achieved, and it was to communications what the CPR had been to Canadian travel. Halifax could now speak to Victoria with the aid of only two intermediate operators.

Regrettably, the basic daytime rate for such a call was $10 — which was too high for most people. For $10 in 1933 you could buy a five-pound sirloin roast, a flannelette night gown, a pair of men's shoes, a windbreaker, a pound of bacon, a dozen oranges, a tailored skirt, a pound of butter, a 20-piece kitchen tea set, and have 50¢ left over for a good movie.

People with jobs lived in mingled dread and apathy.

"We had so little to do that when a job did come along it was an awful effort to do it," remembered Arnold Groleau, then just out of university and later an executive vice-president of Bell. "A lot of people never recovered from that outlook."

The shadow of dismissal hung over everyone. Many employees were supporting wives or husbands, parents and sometimes other relatives on a meagre income. A lost job could affect a dozen people.

Apprentice lineman Gillies McCormick filled his unemployed

time with education. He started with Saskatchewan Goverment Telephones at the brink of the Depression.

"We lived in local hotels, two to a room, 35¢ for meals," McCormick remembered 45 years later, when he was general manager of Sask Tel. "Stayed weekends too, because we worked a six day week. I was usually laid off in the winter, so I finished high school and took courses in vocational school at Moose Jaw."

He coped. Coping and surviving were the operative words for humans and companies. The bad-years' psychology moved through three phases. At first, in spite of the evidence, no one believed the Depression was happening. Then, no one believed it could last. Next year, always "next year," would be better. To believe that was to retain sanity.

When next year proved to be as bad or worse, some gave up hope. Others found in themselves surprising reserves of fight and ingenuity. They learned to live with the bad years. Telephone and telegraph companies did it by milking every conceivable business angle. Each had some version of an "Everybody Selling" campaign, goading employees out to badger their friends, neighbors and total strangers into buying services they couldn't afford.

"It's up to you to see that none of your friends are left out," admonished New Brunswick Telephone Company in 1936. "Sell them a telephone today!"

"Hooray! No More Burned Dinners," cooed B.C. Telephone in 1932. It told how Mrs. Housewife burned her dinner while talking on a phone that was not, alas, located in her kitchen. Now, if she had owned an extension. . . .

In Alberta, if a subscriber cancelled a long distance call, an operator would call back the next day to urge a second try.

Saskatchewan made a pitch straight to the heart on its billing envelope:

Four points to keep in mind during February:

"1. February 14 is St. Valentine's Day."

"2. The year 1936 is Leap Year."

"3. Any proposal can be made (ever so privately) by Telephone and no matter whether he is at hand or far away."

"4. There are cheaper long distance rates every Sunday all day and also after 7 p.m. each weekday."

The companies brazenly capitalized on unemployment. "She had a telephone," the B.C. Telephone advertisement said approvingly, "so she got the job." Bell chimed in with, "In his home a man's telephone should be kept, even if other things have to be sacrificed. If an employer can reach a man readily by telephone, it may make the difference between getting and just missing the job." In fact, employers didn't have to phone for help. The jobless were waiting at their gates.

The Bell could turn any misfortune into an object lesson. An Ontario farmer cancelled his phone in 1931. Soon after, he fell from a haymow and fractured his skull. His wife had to run to a neighbor to call the doctor. The farmer renewed his phone.

"This is a good story," Bell's employee magazine said soberly, "for all other farmers to know, who intend to give up their telephone service."

Subscriber R. D. Croft couldn't *make* the Bell remove his extension. His wife requested the takeout. The Bell grudgingly agreed, but did nothing. Mrs. Croft repeated her order. A Bell voice asked kindly if she realized she was putting Bell employees out of work. Mrs. Croft did, but was not feeling so affluent herself.

After a long harangue the Bell again agreed to remove the phone. But it didn't. She asked a third time. Another polite but stubborn voice told her a horror story of a women who, without that precious extension, fell downstairs and broke a leg while rushing to answer the phone. Did Mrs. Croft want to break a leg? Anyway the phone was paid up until the end of the month; might as well keep it.

"By that time," snapped the lady, "things will be so bad you can take *both* phones out!"

More and more farmers discovered that the cheapest, although not necessarily best, telephone service was the homegrown variety. In southern Saskatchewan 30 farmers banded together on a 50-mile circuit over barbed wire fences, using old radio headphones for receivers and batteries from unused cars. On April Fool's Day 1933 — 25 years after ousting the Bell — Alberta Government Telephones reluctantly began selling its rural exchanges to farmers at five percent of book value: poles at 25 cents each, wire at a cent a pound, wall sets at $7.50.

The government couldn't afford to run them. The farmers could, by keeping their own books, setting their own standards, hanging wire on fences if they felt like it. They formed 600 new mutuals with 6,500 more rural telephones, and names brimming with prairie hope and whimsy: Golden Grain, Golden Meadow, Morning Star, Sunbeam, Rosebud Corner.

There was no government graft or corporate fat in the farmer co-ops. Barwood Mutual wrote its accounts in watered-down ink. Buffalo Lake Mutual's minute book was one of the cheap school scribblers known to every child of that era, with grey ruled paper, math tables on the back and a cover picture of a wholesome farm girl.

The officers consisted of president and secretary-treasurer and there were no struggles for power. President R. O. Sykes of Bearspaw Mutual, after years of thankless unpaid service, sent his subscribers a plaintive memorandum: "During the last two or three years owing to the absence of voters at the General Meeting, I have had to re-elect myself to carry on. I am old now and should get the axe and some younger man take my place."

The hired help was erratic. Fairview Mutual's switchboard operator doubled as weatherman and telegraph operator, at $30 a month. He would obligingly leave his post and walk anywhere in town to deliver a message — but there he could be seduced by strong drink. When this happened his wife sent their hired girl to the deserted switchboard. It happened so often the girl became a first-rate operator.

Among them — farmers, governments, private companies — the lines stayed open. In the blackest of times Canadians could always reach out through telephone and telegraph and figuratively touch hands, help each other, commiserate and exchange grim jokes. It was friendship, and that was their strongest currency in the Bad Years.

# Incident at Moose River

There were few heroes to worship in the '30s. When Nova Scotia's Moose River mine caved in on Easter Sunday, April 12, 1936, trapping three men seemingly beyond hope, Canada stopped in its tracks to watch. Here was a chance for courage and ingenuity to triumph over the rotten luck that had dogged humanity for six years.

When the news first came out of Moose River, it appeared that Dr. D. E. Robertson, the 52-year-old chief surgeon of Toronto's Sick Children's Hospital, lawyer Herman Magill, 30, and mine timekeeper Alfred Scadding were dead. The two Torontonians had just purchased the 60-year-old mine and gone down for a look. Scadding was about to bring them up from the 141-foot level, when the mine buckled with a great "whump." On April 15 black headlines mourned, "HOPE ALMOST GONE." Even if the men had escaped the initial cave-in they surely were starving, suffocating or dying of exposure.

All the same, Nova Scotia miners were tunnelling down toward them and a diamond driller was blindly aiming a communications shaft from an opposite angle. The trio had been lost nearly a week when the diamond driller scored a bullseye. Muffled cries came up the tiny hole. The three were still alive but weak, and water was pouring in nearby. Rescuers sent hot drinks and medication down the hole, but the rubber hose that carried the liquids gave them a sulphurous taste. Scadding later said he could never face tomato soup again.

Now the whole country hung on the rescue attempts. Four expert miners flew in from Ontario but they were not needed. The Nova Scotians had the situation in hand. Draegermen, they were called, after the oxygen equipment they wore, and the name became synonymous with "hero." They worked around the clock. Newsmen gathered from all over North America. Over the new Canadian Broadcasting Corporation the rich baritone of J. Frank Willis broadcast on-the-spot bulletins. Willis arrived on the afternoon of Monday, April 20, and, with the exception of a two-hour rest on Wednesday, delivered news every half-hour until two a.m. April 23. Radio listeners sat up far into the night and doctors reported dozens of "nervous prostration" patients, suffering too much excitement and too little sleep.

Meanwhile Maritime Telegraph and Telephone was quietly installing telephones at the site and setting up facilities for the first telephotographs ever transmitted in Canada. And on Sunday April 19, engineer W. E. Jefferson and shop foreman Bill Boak created their own little scrap of immortality. The trapped men could barely be heard up the drill hole. If they were to be encouraged, counselled and nourished with hope, better communications were essential.

The drill hole was said to be $^3/_4$ of an inch in diameter. Jefferson and Boak later found it was $1^9/_{16}$ inches. In either case, no microphone that small existed. They would have to invent one. Jefferson pulled from his vest pocket a new "penlight" — a flashlight the size of a fountain pen — and dumped the batteries. That slender shell was the beginning. Some kind of microphone had to go inside it.

All afternoon, Jefferson and Boak rummaged through the

workshop, experimenting, discarding, starting over again. By six o'clock their third try worked: a tiny transmitter, pieced together from miniature parts, fitted into the penlight casing, wrapped with friction tape.

Eight hours later the mike arrived at the minehead with amplifier, earphones and heavy batteries. It had to go down the hole undamaged and dry. A doctor donated a rubber surgical glove; one cut-off thumb went over the mike as a waterproof guard. The MT&T crew taped it to a one-inch pipe, to help guide and protect it on the way down. They added a note telling how to unwrap and use the mike, and to that taped a small white stick to catch the trapped men's attention. It was essential that they read first before clawing at the fragile bundle.

At nine a.m. Monday morning the microphone went down. With 150 feet of line paid out, the men above waited. A rattle came through the earphones. The trapped men had found it. The rattle continued; they were unwrapping it. At 9:17 a voice called "Hello, hello, do you hear me up there on the surface?" Success!

It was only a one-way circuit; the rescuers had to shout down their replies. But they could clearly hear the trapped men and could devise a code for answers: a long drawn "yes–yes"; and a short sharp "no." Wives communicated with their entombed husbands. The awful loneliness in the black hole was lessened. For 64 hours the little microphone would keep their hope alive. Conversations, coughing, even Scadding's heartbeat from the mike tucked inside his coat came through clearly. But it was private, despite the turmoil at the minehead. The telephone men refused to allow the press to listen in on the distress below.

On Monday afternoon someone carelessly rapped on the mouth of the drill hole to gain attention below, and severed one of the twin telephone wires. A single strand remained. From then on, only one man was allowed at the speaking hole: a leather-lunged Nova Scotia guide named Boyd Prest, who crouched at his post from 4 p.m. Monday to Wednesday midnight.

On Monday, Herman Magill died and with him a little of the hope for his companions. Rain poured. A tar-paper shack went up over the drill hole. The draegermen pressed deeper. On Wednesday the sounds of picks and drills came through on the microphone. At 11:40 p.m. a voice cried, "They've arrived, everything is hunky dory!" At 12:15 a.m. the microphone was cut off. On the surface men and women wept and miners sang "Praise God from

Whom All Blessings Flow." Below as Robertson and Scadding were helped out, the doctor begged the draegermen not to leave the microphone behind. Later he said "the telephone was the one thing that allowed us to consider any further stay with equanimity."

Telephone men are not ones for histrionics. An MT&T report of the matter concluded laconically, "After about 100 intensive hours starting Sunday morning, Thursday forenoon found the ten of us, who had worked at the mine, well on our way to Halifax." Incident over.

# At War

On September 3, 1939, the day Britain declared war on Hitler, Bell Canada's information switchboard in Montreal was strained to its limits. On a normal day, 40,000 people dialed 113 to ask the time, weather, ball scores or the numbers they were too lazy to look up. On this day 51,000 wanted Information to tell them if there *was* a war, if Canada was in it (she would be, in seven days) or how long it would last. That day set the style for the next six years of war — exhausting demands on communications and people.

The war immediately claimed Canada's best wireless operators. Bill Lockhart, now a major, had seen to that. As the Northwest Territories and Yukon System grew through the '20s and '30s the Signal Corps' expertise grew with it. Early in 1939 Lockhart, convinced war was near, began plucking Signals men from across the land and getting them ready for service. They formed the nucleus of the finest Allied military wireless group in World War II.

They were one of the few Canadian organizations prepared for a war that the country didn't want and hoped would go away. Even into the first winter Canadians viewed it through a haze of unreality. There was no privation at home. The telephone companies were still urging people to use long distance. And now to a 1940 advertisement:

Inset — a clean-cut serviceman in wedge cap, flashing a dazzling mouthful of teeth at a telephone.

Foreground — two elderly women rocking and talking. The copywriters have decked them out in a brogue as thick as porridge. (Why **Scottish?** Do Scots in 1940 still epitomize all that is honest and thrifty?) One old lady speaks. ". . . I was just thinking of him as a wee bairn. . .Then the Braw Laddie called LONG DISTANCE . . . all the way from camp! And he said it didn't cost so much!"

Then Hitler marched to the English Channel and London burned under German bombs. By the time 3,367 Canadians died or were wounded in the catastrophe called Dieppe, Canada had grimly settled down to business. Telegraph traffic doubled between 1939 and 1942. Telephone ads urged civilians to answer that phone quickly, and clear the wires for war talk. In 1942, the Wartime Prices and Trade Board, which rigidly governed life at home, put a lid on residential telephone installations. By December 1943 the telephone industry was pleading with civilians to forego Christmas long distance calls and spare the lines for government and the military.

All companies shared a common problem: business was running wild but workers were scarce because the young men were all in uniform. So the war proved conclusively that women could do most jobs as well as men, and some jobs better. By 1944, a third of CN Telegraph employees were women, compared to 14 percent at war's outbreak. Some were "messengerettes," pretty teenagers mostly, in oxford-grey air force–style uniforms with wedge caps, white blouse, black tie and company crest on the sleeves. For them and for retired employees called back for duty as telegraphers and clerks, wartime was rather a lark.

For most other telephone and telegraph employees there was no romance to war. No bands played, no cheering crowds lined the sidewalks when linemen marched out to battle a sleet storm. The woman munitions maker or ship builder was everybody's darling. Her pert face in close-fitting turban with pincurls peeking out in defiance of safety regulations, and her curves poured into tight-fitting overalls, were a national trademark. Everybody sang "Rosie The Riveter" and chanted "Milkman, Keep Those Bottles Quiet" (because the night shift workers were sleeping by day).

But nobody sang to the overworked switchboard operator, or the deskbound executives under their own brand of shellfire. One senior AGT man died of a heart attack in 1943. His successor was invalided the same way two years later. Both had been working on defence contracts. World War II for telecommunications people was flinging a pole line across Newfoundland for our Allies, the Yanks — one of Bell's major contributions to the war effort — and

Churchill, Roosevelt and Mackenzie King meet the press at the end of the Quebec Conference, 1944. PUBLIC ARCHIVES OF CANADA C 26932.

again 2,000 miles along the Alaska Highway, over rivers, mountains and lakes, in temperatures to 70 below. It was soothing colonels and politicians who banged desktops and demanded more. It was holding a telephone-hungry public at bay with patriotic advertisements. It was carrying bad news more often than good, and standing by, numb and impotent, while bereaved wives screamed and parents quietly wept. The telegraph companies had careful procedures for casualty announcements. A senior agent was required to personally deliver such messages, accompanied if possible by priest or family friend.

As in 1914–18, the Atlantic cable system was invaluable to the war effort and most important of all, as a morale booster to servicemen overseas. Canadian troops abroad, like others, were able to choose from 240 standard cable texts, any three of which could be combined for a flat rate of two shillings sixpence (about 62¢ per message). The 10 most popular texts were: "Loving birthday greetings," "All my love dearest," "Fondest love darling," "Many happy returns," "All my love," "My thoughts are with you," "All well and safe," "God bless you and keep you safe," "My thoughts and prayers ever with you" and "Am well and fit." It served most situations well enough at the price, but had its shortcomings, as in the story, perhaps apocryphal, of the major on active service who cabled home for his bank balance. The numerals cabled back were mistakenly treated as the reference numbers for three standard message forms. The major accordingly received from his banker: "Very happy to hear from you dearest; Am well and fit; Many thanks for your telegram parcel sent."

Maintaining civilian morale was just as important, especially for employers. Bell, in its magazine, *The Blue Bell*, spoke to employees with a friendly little clasp of the arm: "We can't all be soldiers or sailors or airmen or nursing sisters. But we should never forget that this all-out effort to rid the world of tyranny and dictatorship depends to a great extent on the home front." Then it told how Winston Churchill, after the December 1941 attack on Pearl Harbor, had personally phoned Franklin Roosevelt, across the Atlantic.

"Even our great leaders turn continually to the telephone," said *The Blue Bell* with satisfaction.

Of course, they did. So did lesser leaders of governments and military, because *they* could get phones when they wanted them. Red tape magically parted when *they* wanted a long-distance line, whereas one ordinary Edmontonian in 1943 waited so long for a phone connection to Calgary that he finally jumped a plane and flew there.

In 1942 B.C. Telephones told ordinary subscribers there were no more telephones. The same year Bell denied 30,000 applications. Copper, nickel, zinc, tin, all the materials of telephony were needed for war. If they could be had at all, delivery time was months or years longer than normal. A Manitoba Telephones employee remembered "putting supplies away like squirrels, always being doubtful of how inadequate the next shipment might be."

The military appetite was insatiable. By the end of 1941 Bell had installed 114 military switchboards in Ontario and Quebec alone. Hundreds more went into munitions factories, shipyards, aircraft plants and steel mills, to government and to such auxiliary services as Red Cross, Salvation Army, YMCA, War Savings and Victory Loan Committees.

In 1943 and 1944, on scant days' notice each time, telephone and telegraph crews swarmed into Quebec to turn the Citadel and the Chateau Frontenac into miniature wired cities for historic conferences between Churchill, Roosevelt, Mackenzie King and their glittering imperious phalanx of ministers, admirals, generals and field marshals. At one point a Northern Electric crew worked 72 hours around the clock assembling a switchboard, then travelled with it in a moving van from Montreal to Quebec to install it. More than a million words of press news alone were despatched by CN telegraphs during the 1943 conference.

By war's end, CN telegraphs and cables had carried close to 50 million messages. On the actual days that fighting stopped, first in Europe, then in Asia, Canadian telephone switchboards were swamped in calls. By then the files were bulging too, with unfulfilled orders: 5,300 in Nova Scotia and Prince Edward Island; 77,000 in the Bell System; 5,000 in Calgary alone; and so on across the land. The war was over, but for telecommunications there was no peace.

# The Way It Was

Who are these people standing hesitant at the portals of another year? They should be the proudest, most secure Canadians in history. Their land is full of riches. They have acquitted themselves honourably in war. Other nations look on them with dawning respect.

The veterans are home, resplendent in civilian suits with voluminous trousers, acres of lapel and fedoras that swallow up heads still trying to regrow hair. The war brides arrive daily — English, French, Dutch, even German. Romance is everywhere: the front pages this morning picture Prince Philip of Greece bending his aristocratic head over a demure Princess Elizabeth. Rumour says they are betrothed.

The news bears other cheerful tidings. The prevailing cost of a Christmas tree is only $1.25 this season. Sirloin steak is a mere 45¢ a pound and two loaves of bread go for 15¢. A nine-room home in Toronto's Forest Hill Village, with three bathrooms, two stone fireplaces and a panelled library opening onto a flag-stoned patio sells for $23,900.

At noon today, with a rush of nostalgia, Toronto mayor R.H. Saunders sends a telegram to Mayor Sam Lawrence of Hamilton,

commemorating that first message of a century ago. The radio
is full of gentle silly songs: "The Old Lamp Lighter," "I'm a Lonely
Little Petunia in an Onion Patch" and "All I Want for Christmas is My
Two Front Teeth." Canadians are wistfully, almost desperately, trying
to recapture the carefree past.

Alas! As always, there is no going back. Sweet innocence is gone.
Veterans can't afford that $23,000 home in Forest Hill. Low-cost
housing is painfully scarce, and this year's crop of war babies has
raised the population to 12.3 million. Inflation is looming. An ugly
story comes from Quebec: a man has been sentenced without trial,
for distributing religious literature without a municipal license. "The
treatment of Jehovah Witnesses," says today's Toronto *Star*, "becomes
more and more shocking." Was it for this that men fought tyranny and
died?

It has been a year of unrest and revelation — a Royal Commission
investigation of espionage in Canada; the sentencing of Nazi war
criminals at Nuremburg; the first meetings of the United Nations
General Assembly and United Nations Atomic Energy Commission. It
is a time of doubts — of oneself and of the future.

What became of true-blue dependable values? In today's Halifax
*Herald*, "Uncertain" puts a yearning question to Dorothy Dix, the Ann
Landers of the day: "What is the best way to tell whether a man really
loves you?"

"The only sure test that any woman can have is the way he treats
her," Miss Dix replies with authority. "If he is tender, kind,
considerate, if he works hard to make her comfortable and if he is
always thinking of some little way to make her happy, it is proof of
affection that she can bank on. . . .Beware of the glib love maker. It
shows he has too much experience."

Perhaps Uncertain senses in her secret heart that those time-worn
verities will never satisfy the Nuclear Family in the second half of the
century. Why *not* be glib? Why build a life or a world on faith and
fidelity when tomorrow there may be *no* world?

Uncertain remembers the photographs of mushroom clouds over
Hiroshima and Nagasaki, little more than a year ago. And last March,
Winston Churchill, with his uncanny feel for the pulse of history,
added another deathless phrase to the English language. "From Stettin
in the Baltic to Trieste in the Adriatic," he rumbled in the old

spine-tingling wartime cadence, "an iron curtain has descended across the Continent."

An Iron Curtain! Perhaps another war? Uncertain and her countrymen have seen awful leaps of science in six years: radar that reaches far beyond the limits of sight to pick flying objects out of the sky, cameras that see in the dark, bombs that vaporize whole cities. Too much, too soon.

So here on the brink of the Nuclear Age, with its wonder drugs, miracle fabrics, frozen dinners and air travel as common as yesterday's stroll to the corner store, all the Uncertains of Canada gingerly prepare for another Christmas. Does any of it, especially "peace and goodwill," have meaning anymore?

These ordinary folk can only go stubbornly about familiar tasks: decorating the $1.25 Christmas tree, paying the bills, raising families, holding jobs, grappling with inflation, recession, depression, wind, fire, drought and flood — natural enemies that they at least can understand. And they can only pray — some still pray — that the new science, irrevocable, unstoppable, will do more good than bad.

# Chapter 17

## The Flood

To battle-weary veterans, barely five years back from overseas, it was war all over again: shattered towns, truckloads of weary frightened refugees, sandbagged defences, and an enemy creeping forward, circling behind, cutting off retreat. Except the enemy was water. This was southern Manitoba in 1950, and the Red River was on rampage.

The farmland around Winnipeg is an ancient glacial lake bed, soft rich earth, table flat from horizon to horizon. It is the "typical" prairie that visitors expect but rarely see in the West. It is also prime flood country. Often before, the Red had jumped its banks, and as recently as 1948, but for sheer chaos nothing could match the flood of 1950.

Spring came late to the Red River Valley that year. Heavy rains had saturated the land the previous autumn. A record snow topped the soggy soil. Now, with April thaw, the Red rose to a torrent in its eternal run from North Dakota and Minnesota to Lake Winnipeg.

On April 11, provincial government engineers warned that the flood danger was "very great." Up and down southern Manitoba, party lines jangled incessantly as operators called the alarm. Valley

233

farmers wearily packed their families and herded their livestock to high ground as they had done before. Truck convoys began hauling sandbags to the first line of defence, Emerson, a small town at the international boundary.

The Emerson telephone office barricaded itself for a fight. Pumps went up on a high platform behind the building. Sandbags surrounded every wall. Even the doors were sealed halfway up; operators crawled in over the bags beneath a sign warning "Watch Your Head."

The river began spilling its banks on April 20. Emerson people stockpiled food, moved furniture from ground floors and ripped up the shiny new hardwood they had installed after the '48 flood. The telephone girls walked to work in hip waders. By April 22, two-thirds of Emerson was under two feet of water.

The next day the operators set up housekeeping in the exchange. For recreation they took boat rides. Emergency phones were installed in a shack on high ground in case — impossible as it seemed — the flood jumped the five-foot sandbag buffer.

By April 30 Emerson's main street was a lake. A CNR overpass, with clearance for tractor trailers in normal times, was barely above the lake's horizon. The water now stood 46.5 feet above datum (flood stage).

At 3:25 a.m. the next day the telephone exchange's foundation gave way with a rumble and splash. Protective sandbags slipped out of sight and icy water welled over the floor. Bleary-eyed operators scrambled from their cots to the counter top, pyjamas rolled above their knees. A Red Cross patrol boat hauled them away, wet and barefoot, for sandwiches and hot coffee. For the next seven weeks three MTS men kept the emergency exchange going with charming informality: "You wanta number?" and "Put a quarter in the pot, boy!"

While the Emerson operators were being fished from the drink, a mass evacuation was on at Morris, 30 miles down river. The Red Cross moved nearly 1,200 people, while nine operators and two maintenance men stuck to their jobs. At that point the water was only two feet deep around the telephone exchange but still rising. Three CN Telegraph men, on an inspection visit from Winnipeg, rowed down Main Street where the water was 10 feet deep and crawled into the Morris Hotel through a second storey window.

The telephone girls were now living in a trailer. As the water rose the trailer was raised on oil barrels, and the girls entered over

Sandbags piled high to protect an exchange from flood waters in Winnipeg, 1950. MANITOBA TELEPHONE SYSTEM.

Electric and telephone poles partially submerged by the flooding of the Red River, 1950. BELL CANADA TELEPHONE HISTORICAL COLLECTION.

a wooden ramp. The water kept rising and the ramp began to float. The exchange itself was sandbagged to 5$^1/_2$ feet but the Red was building against the outer walls. To ease the pressure, the MTS maintenance crew let water into the basement, then gradually into the main floor. The operators stayed at their switchboards, perched on elevated chairs. Since Morris is a main route the telephone girls were busy.

"The rush of calls, and the water gradually creeping up on us, strained nerves almost to the breaking point," chief operator Pat Stanley remembered afterward. There was a little comic relief. Operator Alice Penner, walking the plank to the trailer, fell in water to her neck but held a handful of cookies high and dry.

On May 11, the flood burst in and the girls got out. Morris was now the centre of a shallow prairie sea, whipped into whitecaps by wind, rain and sleet. The first boatload of evacuees had to turn back for a larger craft. Six operators finally reached Winnipeg's St. Regis Hotel late that night in rubber boots and parkas, exhausted after a 50-mile trip over tossing waters.

By then 550 square miles of Manitoba farmland was inundated and Winnipeg had been under siege for 20 days. On May 12 the river level at the St. James Street pumping station reached 30 feet above datum. The Army was in charge of flood control. Muddy chains of men, women and teenagers were stubbornly throwing up 30 miles of sandbag dykes. One-tenth of Greater Winnipeg was under water and 8,500 telephones were knocked out.

At the Canadian Pacific Telegraphs headquarters at Portage and Main, water crept into the pneumatic tube systems. To keep a link with the outer world, linemen threw up 200,000 feet of insulated wire. Five thousand telegrams a day poured in from anxious relatives and friends across Canada and messengers, with volunteer help, delivered them — sometimes by canoe.

The flood had caught Manitoba Telephones midway through the postwar communications boom. Between 1945–55 the company installed more telephones than in all the years since Horace McDougall brought the first box sets from Brantford. Operators were scarce and MTS was in the midst of the biggest training program in its history. Now, operators cancelled holidays, worked overtime and slept at exchanges (like thousands of other Winnipeggers, many of them were driven from their homes). Even so, as one suburb after another was evacuated, the volume of calls was overwhelming.

On May 12 MTS banned all calls from outside Winnipeg, except on a flood emergency basis. Companies of the Trans-Canada Telephone System and American Telephone and Telegraph cooperated. Winnipeg's radio stations, operating around the clock, helped ease the load by broadcasting much of the news that outsiders wanted. Even so, on May 13 and 14, local telephone traffic was 99 and 153 percent above normal.

By mid-June the Red was tame again. The people had won. It had been catastrophic but it would have been immeasurably worse without telephone, telegraph and radio to sound the alarm and marshal the defences. Much of the city and countryside was in ruins but the human spirit was intact. The six tousled muddy operators from Morris, whose ordeal ended in Winnipeg on the night of May 11, were a case in point. There were no hysterics on arrival. Their main concern was in looking like women again.

"Where can we get our hair done?" they chorused. "We haven't washed it in three weeks."

# The Corporal, the Sergeant and the Eskimos

In the postwar years Canada discovered her North. At Aklavik, where in Hugh Young's day the mail came twice a year, telegraph and telephone became as commonplace as in Vancouver or Montreal. At Frobisher Bay, jackets and tie were *de rigueur* in the Rustic Room cocktail lounge.

Back from the settlements, though, life went on as it always had. Which is how a corporal, a sergeant and some enlisted men of the Royal Canadian Corps of Signals came to save a dwindling Eskimo culture almost as old as mankind.

In the summer of 1949, Cpl. Joe MacIsaac and five other Signal Corpsmen left Edmonton for the bleakest posting in the Northwest Territories. The federal meteorological division had persuaded the Department of National Defence to put a weather reporting station in the Barren Lands. MacIsaac and company were bound for Ennadai Lake, 250 miles northwest of Churchill, Manitoba.

It was by no means the most northerly posting, but others had such amenities as an RCMP detachment, a Hudson's Bay store and a Catholic mission. Ennadai had nothing. MacIsaac and his party greeted the assignment phlegmatically, with the routine griping and cursing of soldiers anywhere anytime. They went north in the Forties' best style: to Winnipeg aboard a plodding prop-driven North Star, to Churchill by rail on the CNR's weekly "Muskeg Special"; to Ennadai Lake in an RCAF amphibious Canso.

The Barrens, though not truly barren, are strange to a southern eye. They are flat, with myriad lakes, endless miles of mosses, lichens, Arctic flowers and low shrubs in summer, and endless vistas of snow in winter. Around Ennadai, the only human life was a nomadic band of Eskimos, the Kazan River Group — small dark people living off the land, totally unaware of the outer world. Because of them, this would be no ordinary posting.

Amid rain and hordes of black flies and mosquitoes, the Signals men flung up a combined radio station and barracks, 68 feet by 24, and three auxiliary buildings. On October 8 they beamed out the first weather reports, part of the national weather service and a valuable aid to the increasing air traffic in northern skies. Every year the partnership of aviation and communication was opening the North a little wider. New oil exploration was inching into the Territories. Defence warning towers would soon probe the silence.

The 47 Kazan Eskimos, 25 miles from Ennadai Lake camp, were back in another age. Elsewhere, native people were adopting white men's soft bread, candy, Coca Cola, liquor, portable radios and frame houses. Not so the Kazans. Their lives revolved around the caribou. They dressed in untanned caribou skins, which lent a ripe body odor; fed themselves and their dogs on caribou meat; lived in skin tents in summer and paddled skin boats. When the annual caribou migration bypassed them in the winter of 1949–50, the Kazan Group was destitute.

Left on their own, most of them would have died. Many were clinging to life by boiling and eating old caribou robes and the inner liners of their skin parkas. Their precious sled dogs were dying. When the RCMP at Churchill and the RCCS at Ennadai Lake heard of their plight in April, a mercy flight brought in 250 pounds of flour, sugar, tea and dried milk. But the Kazans would have to be moved to Nueltin Lake, a hundred miles southeast, where fish and caribou were plentiful.

While the Mounties arranged an airlift the Signal Corps rounded up the scattered band. The Kazans revelled in the food and fringe benefits. One elderly woman discovered that if she sang a song the soldiers would give her a cigarette. She was no Maria Callas. "She stops singing as soon as she gets a smoke," wrote MacIsaac in the monthly log, "and, believe me, it's cheap at the price."

As the families checked in, MacIsaac noticed one man was minus his stepson. When asked, the stepfather pointed vaguely back into the Barrens. MacIsaac thought little of it but another Eskimo, known to the soldiers as Ang-ma, smelled trouble. The stepfather had an unsavory reputation. Ang-ma retraced the trail. Miles back he found the boy, semiconscious and too weak to walk. His stepfather had been systematically starving him, to hoard food for himself.

Ang-ma lifted the boy and staggered back toward camp but he, too, was weak. Finally he hurried back alone for help. By 10 o'clock that night the Signalmen had brought in the unconscious youngster and radioed for medical advice. Instructions came back promptly: feed him water, salt and sugar, then tea and soup. By two a.m. the patient was sitting up, asking for a cigarette. Within two days he was on a solid diet.

On May 2 and 3, all 47 Kazans and their dogs were flown to Nueltin Lake. Twenty-five days later one was back by dogteam; he didn't like the new place. Soon after, the errant stepfather returned, for the same reason. By November all the Kazans had come back to familiar territory, bringing their familiar problems along. This time the government provided rifles, ammunition and traps. The Signalmen, between weather reports, showed them how to bale furs and ship them to Churchill. The police sold the pelts and sent back food and ammunition.

The Kazans grew fond of their new friends. When food was scarce the soldiers handed out emergency rations. When stomachs ached or fingers were infected, first aid was close at hand. Sometimes the kindly soldiers, who must have wondered whether they were working for the Army or the Eskimos, hitched their caterpillar tractor to a heavy caribou and hauled it into the Kazan camp.

Naturally, when an old woman died suddenly in May, 1954, her worried neighbor ran to Sgt. Fred Waite, the noncommissioned officer now in charge. With her fragments of English and his stray word of Eskimo the message got through: many people sick. Waite rode out to camp. Influenza was epidemic. Already one fresh grave lay under its stone cairn.

Waite radioed for medical aid. All aircraft were socked in by bad weather so the Churchill doctor gave the sergeant a crash course in influenza treatment via radio. Armed with the station's modest medical supplies, Waite gave shots of penicillin, forced aspirin down throats and poured eggnog into the old and frail. Then *he* caught the 'flu, but kept going despite a temperature of 103.

"The hardest thing I did," Waite remembered later, "was to give *myself* a shot. We only had one needle and it was getting dull. . . ."

Waite saved all 22 of his patients. Afterward he was commended for "prompt action and sound judgment in accordance with the best principles of medical practice."

That September, a Signals history noted, ". . .with no noticeable weeping or gnashing of teeth, the Signals Territorial Eskimo Medical Clinic, otherwise known as RC Signals Radio Station, Ennadai Lake, was turned over to the Department of Transport. . . ."

The Kazans moved on too. The federal government transferred them east to the shore of Hudson Bay. There they live today, their very existence a monument to the work of Marconi, Fessenden and the Signal Corps.

# The 30 Million Dollar Misunderstanding

The real war of 1939–45 was barely over when the Cold War began. Russia the ally was suddenly the enemy, minutes away by bomber over the top of the world. Canadians built bomb shelters and hoarded canned goods. Cities formed evacuation plans and held clumsy evacuation exercises. The entire continent frantically looked to its defences.

Out of this came the Mid-Canada Line. It was a brilliant technical feat but the achievement was smirched by waste, acrimony and political in-fighting. In the end the Mid-Canada was an object lesson in the mismanagement and frustration that tends to haunt any multidepartmental government project.

In 1954 Clarence Decatur Howe, minister of Defence Production, called Bell Telephone officials to his office on Parliament Hill.

Howe, with granite face and will to match, was one of the two or three best-known politicians in Canada and easily the most powerful minister in the St. Laurent cabinet.

He was anything but the best loved. Howe was the supreme autocrat. He bludgeoned his way through government, creating private empires, and in the House showed massive disregard for the parliamentary process. Once he answered Opposition criticism with, "If we have overstepped our powers, I make no apology for having done so."

Whatever else one said or thought about C. D. Howe, he got things done. Now, he told the Bell, Canada was going to build a middle-distance warning line. "Mongoose," it was called, in the mystic code that bureaucrats and the military adore. It would come to be known as the Mid-Canada Line, extending 2,800 miles along the 55th parallel. It would supplement the existing Pine Tree Line in the south and a Distant Early Warning Line to be built by the Americans north of the Arctic Circle.

Technologically it would employ the Doppler effect of physics: if a source of sound is moving toward a listener, the sound waves are shortened and the pitch is higher. The reverse occurs when the sound source moves away. Researchers, particularly at McGill University, had applied the principle to aerial detection, by using ultra–high frequency and radio waves. Twin bands of continuous-wave Doppler radar from the Mid-Canada's 102 stations, probing beyond the maximum altitude of known aircraft, would pick up any approaching flying objects. It would even distinguish between bombers and Canada geese.

Howe was looking for a nation-wide agency to mastermind the project. The Trans Canada Telephone System, able to operate in all parts of Canada, was a logical choice. Furthermore, Bell was a major partner in the TCTS and Howe admired Canada's largest telephone company for a couple of reasons. Up the Labrador coast, Bell was building for the government the world's first tropospheric scatter system. "Pole Vault," as it was known, would bounce high-power signals against the troposphere (that segment of the atmosphere extending up to about seven miles). Enough signals coming down would be captured by large aerials at ranges of 150–220 miles. It was a breakthrough in communications technology and Bell was doing the job quickly and efficiently.

Howe was also aware, to his chagrin, that Bell Canada had once offered him good advice that was ignored. In 1950 the Royal

Canadian Air Force undertook ADCOM, a microwave air defence network through Northern Ontario and Quebec, part of the North American System. Microwave was then in its infancy. Bell recommended that the RCAF rent its circuits from the common carriers. The air force chose to build its own system.

Two years later Alex G. Lester, a 30-year Bell man on loan for six months to Defence Production as associate director of electronics, realized that ADCOM had gone awry. Lester bore a striking resemblance to Jack Webb, the star of a popular TV detective series in the 1950s and, like the laconic Sgt. Friday of *Dragnet*, he just wanted the facts.

The ADCOM facts, as Lester recalled them years later: "The initial equipment didn't work properly and the system was planned and engineered on a committee basis. It started off with an estimated cost of about $3 million. By 1952 it was up to $10 million. I tried to stop it. I had a letter ready for Mr. Howe's signature to send to Brooke Claxton, Minister of National Defence. But Claxton got to Howe first with a letter saying that he had authorized the thing to go above $10 million."

The cost went to $22 million before the system was fully operational. Eventually, at the RCAF's request, Bell took ADCOM over for $2 million.

There was no use crying over spilt millions, nor was it Howe's style. (He had already been castigated in 1945 for his breezy reference in the House of Commons to a $7 million estimate for winding up war contracts.) Now, however, he hoped to avoid more such blunders with the Mid-Canada line.

Howe's choice of TCTS, with Bell as project agent, did not endear him or the telephone company to the military. The latter considered it an intrusion. Yet even that problem might have been surmounted if authority had been clearly defined.

Instead, it was a hopeless muddle of too many chiefs. Although the Department of National Defence was clearly the prime customer, Defence Minister Ralph Campney evidently had no say in the choice of Bell. Howe's Department of Defence Production, as procurement agency, hired the telephone company and awarded major contracts for equipment. Defence Construction Limited, a Crown Corporation, awarded construction contracts and was responsible for actual construction with Bell as its agent. The Department of Transport controlled transportation. The RCAF was design authority.

Shortly after the project began, Bell Telephone — initially assured that it was to be prime construction authority — was named "management contractor." It now had responsibility but little authority. As the newly appointed general manager of Bell's special contract department, Alex Lester was expected to get Mid-Canada built. His credentials were impressive. An Army signals officer during the war, Lester had attended the National Defence College, supervised the building of Pole Vault and had been chairman of Trans Canada Telephone System's engineering committee. None of those was as difficult as Mid-Canada "in which 35 percent of my time was spent in warding off government people and the other 65 percent in getting the job done."

The terrain alone was challenging enough. Although not really a frontier by today's standards, it was farther north than most Canadians had been in 1954. A senior air force officer displayed his ignorance of the situation with, "I think construction procedures and techniques in the Arctic present no special difficulty. Each job presents its own problems, but these can be dealt with on the spot by the competent engineer." He was wrong on two counts: the 55th parallel is nearly 800 miles **south** of the Arctic Circle, but it did indeed present "special difficulties."

In some respects the Mid-Canada route was more troublesome than the true North because the weather at that latitude is less consistent. Spring thaw and autumn freezeup brought transportation to a standstill for two or three months a year. There were muskeg patches, impassable to vehicles in summer. Survey crews had to be lowered from helicopters in rope slings. Forests had to be cleared, roads built and supplies hauled over vast distances, with none of the northern expertise or specialized equipment Canadians would possess even a decade later. All of this had to be done by January 1, 1957, a little more than two years.

The need for a single authority immediately made itself felt. From meeting rooms down to construction sites, the participants got on each others' nerves. One senior air force officer won a lasting place in Bell men's memories by stating flatly that he knew more about construction than anyone in Canada.

At the first meeting in October, 1954, Lester asked for various plans and specifications. He received the last of them in the spring of 1957, after the line was completed. Other plans were late reaching construction sites because "they were wrong when they reached us and had to be corrected. Partly that was from asking for too much in a hurry. But the competence of the design engineers was by no means uniform."

Bell handled day-to-day transportation and other small contracts but was not allowed to award major contracts; the government did that. Lester emerged with a sour view of the Canadian construction industry: "I expected to find real competence in the people running the jobs. I didn't find it. You seemed to have to be on top of them all the time. The details and bookkeeping were sloppy. Jobs were done more expensively than necessary." (To be fair, the construction contractors would undoubtedly have said that if Bell had driven with a looser rein, they could have worked to better advantage.)

Expense was a sore point, and rightly so. Early estimates had hovered around $100 million. Bell came on the scene with an estimate of $161 million, quickly revised to $169 million. Lester admitted later "we stayed with that too long." Eventually the estimate went up to $206 million. The final cost was $228 million, including $15 million for RCAF helicopters.

No provision was made in early estimates for the purchase of helicopters, scows and barges, or for rental of additional helicopters. The aggregate area of buildings was increased 25 percent over the original plan. Supplies were lost. A fire at the Knob Lake camp wiped out the quarters for 200 men. No one had calculated the extra cost of a hurry-up job along the 55th. Some supplies had to be flown in by winter to frozen lakes, unloaded in gales of up to 100 miles per hour, and cached. Others were freighted by tractor train over a 300-mile winter road. Still others were shipped in summer via Hudson Bay, through squalls and shrouds of fog.

Initially, for the eastern end of the line, fuel had to be shipped in bulk to Sept-Îles, Que., sent in drums aboard a train to Knob Lake, poured into the fuel tanks of Canso aircraft and siphoned out into drums again at the campsites.

Men stood idle waiting for essential supplies. Supply ships were stuck in the ice of Hudson Strait for weeks, and one ship was crushed and sank in James Bay while wintering there. In total, transportation represented $42 million of the overall project cost of $228 million.

In one instance the intricate process of choosing a supplier of diesel engines took so long (50 requests to tender sent out by the government, with 70 bids in return) that the final 125 units of a 300-diesel order had to be airlifted from England to air strips near the line, so they could be hauled to sites while the ground was frozen. Otherwise the whole project would have been delayed a year. That little caper cost $2,000 per diesel airlifted.

"The government process is inherently a slow one," Lester concluded in retrospect. "I've met some very solid people in government agencies. But the system of checks and balances makes it very difficult to get approvals."

Presumably, the crisscrossing government agencies were attempting to safeguard the public interest. Yet the Canadian taxpayer was left in a familiar stance — bleeding heavily from the wallet. The public interest would have been better served with fewer watchdogs.

This multiplicity of agencies and confusion in responsibility bred waves of bad feeling. The RCAF felt that it could have run the show itself, working directly with the construction contractors. Defence Production was equally sure that it should be the guiding light. The Bell, wishing a plague on both their houses, was determined to get the job done right according to its own methods. Strong personalities there were, both in government and in Bell. Personality clashes there were, but despite all that, the line was built.

The western half was finished on deadline, in January 1957. The remainder was operational later that year. Early in 1959 an RCAF advisor, who in Bell's opinion had become something of a troublemaker, circulated a memorandum fiercely critical of the telephone company. Lester received a copy and appended some tart marginal notes, including, "I would say that this whole report can be construed as a monument of Air Force impertinence and harmful interference."

The document found its way to Arnold Edinborough, editor of *Saturday Night*, who blew the lid off in a two-part series. Although his articles lacked full appreciation of the northern conditions, and leaned heavily upon one set of allegations (many of which were later refuted) he made a valid point: haste and divided authority had caused an estimated $30 million worth of waste. Seventeen years later, Lester acknowledged, "I wouldn't argue that the job could not have been done for $30 million less."

Edinborough made other telling points: "One is left wondering why such a muddle was allowed to develop in the first place, and why, once it had developed, strong action was not taken. Mr. Campney knew about it. . .but he did nothing. . . ."

Edinborough's articles caused a flurry in the House of Commons, but the fuss and the wasted public funds were soon forgotten. The pity was that the admirable parts of the Mid-Canada project were not longer remembered. For all its mistakes, the job contributed immeasurably to Canada's knowledge of the North. An official National Defence memorandum later rated it a "truly remarkable achievement."

The Line served its stated purpose for the prescribed eight years (at a maintenance and operation cost of $15 million a year). Its presence as part of NORAD (North American Air Defence) no doubt helped to serve as a deterrent to aggressors in the anxious '50s and '60s, including the tense days of the Cuban missile crisis.

Perhaps many Canadians slept more easily because of the Mid-Canada Line. And in the end all the waste and bitterness could not diminish the effort of the hundreds who worked their hearts out, and a few who died on the job, to help make their country safe.

# Chapter 18

## Age of the Wizards

A t war's end the telephone and telegraph industry still had one foot in the horse and buggy age. It depended on poles, wires and cables to carry messages. Storms could still isolate a neighbourhood, a city or half a province for days on end. And the most elaborate wiring systems could not handle the demands of the late 20th century.

Canada was starved for communications. Bell Canada, for example, began 1946 with 77,000 telephone applications and ended the year with 84,000. The volume of long-distance calls, which had doubled during World War II, was about to double again. Bell's phones in the first postwar decade would double too, from one million to 2,300,000. Something radically new was needed. Indeed, it was already on its way, a quarter century of electronic legerdemain. Canada's littlest province led the country into the age of wizards.

For years Prince Edward Island had put up with stop-and-go telephone communications to New Brunswick and Nova Scotia, via the submarine cable under Northumberland Strait. Waves and ice chafed the cable against rock ledges and broke the connection. The nuisance ended forever on November 20, 1948, when Premiers

Walter Jones of P.E.I., and Angus L. Macdonald of Nova Scotia had a conventional telephone conversation *without wires*.

Their words jumped between towers near Charlottetown and New Glasgow, over the world's first commercial microwave for voice transmission. Storms could not touch them. Moreover, this new electronic wonder had 24 channels, compared to seven on the old cable.

But what *was* microwave? Not one Canadian in a thousand had a clue. To grasp its principle, laymen had to understand the rudiments of radio waves as discovered and elaborated on by Rudolph Hertz, Reginald Fessenden, Marconi and their successors.

Radio waves are characterized by *wavelength* — measured in miles, inches or centimeters — and *frequency* — the number of waves in a given time, measured in cycles per second, or "hertz." The longer the wave, the lower the frequency, and vice versa. A 10 khz (10,000 cycles per second) frequency has a wave length of 18.6 miles; a 3,000 khz frequency has a wave length of .062 miles.

By visualizing the radio wave spectrum as a kind of multilayer sandwich, the frequencies and their uses come into focus. Up to 30 khz is Very Low Frequency. Following it comes Low Frequency, 30 khz to 300 khz, and Medium Frequency, 300 khz to three megahertz, (one megahertz being a million cycles per second). Ordinary AM radio broadcasting fits into the latter band, from 525 khz to 1,605 khz.

Next comes High Frequency, up to 30 mhz, followed by Very High Frequency, up to 300 mhz. The latter carries today's basic television channels and FM broadcasts. Television is also carried in the lower ranges of Ultra High Frequency, which runs from 300 mhz to three gigahertz (one gigahertz being a billion cycles per second). Beyond that are Super High Frequency, to 30 ghz, and Extremely High Frequency, to 300 ghz.

From one ghz and up is the preserve of microwave. Shortly after World War I, radio technicians learned that these extremely short "micro" waves (30 centimeters or less) have special properties. Unlike longer waves, they bounce back from solid objects in their path. Out of this came "radar," an acronym for "radio direction and ranging." The man who did the foremost work in radar — and some credit him with discovering it — was Robert Watson-Watt, the apple-cheeked son of a poor Scottish carpenter. Watson-Watt called radar "a triumph of pure reason over a mass of

The microwave tower on Pyramid Mountain, Alta. Because microwave is a "line of sight" system, mountain towers have to be on the peaks. CANADIAN NATIONAL.

unrelated facts which were known to thousands of people."

This invisible eye-in-the-sky could detect and identify flying objects. Because of it, RAF Fighter Command in World War II was able to spot German aircraft soon after take-off across the English Channel, and get a fix on their height, speed, type, number and direction. Without radar, the Battle of Britain would surely have been lost.

Radar equipment was mass-produced by a wartime Crown Corporation in Toronto's suburb of Leaside. Watson-Watt called Canada "the radar arsenal of the western world." After the war, microwaves came home to work for peace. They could carry many hundreds of telephone channels plus black and white or colour television. Unlike longer waves, however, they followed a line-of-sight path and could be blocked by surface objects.

Soon after Prince Edward Island set the pace, Bell built microwave systems between Buffalo, Toronto and Montreal. The new medium was well suited to the new broadcasting wonder, television. Indeed cross-country microwave seemed the solution to Canada's entire communications traffic jam.

There was much soul-searching over the cost. Every company was wallowing in postwar expenditures that boggled the mind of men raised in the Depression. When Bell's construction bill hit $96 million, Alex Lester wrote an impassioned letter to employees, imploring them to "spend every dollar as if it was your own." It had reached that level, from $18 million, in less than 10 years.

Nevertheless Bell and the CBC pushed for microwave and the telephone industry, not without qualms, went along with it. By 1958 a $50 million electronic highway, the longest microwave network in the world, stretched 3,900 miles across Canada. Its towers went atop buildings and mountains, through forests and over the obdurate Canadian Shield, tossing words and data across land that defied conventional pole lines. Signals came down from each antenna through a hollow metal tube called a waveguide (microwaves lose too much power if passed through wires). A repeater in each tower strengthened the incoming signal and passed it on.

Ultimately, each microwave channel simultaneously carried more than 1,200 telephone channels or their equivalent in tele-graph, data, network radio and TV, Telex and TWX (customer-dialed teleprinters) and computer communications. By the mid-'70s teleprinters and the increasing use of telephones had revolutionized the telegraph business. Telegrams were phoned to their recipients. The telegraph messenger was as rare as the whooping crane.

Other antiquated and inefficient systems were vanishing as Canada joined hands anew with the whole world. Prior to 1950, Cable and Wireless Limited, with cable terminals in Newfoundland, Nova Scotia and British Columbia, and Canadian Marconi Limited, with a central telegraph office and sending and receiving stations in Quebec, were Canada's tenuous links with other continents. Three telephone and 13 telegraph circuits provided radiotelegraph communications with the United Kingdom, Australia, Barbados, St. Pierre and Miquelon and radiotelephone service with the U.K. and West Indies which were often slow and erratic. With the formation in 1950 of the Crown agency, Canadian Overseas Telecommunication Corporation, the world began to shrink. "Via Canadian," shouted the new message blanks in bold red letters.

A new receiver and transmitter in British Columbia gave Canada direct communications with Australia, New Zealand and Japan instead of routing via the United States. The same year, 1956, the world's first long-distance multipurpose submarine cable went down between Scotland and Newfoundland, with COTC as one of four international joint owners. It employed coaxial cable which has, instead of pairs of wires, a hollow half-inch copper tube as one conductor with the second conductor, a heavy insulated wire, supported inside it. The cable reduces interference and increases the range of useable frequencies.

The new cable gave Canada 6 telephone and 12 telegraph circuits to overseas points. It also provided picture transmission, broadcast programs and the first international Telex system. The effect on telephony in particular was phenomenal. Tedious days of waiting for good radiotelephone atmospheric conditions were now almost a thing of the past. As demand exceeded capacity, COTC installed equipment to bring the telephone circuits up to 20.

Five years later, a new cable, CANTAT (Canada Trans-Atlantic Telephone) was laid between Scotland and Corner Brook, with an ultimate capacity of 80 voice circuits. Now Canada had direct telephone, telegraph and Telex circuits to Norway, Denmark, Sweden, the Netherlands, France, Germany, Switzerland and Italy without the previous time-consuming switch via London. Canada-England telephone rates were cut by 25 percent.

Step-by-step electromechanical switching equipment is still the most common switching equipment in use in Canadian telephone exchanges today. BRITISH COLUMBIA TELEPHONE.

A typical crossbar central office showing aisle of crossbar switch units. Canada's first No. 5 crossbar system went into service at Chatham, Ont., in 1956. BELL CANADA TELEPHONE HISTORICAL COLLECTION.

A handful of these control centres monitor routing of long-distance traffic. BELL CANADA TELEPHONE HISTORICAL COLLECTION.

Push-button electronic consoles are replacing the familiar plug-and-jack switchboards of old. BRITISH COLUMBIA TELEPHONE.

New techniques, such as burying cables, help to minimize visual pollution of the environment and also to avoid interruptions due to bad weather. This machine digs the trench and then pays out the cable. BELL CANADA.

Two years later, in 1963, COTC was one of four partners in the laying of COMPAC, a 6,725 mile submarine cable system extending from Vancouver Island to Hawaii, Fiji, New Zealand and Australia — the first truly reliable high-quality communications service between the countries concerned. After three months of operation it raised COTC's telephone traffic revenue by 222 percent over the same period a year before.

In 1966 Canada became a joint owner of SEACOM, a cable link through southeast Asia. Now the cable system almost girdled the world, but the final connection by way of India, Africa and the United Kingdom was never undertaken. The age of the satellite was near at hand.

Meanwhile, in other fields of communication back in Canada, technology bred more technology. The invention of transistors in 1948 caused the steady disappearance of tubes for most electronic applications, especially in switching and computer circuits. Telephone switching was transformed. In the old system, lifting a receiver off the hook activated the searching mechanism of the caller's circuit. Each digit dialled moved a corresponding switch to a given position. All the switches used in calling the number remained tied up for the duration of the call.

In the mid-'50s, crossbar, a kind of electromagnetic computer, was introduced to Canadian telephony. It separated the switching and dialing process, simplified it and speeded calls. A later generation of semielectronic switching systems, half the size of the newest crossbars, had a built-in self-testing system and a modular design that could be expanded to almost any need.

The switchboard operator herself no longer stooped under six pounds of headset; her paraphernalia of the '70s weighed 1.3 ounces. Direct Distance Dialing, which came to Canada in the late 1950s, dispensed with the operator altogether on self-dialled long-distance calls. The push button telephone speeded up calling and permitted data to be coded into a telephone system.

The technique of sending signals was likewise caught up in the postwar revolution. The old way was "analog." A voice message or signal went into and through the telephone network as an electrical wave representing the original signal, and came out the same way at the receiving end. What went in was analogous to what came out. It was essentially the form Alexander Graham Bell devised, and it was susceptible to interference and distortion.

Now came a "digital" technique, borrowed from a combina-

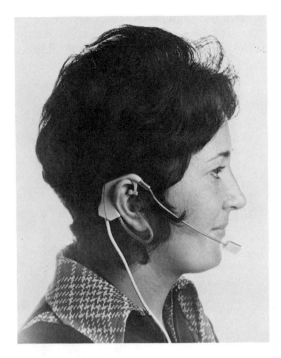

The Venture 1 headset, designed in Canada by Bell-Northern Research, was introduced in 1972. It weighs less than 1 ounce. By contrast operators of the 1880s wore the Gilliland Harness (below) which weighed 6½ pounds. BELL CANADA TELEPHONE HISTORICAL COLLECTION.

To the consumer the telephone in the home is the most visible part of the whole system. After a century of research and development the telephone bears little resemblance to Alexander Graham Bell's early experimental sets.

1877. Canada's first commercial telephones connected the Prime Minister's office and the Governor-General's residence. BELL CANADA.

1880s. Blake magneto wall telephone. BELL CANADA.

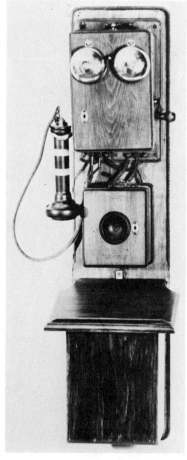

1880s. Improved version of Duquet's combined handset. BELL CANADA.

1878. Hand telephone, used both as receiver and transmitter. BELL CANADA.

Automatic Electric Company dial telephone, installed in Edmonton, 1908. ALBERTA GOVERNMENT TELEPHONES.

1924. First dial phones in Bell Canada system. BELL CANADA.

1927. Combined handset came into general use. BELL CANADA.

1937. The bell was hidden in the base of the telephone. BELL CANADA.

1968. Contempra phone, available with dial or touch-tone on the handset. BELL CANADA.

tion of old (telegraph) and new (computer) technologies, the latter with its system of binary numbering. Ordinary numbers are expressed as combinations of 10 symbols. The binary system uses only two: 1 and 0. Electrically, they can be expressed as "pulse" or "no pulse," respectively. Any number can therefore be translated into a series of infinitesimal pulses and pauses. More and more, voices, data, music or TV go over the network in "pulse code modulation."

All kinds of information can be leavened together, making maximum use of the space, yet everything is neatly sorted out at the receiving end, and recipients hear a friend's voice, see a telecast or read data in the normal fashion. The system is cheaper, has better quality transmission and can be readily expanded. Bell introduced the first pulse code modulated system to Canada in 1965.

The age of the wizards produced no lone wolves like Alexander Graham Bell or Reginald Fessenden. It was an age of teamwork and of a skill that the genius Bell never possessed: business management. Every technological advance represented not only inventive minds but the unromantic task of planning and managing: looking ahead not one year but 5 or 10, balancing costs against possible return, forecasting needs so the communications system would not break down, trying to find capital to fill those needs.

In this industry, as in others of the late 20th century, the comforting human touch seemed long gone. Machines were replacing people. As dials spread through rural areas, a strange silence settled on the party line. The honourable sport of rubbering was no more. Alice Jones, a former Shelburne, N.S., operator, penned words of lament for that vanishing species, Central:

. . .Central, I'm going next door,
Just to have a cup of tea,
You can reach me over there
If there are any calls for me.
Operator, why is that TV station off?
It's been off since yesterday you know.
If you don't get it fixed before long
I'm gonna miss my favourite show!
How long does a hen have to sit
On an egg before it starts to hatch?
Operator, give me a ring at 5 in the morning
My clock is broke and I have a train to catch. . .

Yet the story of Addie McCormack proves that human hearts still beat in the age of wizards. In 1916, as Addie Stacey then, she joined the Bell in Ottawa. The winsome redhead with the big smile was only 16 so she lied about her age to get the job. Her three sisters worked for the Bell; Addie never dreamed of breaking the family tradition.

She was a born operator: even tempered, cheerful and unbelievably true to her company. Within 11 years she was a chief operator. She liked to remind her girls that they bore the same responsibility as a soldier, fireman or policeman. The public depended upon them to be on duty. She told stories of operators who had stuck to their posts through fire and poisonous gas fumes. Maybe it was old-fashioned loyalty but for Addie there was no other way.

"Addie always tried to make the job sound important," another operator said.

She left the Bell in 1933 to marry a widower, help him raise two sons and bear one of her own. One, Donald, was a fireman. His mother always telephoned after he had been on a call. Sometimes she appeared on the scene with sandwiches and hot coffee for the firemen. At Christmas she made up parcels for poor families, left them at their doors, rang their bells, and quietly walked away.

In 1957, now chubby and motherly with a grown family, Addie McCormack went back to her first love. She was working the switchboard in the Beacon Arms Hotel on the afternoon of July 30, 1964, when a runaway fire flashed through the building. Only 60 of the 130 registered guests were in the hotel but Addie had no way of knowing that. She refused to leave, and kept methodically ringing the rooms. Fifty-eight of the people escaped. When firemen finally got through the flames and smoke they found her body beside the switchboard. Every jack was plugged in. Addie McCormack had been working the telephone with her last breath.

# "We Have Ignition. . . We Have Liftoff!"

*"T minus 22 minutes and counting. . . .We remain on schedule for liftoff at 7:29 p.m. Eastern Daylight Time. This is Delta Launch Control. . . ."*

*May 7, 1975. The crowds here at Cape Canaveral keep an ear tuned to the laconic voice from Mission Control and an eye on Complex 17. Even from four miles away the metallic green Delta launch vehicle is a huge gleaming finger pointing 119 feet into the overcast Florida sky. From closer view, a Canadian flag against a blue background stands out boldly on the Delta's sleek sides, beneath the white words "Telesat Canada." Hidden in the dark green nose cone is Anik III, a $10 million, 1,265-pound communications satellite. Tonight the Canadians, those outer space veterans, those pacesetters in satellite communications, are getting ready for another launch.*

Canada joined the space club in 1962. To that point only America and Russia had satellites in orbit. Canada's Alouette I, launched that year, and its successors, Alouette II and ISIS I and II, were scientific satellites. They probed the ionosphere, measured cosmic noise and examined the sun's effects on the earth's atmosphere and on radio transmission.

They were extraordinarily successful, and they helped Canada reach another fundamental decision in the late '60s: to get into satellite communications. It was a new, relatively untried and enormously expensive science. It seemed a heady undertaking for a middle power of less than 20 million people. Yet it also seemed made to order for a nation of vast distances, harsh weather and sparse population. It could bring telephone, television and all the telecommunications services into the farthest reaches of the Canadian North.

In 1969 Telesat Canada was incorporated as a private commercial venture, jointly owned by the Canadian Telecommunications Common Carriers (CN, CP and the major telephone companies) and the federal government. Communications satellites were not new by this time. The U.S. had launched TELSTAR in 1962. Early Bird, launched in 1965 for INTELSAT, became the first commercial communications satellite in geostationary orbit. The Russians had six satellites orbiting the earth: as one vanished over the horizon, Soviet earth stations locked onto the next behind it.

Canada would be a little different. It would produce the world's first *domestic* geostationary communications satellite. Its Anik (Eskimo for "brother") would ride the equator, seemingly motionless. In fact, its speed — 6,900 miles per hour — would match the speed of the turning Earth. Its electronic umbrella would cover Canada from sea to sea, and from the U.S. border to the 80th parallel. It could relay telephone, television, Telex and data signals from any point in Canada to any other point, flawlessly (or as flawlessly as the ground services permitted), 24 hours a day.

*"T minus 12 minutes, 53 seconds and counting. We remain on schedule. If the flight goes as planned this will make the 101st successful Delta launch. . . ."*

*The Delta is a U.S. vehicle. Few nations have the capability to produce this 146-ton monster with its 390,000 pounds of thrust. And the launch as usual goes from Cape Canaveral. But the Americans are doing it to Canadian specifications, and for a $10 million fee. In the control room Robert Chinnick, Telesat's vice-president of engineering and operations, watches proceedings with his usual deceptive calm. Others of the 12-man Canadian team are with him, as they have been for five weeks, helping get Anik III ready to fly.*

*At 333 River Road in Ottawa, in a control room like the rooms millions of Canadian moon-shot viewers have seen on TV, Telesat Mission Director Harry Kowalik chews fretfully on an Old Port cigarillo. He and 50 other Canadians in Telesat headquarters are tied in to the Cape, and to tracking stations at Allan Park, Ont., and Guam in the Pacific. Exactly 26 minutes after the liftoff, when the satellite separates from the rocket's first stage, they will take charge of Anik III.*

The problem and challenge, the Canadians discovered in the early '70s, was that there was no precedent for the domestic satellite system they were about to attempt.

Neither TELSTAR nor the Russian satellites were in synchronous orbit. That gave them considerably more flexibility. Their earth stations would "track" the satellites, no matter what the latters' positioning.

But tracking stations are highly expensive and their mechanism tends to break down in severe northern climates. So Anik I and its successors would beam down to fixed earth stations, from a precise position in space. They would have to be controlled to within .1 degree tolerance. As it turned out, Kowalik and the team of brilliant whiz kids he gathered around him achieved even tighter tolerances of .05 degrees.

*"T minus 9 minutes, 54 seconds and counting. All continues to go well in the blockhouse at Complex 17. . . ."*

*Whole families, clad in shorts and bikinis in the 82-degree heat, are streaming into the public viewing area now, with their ice cream cones and portable radios. If they could see inside the Delta nose cone they would view the guest of honour for this occasion: Anik III, a drum six feet in diameter and five feet high, topped with a 60-inch dish antenna. Its skin contains 20,000 solar cells that will power it while aloft (except during eclipses twice a year, when on-board batteries will take over). It has 12 radio frequency channels, each capable of carrying one colour TV program and associated audio or up to 960 simultaneous telephone conversations.*

*Anik III came from Hughes Aircraft in California in four boxes, packed with dry nitrogen to keep out humidity. The packing boxes alone are worth $50,000 each.*

In November 1972, less than 1,200 days after Telesat was incorporated, Anik I rose from Cape Canaveral. It began in an egg-shaped orbit — 22,800 miles from earth, at its high point or apogee, 105 miles away at its low point or perigee. Some 70 hours later, a ground-controlled burst from its apogee motor kicked it into circular orbit around the equator. More nudges from the control system and Anik I took its place at 114 degrees west longitude, due south from Calgary. Every synchronous satellite (and there are now many) is assigned a specific "parking space" around the equator. Canada opted for three of the coveted spaces.

Anik I's positioning had to be incredibly precise, to hold it within the beams of the earth station antennas. To correct any error in direction would draw from the spacecraft's precious seven-year hydrazine fuel supply, needed to correct the normal gravitational pull of sun, moon and earth, forever tugging at Anik out in space.

*"T minus seven and holding. This is a planned hold and is of 10 minutes' duration, an evaluation period to make certain the rocket and spacecraft are ready for launch. . . ."*

*They should be ready. Three days ago Bob Chinnick and the mission director at the Cape went over literally hundreds of individual items that had already been examined in the previous five weeks. "That's why you need so bloody many people," Chinnick sighs. "Checking and re-checking to meet the specifications."*

*The slightest deviation from norm must be examined. Anik II's launch was held up a day because a tape was missing. The tape, wrapped around some cables, was not critical, but why was it missing? No one would admit having removed it. Maybe something else was wrong. The crew spent all night rechecking the systems, which turned out to be flawless. "That's what they call tender loving care down here," Chinnick says. "It produces a successful launch."*

Sixty-three days after Anik I left the ground it was in use. Signals, with an equivalent strength of 200 megawatts, were flashed from earth stations to the satellite, 22,300 miles in $1/8$ of a second. By that time the signal had slimmed down to two millionths of a millionth of a watt. The satellite boosted it to the equivalent of 2,000 watts. It flashed back, dwindling to 40 millionths of a millionth of a millionth of a watt. Sensitive receivers on earth picked it up and boosted it to levels suitable for retransmission.

On January 11, 1973, telephone service via Telesat was begun between Frobisher Bay and Resolute in the high Arctic, and southern Canada. The satellite also took on some of the Toronto-Vancouver service for CNCP Telecommunications and for the Trans-Canada Telephone System. A few weeks later telephones went to Pangnirtung, northeast of Frobisher, and Igloolik on Melville Peninsula above the Arctic Circle. Now these remote northern villages could do what southerners had so long taken for granted: pick up a phone and call any other subscriber in Canada.

By spring 25 northern communities received their first television, via satellite. Before, the best such communities got was a package of video tape recordings flown in on a round robin basis. They'd see news or public affairs as late as six weeks after the event. By autumn of 1973 a Frobisher Bay man gloated, "It's just unbelievable! This year the Grey Cup live and in colour. Last year, it took days after the game just finding out the score!"

*"T minus six minutes and holding. . .this is an unscheduled hold . . .the countdown is being delayed due to the presence in the offshore impact zone of some pleasure boats. Safety officials are attempting to clear the area and the countdown will be resumed as soon as possible. . . ."*

*Moments like this turn mission directors grey before their time. It will not take long to shoo the boats out of danger, but any delay is bad. The weather is not ideal tonight: scattered cloud at 3,200 feet, overcast at 30,000 feet: thunder clouds building over the Gulf of Mexico. A lightning storm could cancel the space shot.*

*Also, Anik has a limited "launch window." Tonight it must be fired into orbit between 7:29 and 8:33, if it is to assume orbit in proper conjunction with the position of the sun. How maddening if a bunch of Wednesday night sailors stall a $20 million shot into space!*

Not all of Telesat's crises were on the launching pad. The corporation was criticized at times for trying to make a profit although that is part of its mandate. It was blamed for the poor quality of telephone service in some northern communities (although the service on *ground* lines has nothing to do with the satellite). Northerners complained about television programming — again, not a Telesat function.

There were unfavourable comparisons between Telesat and the federal government's experimental Communications Technology Satellite, launched in 1976. This was an apples-and-oranges comparison. Telesat is a commercial venture serving all of Canada, 24 hours a day. CTS, built and launched with $100 million of taxpayers' money, was designed for specific and exotic experiments in tele-education, telemedicine and community development.

Yet again, Telesat was criticized for having the spacecraft built by an American firm. In fact, Hughes Aircraft tendered the lowest bid, coupled with its solid history of spacecraft achievement. However, major subcontracts went to Spar Aerospace Products of Toronto and Northern Electric of Lucerne, Que.

The path of communications never ran smooth and Telesat — as part of a new, expensive and mysterious branch of technology — was no exception.

*"The count has been resumed and now stands at T minus 5 minutes, 44 seconds and counting. . . ."*

In 1974 Anik II took its place over the equator at 109 degrees west longitude. It was nearly on line with Battleford, Sask., where a mere 96 years before, the first feeble telegraph signal came over the flimsy government line. Satellite communication was already paying dividends in the North. Radio and radio-telephone are highly susceptible to atmospheric interference. Prior to the Aniks, northern communities could be cut off from the outside world for minutes, days or weeks. Now their telephone systems were as reliable as the ground lines and the telephones themselves. A village could instantly call for a doctor or an urgently needed spare part for a heating or lighting plant. A federal government man in Frobisher heard of an oil spill in Resolute. He phoned across Canada to Yellowknife and mobilized a clean-up operation within hours. In the old days it would have taken longer to even *hear* about the spill.

By summer, 1974, Pangnirtung had ordered 300 colour TV sets.

TV reception, although limited to a single CBC channel, was as clear as any in the South. What was TV doing to the Eskimo culture? Probably a little more bad and a little more good than to more advanced communities in the South. It was one part of the violent traumatic change overtaking northern people. TV couldn't be kept out; people wanted it. It brought with it the potential for great good, with great onus on its programmers.

*"T minus 4 minutes, 44 seconds and counting. . .T minus three minutes and counting. . . .All systems are go. . . ."*

By late 1974 the first two Aniks were well used. Some spare channels were leased, short-term, to the U.S. Close to 50 earth stations across Canada were relaying every conceivable kind of telecommunications from Igloolik to Montreal. An Imperial Oil crew on Richards Island at the brink of the Beaufort Sea, was direct-dialing its Calgary office from a portable earth station. A similar "transportable" station on Melville Island was serving Panarctic Oil. These mobile facilities would be increasingly valuable to other mining and petroleum exploration parties, and for TV actualities from any corner of Canada.

Telesat was now committed to its third and last "parking space." Anik III was needed as a back-up for Anik I and Anik II. Anyway since a satellite's life is only five to seven years (the fuel is burned and the batteries and solar cells deteriorate), Anik III would eventually replace Anik I.

*"T minus 15 seconds. . . .Stand by. . . .T Minus 10–9–8–7–6–5–4–3–2–1–zero. . . .We have ignition! . . .We have liftoff. . . !"*

*Flame blossoms at the Delta's base, a miniature fireball, a searing white light. The rocket lifts slowly, fighting the pull of gravity, then faster, faster, knifing the sky. Now, coming in late, as sound always does, its thunder crosses the distance.*

*The crowd cheers and claps. In the NASA Mission Control room, men who have seen a hundred launches yell wildly, "Go, go, you bastard, go!" One of them blinks back tears. It is not uncommon, nor unseemly, to weep during a launch. The rocket soars, thick smoke pluming behind it. Then it vanishes into the overcast.*

*". . .Plus 15 seconds, all looking good, flight going well, all systems looking very good. . .T plus 30 seconds. . . ."*

*It is a perfect launch. Smiles and cigars go around the control room.*

*At 3 minutes, 56 seconds, the rocket's first stage falls away on schedule. Now Delta and Anik III are 83 miles high, 223 miles downrange and travelling 2,710 miles an hour. The crowds drift home. The scores of spacecraft workers go back to town for a postlaunch party.*

*Long before they settle into the drinks and canapes — 25 minutes and 16 seconds after liftoff to be precise — Anik III has shed all its Delta stages. Telesat Satellite Control Centre in Ottawa takes charge. Anik III begins its blooping orbit around the earth.*

In time all three Aniks will be replaced in their same parking spots by more sophisticated generations of satellite. In time all the channels will be used for Canadian needs. One day every Canadian may have a rooftop antenna, taking signals directly from the satellite, for a choice of perhaps 50 TV channels, or a host of other communications services undreamed of in 1975.

*May 10, 1975. Anik III's apogee motor fires, on signal from Satellite Control. The satellite assumes a circular path around the equator. Now, delicately, the men in Ottawa jockey it precisely into place — and all this with invisible radio waves directed over 22,300 miles to a mere pinprick in space. Anik III hovers obediently at 104 degrees west longitude, on a direct line with Regina. Its time has come, out there in the yawning distance, to serve Canadians on earth.*

# Chapter 19

## The End of Distance

A mere 130 years from the first faltering message between Toronto and Hamilton, technology had put an end to distance. Those simple folk of 1846 who found the telegraph so difficult to comprehend would have cried "Witchcraft!" if they could have seen their great-grandchildren's Canada. Much of its electronic wizardry had come within the memory of living men. Adults who as children had never heard of television — and, if they were Depression products, may have grown up without telephone or radio either — now heard voices and saw images rebounding through the inky distances of outer space.

By 1976 the Brothers Anik were watching over us, 22,300 miles above Earth, relaying signals in fractions of seconds across the length and breadth of Canada's 3,851,809 square miles. Although the sun, moon and planets tugged and jostled the Aniks, earth-bound Canadians held them on their marks in space like well-behaved pets.

Signals and voices rebounded from other satellites around the world, and through cables snaking under the Atlantic and Pacific. Telegraph and telephone microwaves spun their invisible webs

The satellite earth station at Lake Cowichan on Vancouver Island. This links the Canadian telecommunication system with the international satellite system. TELEGLOBE.

CN Telecommunications scatterwave station at Hay River, Northwest Territories. This system links a number of far northern communities. CANADIAN NATIONAL.

from St. John's to Victoria, from the 49th parallel to the High Arctic. Inuvik, near the Beaufort Sea, was becoming a lively market for colour telephones. High frequency radio and satellite signals reached into even more remote corners of the land. Coast-to-coast and south-to-north, radio and television followed the electronic paths.

Day and night these vital links carried a torrent of entertainment, business and friendship. They saved lives and made lives more liveable. They represented a total capital investment of $12 billion, annual revenues of $3 billion and a work force of 96,000 earning close to a billion dollars a year. Without them Canada would not function in modern society.

By 1976 the industry that had struggled so long and hard for a national identity was almost totally Canadian owned. In the previous year, Bell Canada ended its licensing contract with AT&T in the United States. More and more, Canadians depended on Canadian technology. Northern Electric, renamed Northern Telcom in 1976, was this country's major manufacturer of telecommunications equipment, and the second largest in North America, with annual sales of more than $1 billion.

CNCP Telecommunications, a joint operation, dominated the telegraph sector. The two had joined wires in the 1930s to originate a transcontinental network for the Canadian Radio Commission (forerunner to CBC). In 1953 they joined again to provide TV network service between Toronto and Windsor, and again in 1956 to launch Telex. By 1969, rising costs forced them to combine their telegraph business.

A few independent railroads offered public telegraph service in limited areas: the Ontario Northland (whose Ontario Northland Communications system originated shortly after the turn of the century, to assist construction of the railroad), Quebec North Shore and Labrador, Algoma Central, British Columbia Railway and the Northern Alberta (jointly owned by CNR and CPR).

Of approximately 850 telephone companies going into 1976, 6 controlled 95 percent of Canada's telephones. The Bell group dominated 68 percent, through direct operations in Ontario, Quebec and the eastern Northwest Territories, plus majority holdings in Northern Telephone Limited, Télébec Limitée, Newfoundland Telephone Company, the New Brunswick Telephone Company and Maritime Telegraph and Telephone. MT&T in turn owned 56 percent of the Island Telephone Company in Prince Edward Island.

Roughly 99 percent of Bell shares were held in Canada. Its American "parents" of years past were no more. Indeed, Bell was actively nourishing Canadian ownership: its controlling interest in Northern Telephone and the New Brunswick Telephone Company, and its majority holdings in MT&T, were brought about to prevent possible takeovers by U.S. companies.

The three prairie systems comprised Canada's second largest "group" by nature of their provincial government ownership (they were not, of course, actually affiliated). Their 1.8 million phones represented 13.5 percent of the national total. General Telephone and Electronics Corporation of New York indirectly controlled another 12 percent through its subsidiary, Anglo-Canadian Telephone Company. Anglo-Canadian held 51 percent of the British Columbia Telephone Company (which in turn owned the Okanagan Telephone Company) and 54 percent of Québec-Téléphone — the major indigenous company of French-Canada, and the grownup son of Dr. Demers. It served a vast tract of Quebec province on both shores of the St. Lawrence estuary, from its Rimouski headquarters to Blanc-Sablon, plus other pockets of territory around Quebec City.

Québec-Téléphone emerged under that name in 1955, after a succession of corporate mergers and acquisitions. Its main architect in this century was Jules-André Brillant, a prominent Quebec industrialist. Brillant, whose interests over the years included banking, electric power and broadcasting, began putting together a modest telephone empire in the late '20s. It included the offspring of La Compagnie de Téléphone de Métis. Appropriately, Brillant was born in Saint-Octave-de-Métis, where, when he was nine years old, the telephone arrived courtesy of Dr. Demers.

Although these companies controlled most of Canada's telephones by the mid-'70s and although "Central" was then virtually extinct, the independent telephone companies were an endangered but still healthy species. The Canadian Independent Telephone Association with 70 systems, mostly in Ontario and Quebec, included such disparate members as the Thunder Bay municipal telephone company with 70,000 phones, edmonton telephones with 305,000 and the Emile Vézina company of eastern Quebec with 54. Saskatchewan had some 735 independent rural companies.

Canadian National Telecommunications provided public phone service to 71,000 subscribers in Newfoundland, northern

B.C., the Yukon and the Northwest Territories. CNT had long since taken over northern communications from the Royal Canadian Signal Corps. It had pushed microwave from Grande Prairie, Alta., to the Yukon-Alaska border, and a pole line along the Mackenzie River to Inuvik — indeed, the last great pole line probably ever to be built in Canada. The builders had a new trick to make a line stand up in swamp and muskeg: the poles were tripods. There was only one hangover from the wretched government telegraph of the 1870s: where the line ran through Wood Buffalo National Park, itchy buffalo rubbed the poles down, exactly as their forefathers did on the prairie long ago.

In 1966 CNT also hitched up a northern health services radio-telephone network connecting 15 isolated settlements with nursing stations. On opening day it saved a life. The school-teacher/operator in Pelly Bay picked up a distress call from Thom Bay, 80 miles north over Arctic wilderness: a pregnant Eskimo woman was hemorrhaging. Quick work by radio-telephone got a mercy mission into Thom Bay. The baby died but the mother survived.

All together these systems by the mid-1970s gave Canada 13,142,000 telephones, amounting to 57 per hundred population. Canadians logged 21 billion phone calls along the network of the Trans Canada Telephone System — a consortium of the major telephone companies operating about 91 percent of the phones in the country. The system was, of course, available to every telephone system in the land and it gave Canadian telephone users what amounted to one high quality country-wide service. Despite the inevitable pain of rate increases, the cost was reasonable, compared to most other countries. Whereas a European industrial worker laboured five to twelve hours a month to pay for his basic telephone service, his Canadian counterpart worked only 1³/₄ hours to pay for the same service.

By the mid-'70s Canadians also indulged in two million overseas telephone conversations. Their telecommunications link to the rest of the world was Teleglobe Canada (formerly the Canadian Overseas Telecommunication Corporation). By 1976 Teleglobe provided Canadians with telephone, telegraph, teleprinter, video and data transmission services to virtually every other country in the world through networks of submarine cables and satellite.

As a charter member in 1964 of the International Telecommunications Satellite Organization (INTELSAT), Teleglobe is hooked into three orbiting international satellites. Through them Canadians have watched such international events, live, as the Canadian-Russian hockey tournaments, while viewers abroad saw the 1976 Olympics in Canada.

Since its inception Teleglobe has helped install six submarine cables. The *piece de resistance* was CANTAT 2 in 1974, a cable that would have made Fred Gisborne's eyes pop: 1,840 circuits, greater capacity than all the other existing trans-Atlantic cables combined.

CANTAT 2 crossed the Atlantic with almost ridiculous ease. Two ships laid 2,800 miles of 1.47-inch-diameter coaxial cable in eight separate operations, finishing five days ahead of schedule. A 16-ton underseas plow cut 146 miles of trench over the continental shelf, heavily travelled by fishing vessels, and buried the cable 18 inches under the ocean floor to protect it from trawlers. A mini-submarine followed to bury the 10-foot electronic repeaters, spliced in at six-mile intervals, because they were too big for the plow. Television cameras monitored part of the operation. A navigation satellite helped guide one of the ships on a true course.

Teleglobe is coowner of CANTAT 2 with the British Post Office System. It is also Canada's representative on the 24-member Commonwealth Telecommunications Organization and on several other international bodies. And, along with 20 other carriers in Canada, it is a member of the Canadian Telecommunications Carriers Association, formed in 1972 to promote development and improvement of the industry, and to coordinate relationships with governments, press and public. In 1907 Canada joined the International Telegraph Union; today it is the International Telecommunication Union. One function of this oldest member-organization of the UN family of specialized agencies is to allocate bands in the radio-frequency spectrum to particular telecommunications services.

Complex as all this may appear, the system works rather well. For example: a Telex from Ottawa to Vancouver flashes from the customer's premises to the CNCP Ottawa Telex centre, follows CNCP routes across the country, and travels over B.C. Telephone wires to the customer. A telephone call from Halifax to Baffin Island may go via Maritime Tel and Tel and Bell Canada to Ontario, where Telesat's Allan Park earth station beams it to an Anik. The words rebound to an earth station near Frobisher and travel to the recipient over a Bell telephone line. All of this happens as quickly as humans can dial, plus the necessary seconds to pass through circuitry. Distance no longer exists.

Facsimile transmission of weather maps aids in forecasting. CANADIAN NATIONAL.

The Public Message Service Centre in Toronto, where telegrams are taken over the phone, typed, and checked on a video display unit. Today most telegrams are phoned in rather than filed in person at the counter. CANADIAN NATIONAL.

Teleprinter services provide rapid transmission of typewritten messages. CANADIAN NATIONAL.

# Monopoly and Controls

By 1976 Canadian telephone and telegraph service was dominated in every region by one company system or a consortium. (Telex, TWX, data, TV and radio program transmission were provided in competition by CNCP and TCTS.) The monopoly aspects sometimes grated on the country's remaining free-enterprisers, particularly during rate increases. Who was safeguarding the consumers' interests? Would the industry be better run with more competition?

The case for a well-regulated monopoly in communications had been rather thoroughly stated in years past. The eminent John Stuart Mill in the mid-19th century wrote of public utilities in general: "When a business of real public importance can only be carried on advantageously upon so large a scale as to render the liberty of competition almost illusory, it is an unthrifty dispensation of the public resources that several costly sets of arrangements should be kept up for the purpose of rendering to the community this one service. It is much better to treat it at once as a public function, and if it be not such as government itself could beneficially undertake, it should be made over entire to the company or association which will perform it on the best terms to the public."

The telephone and telegraph are indeed public utilities and with the telephone in particular there is an additional and compelling reason for monopoly. As history has demonstrated, it is inefficient and costly to have competing telephones in a given community, each with its own set of subscribers and rates.

"It is sensible to have the telephone system a monopoly for efficiency's sake," writes historian Harold I. Sharlin in *The Making of the Electrical Age*, "but whether it is to be a state-owned monopoly or a privately owned one depends largely on whether the goal is lower rates (state owned) or aggressive extension of the system (privately owned). Both types of monopoly exhibit an unfortunate tendency to resist change."

Sharlin's statement must be qualified on several counts. In Canada, government-owned systems *have* aggressively extended their service although, in the beginning at least, they offered no particular improvement in rates. At the same time, any comparison of rates must recognize that government systems as a rule pay no taxes while investor-owned companies do. Therefore, taxpayers indirectly help subsidize the government-owned system.

Whatever the form of monopoly, users share a legitimate concern: that telecommunications companies be run as efficiently as they would under the forces of competition. To help achieve this, various regulatory bodies oversee the companies' activities, including rate increases.

The 1905 Select Committee that put C. F. Sise on his mettle brought about an amendment to the Railway Act. It placed Bell and other federally chartered companies under a regulatory Board of Commissioners. This was supplanted by the National Transportation Act of 1967 and the Canadian Transport Commission. The latter body ruled on rate increases for Bell Canada, British Columbia Telephone Company, CNCP Telecommunications and a few others, until this function passed on to the Canadian Radio-Television and Telecommunications Commission.

Other systems have other watchdogs. SaskTel for example, is controlled by its government-appointed directors, the Minister of Telephones and a select standing committee of the legislature. All of the 26 municipal systems in Canada are regulated by provincial statutes governing municipal affairs.

To the consumer of the mid-'70s, hard-pressed by inflation and increasing costs (including telecommunications rates), the regulatory bodies were too lenient. Certainly, constant press and public vigilance toward the monopolies *and* their regulators is imperative. Nevertheless, a 1970 federal report on telecommunications in Canada offered a caution.

"There appears to be some danger in adopting a too meticulous approach to regulatory legislation," the report said. "If an attempt is made to establish statutory criteria governing every conceivable aspect of the public interest in telecommunications, the outcome may be disappointing. Perhaps the most likely result would be the creation of administrative machinery so ponderous as to bring both regulator and regulated almost to a halt. At the very least, there is danger that excessively prescriptive legislation may impel the regulatory body to concern itself, or even interfere with, matters that more properly fall within the responsibilities of management."

It is axiomatic that subscribers *always* think telephone rates are too high. "Nobody loves the telephone company," observes Tony Cashman, Alberta Government Telephones' historian. Yet the average Canadian has no inkling of the high quality of Canadian service, compared to communications in other countries, nor the high capital cost of that service. The telecommunications companies are largely to blame for this public ignorance.

The amount invested per telephone in Canada during World War II was approximately $236. By 1975 it was more than $800. The technology of connecting and switching becomes ever more complex and costly, as telephone population increases. Physical plants alone run to multimillions. For example, in 1975 *one* Bell Canada building, handling long distance plus the telephony of downtown Montreal, held $85 million worth of equipment. The communications companies have failed to tell this story, emphatically and dramatically.

Nor do Canadians realize how lucky they are to be able to dial and — assuming the other party isn't on his line — get through immediately, and hear and be heard clearly. This simple act is impossible in many other parts of the world. In 1975 a diplomat had to fly from Vienna to London in order to get a telephone connection with Saudi Arabia.

Canadians have every right to expect the almost flawless service that they take for granted. But by 1977 this, like everything else, was inevitably costing more money.

## Thinking About Tomorrow

"I would hope," remarks Alex Lester, the retired Executive Vice-President of Bell Canada, "that future generations do not spend *all* their time communicating. I would hope they'll do a little *thinking* in between." The 1969–70 federal study of telecommunications chimed in with a similar prayer for any future "wired city" (that phrase being the futuristic shorthand for a metropolis packed with electronic wonders). Such a city, one delegate suggested, "should include silent rooms where citizens could go to escape from communications systems."

Nevertheless, although distance had dwindled to microseconds, communications had not reached the saturation point in the mid-'70s. The industry went into the last quarter-century thinking furiously about tomorrow.

Technologists tend to vault far ahead of the public and sometimes fall on their faces. A classic example was Picturephone, touted in the late '60s as a boon to all mankind. It was available for a price — but people didn't want it at that price. The complaints were various — picture too small; possible loss of privacy — but its basic flaw, as the communications deep thinkers finally figured out, was a lack of "shared visual space." It permitted no interaction. No user could point a finger at the other's nose. It was like talking to a TV set over telephone lines.

So, futurism must be tempered with reality. What are the real probabilities for tomorrow? To consumers, *how* the message gets there is of minimal interest, but to technologists the most exciting prospect for the 1980s was "fibre optics" whereby light is transmitted through highly refined glass fibres, each the diameter of a hair. Because of their size, flexibility and relative immunity to surrounding environment, fibres can be bundled into thin cables handling an enormous amount of video and digital traffic — in the order of several thousand voice channels or a TV channel, per fibre. Beyond that is the laser beam, expected to accommodate seven million telephone circuits or the equivalent in data or television.

Business users of the mid-'70s were already revelling in a data transmission revolution. In 1974 Canada set up the world's first digital data transmission service available on a commercial basis. It was followed in 1976 by "packet-switching" services, in which all information was transmitted in standard-size batches along the digital networks. This was to data communications what the telephone network was to voice: a basic route connecting many users to many computers, the most advanced of its kind in the world.

The development of digital data services, high speed facsimile and optical scanning devices led the Canadian Post Office to contemplate electronic mail by 1985. The so-called "superphone," dreamed and talked about since the 1960s, became reality on a limited scale by the mid-'70s. Spot experiments with push-button telephone shopping and install-your-own-phone (to a jack installed by the telephone company) were underway in selected areas. With full computerized switching the telephone system would be able to forward calls automatically from one number to another if desired, turn on the lights or turn off the oven at the touch of a distant button, ride herd on a busy line until it was free, and a host of other electronic tricks.

By 1990, predicted Gordon Thompson, a senior scientist with Bell-Northern Research — Canada's largest industrial research organization — Canadian householders may enjoy fully digital telephone systems. This means they may be able to receive pictures — not television, but sketches, line drawings or cartoons, possibly in colour — over the telephone line. Most people may have a telephone video "scratch pad." Dubbed "Scribblephone" in 1976, it would permit users to write, erase, read, talk and listen simultaneously. It would be as good as face-to-face communication, for any game playing or other exchange of verbal and written information.

Future telephone users will shop by phone, as they do now, but probably not exclusively. They'll always want to go to the store, if only for the sensual experience. BNR's Thompson calls stores "our contemporary art gallery. It's a social event to go shopping."

Similarly, Canadians will probably still choose to go to a place of work, although likely to a convenient suburban work centre rather than a distant conventional office. They'll sit at audiovideo consoles with view-screen and keyboards, drawing work files and other data from computerized libraries. As they dictate into the machine, a printed copy will roll out at the other end. They will communicate with fellow workers anywhere along the line, by voice or by print on the viewscreen. But most of them *will* want to get out of the house.

Many will also insist on business trips. Two-way video conferences were technically possible by the mid-'70s but research by Bell Canada and B.C. Telephone, among others, uncovered several interesting facts:

- Two-way audiovideo conferences were effective with small groups; with larger groups they tended to become one-way lectures.
- Some people will always rationalize a business trip regardless of its inefficiency.
- Some men don't like to communicate by video screen: it makes them look (and therefore feel) small.
- Cross-country time zones pose a problem for cross-country video meetings.
- The old-style face-to-face meeting will endure to a lesser degree, because people like its privacy and its synergism.
- There really *is* a force field around individuals, and as yet telecommunications has not captured it.

All of these predictions are logical extensions of today's techniques. To them, Gordon Thompson of Bell-Northern Research adds a new concept. He sees the wired city as "one of the most significant wealth-generating mechanisms in tomorrow's world." Thompson is one of a new breed of telecommunicators. From his Ottawa office — a mad and fascinating jumble of memorabilia, communications gadgetry, chairs, low tables but no desk — he visualizes the total environment in which future Canadians will live and communicate.

Already, Thompson points out, a large portion of Canada's labour dollar goes to bureaucrats, researchers, journalists, educators and others in various aspects of information. But this is basically salaried labour, not wealth-creating, and the productivity, notably among government bureaucrats, is "abysmally low."

Thompson sees tomorrow's "information marketplace" as an opportunity for ordinary people to create capital by peddling their creations — music, essays, poems, stories, theses, games, jokes or other leisure-filling diversions — to an enormous national or international communications bank. They would pay a monthly fee for the privilege. If they fell behind on payments or the demand for their product was minimal, it would be withdrawn. Users would plug into the system for the subject of their choice, after consulting the system's catalogue for a fee (there would be catalogue "authors" too) and pay a fee for audio recordings, video information and printouts.

Thompson and other proponents of the information marketplace are probably a little naive in suggesting that it will free "50 to 80 percent" of tomorrow's Canadians from the bonds of wage earning. But it could remove the barrier of costly inefficient antiquated methods of publication and distribution between users and creators. And in tomorrow's Canada, leisure time will be filled with a multitude of new diversions. The information marketplace is possible, perhaps even probable. So are the telecommunications predictions in the little scenario that follows. The technology for all of them is at hand. They need only our will to make them come true.

# The Way It Could Be

A dismal grey morning it is, as John Daedalus discovers, drowsily fumbling for a button among his bedside controls. At his touch the Polaroid window glass clears to reveal a city silvered with sleet. Daedalus shivers, shuts it out again and flicks on his wall-holograph scene of a summer sunrise from Telegraph Hill. Immediately the sentimental Newfoundlander feels better. He frequently wonders what he is doing here in Oshtowin anyway. It was congested enough in the old days, the string of cities from Oshawa to Windsor. Now. . .well, the megalopolis is where the action is, everyone says so, and Daedalus enjoys that part of it.

Over his all-purpose diet-drink breakfast he idly watches the news on the four-by-ten-foot wall television. Not much happening. The 15 Senators of the Royal Commission, newly appointed to explore ways of celebrating Century 21, are complaining that three years aren't enough for a thorough study. The Prime Minister herself has denounced the latest recommendation from the Committee for an Independent Canada, that all Americans in Canada be required to wear the Stars and Stripes sewn to the backs of their coats. The Argonauts have finally made it to a Grey Cup playoff, in the Oshtowin Bowl on New Year's Day.

Miniature TV sets, no bigger than the transistor radios of olden times, are on sale. Daedalus promptly orders one for his nephew in St. John's, keying the order number and his personal code —

DAE-873-429-114 — into the telephone console. Computers will take care of the order and delivery, including a gift card with the facsimile signature "Merry Christmas from Uncle John."

Back to the television. No need to hurry. Like many Canadians, Daedalus works to his own timetable. Good! A commentator is inviting viewers to play ParticiPhone, the gadget that lets them "vote" on any subject, producing a national consensus within minutes.

"As you know," she is saying, "the continuing debate in education this month is whether grade school field trips to the Moon should be financed from public funds. The cost is high, there is still moderate risk to the journey, but the learning experience is rich. What is your opinion? Yes or no? At the sound of the tone, you will have 10 seconds to register your opinion on ParticiPhone. It will assist our educators in forming policies. I will report the computer-tabulated results at the end of this telecast. . . ."

Daedalus hurries to his telephone accessory, the size and shape of the old-fashioned cigarette packages (before cigarettes were banned), with simple "yes"/"no" buttons. Every Canadian with a telephone has ParticiPhone. After all, the device was invented in Canada more than 20 years ago (its originators at Bell-Northern Research called it "in-casting" or "vote-a-phone") and it costs the subscriber nothing. The broadcasting industry foots the bill.

And it is such fun! Entire television game shows are built around ParticiPhone, with millions of viewers joining in. Commercials are keyed to its instant response from potential customers across Canada. Long ago, ParticiPhone did away with broadcast rating systems, and resurrected many programs that the old-fashioned ratings had killed. ParticiPhone is beloved by all, except former political pollsters, now on welfare, and hundreds of university professors whose lucrative second careers as broadcaster-pundits suddenly fell apart. ParticiPhone revealed that academics hadn't the slightest idea what the masses *really* were thinking.

At the tone, Daedalus presses the "yes" button. To a 30-year-old bachelor the question is of marginal interest, but if a trip to the Moon will enrich the kids, he's in favour. He likes children, although he doesn't believe in marriage. . . .Which reminds him. He phones his sister in St. John's. "I've sent Gerry's present," he says, "but what'll I get for Ginny?"

"She wants one of those new dollhouses."

"Like this?" Daedalus seizes a stylus and doodles the flowing lines of a 1996 apartment module on his Scribblephone pad. The line drawing grows on his own and his sister's screen as they watch.

"No, no, one of the old styles. . .you remember. . .like this. . . ." His sister rubs out the curving lines, adds a peaked roof, gables and a chimney. "See? All the kids want these. They say they're quaint!"

"Got it, thanks," says Daedalus. "Talk to you later."

Next he punches into Computer Canada for a statement of his account. Good news: the national banking system (all in the form of computer credits and debits) reports that his royalties took a gratifying jump in November. Daedalus is a university botanist by profession but, like many Canadians, he has a profitable sideline filed with Canada Bibliographic, the national reference library, for the payment of a small monthly fee.

Most of his 38 million fellow Canadians are urban dwellers like himself. That's why his audio lecture, supplemented with color video line drawings — "Indoor Gardens for the Megalopolis" — is a modest best-seller. Every time someone plugs into Bibliographic to use the Daedalus material, royalties click into the Daedalus Computer Canada account.

Even more astonishing is the way the counter-culture keeps plugging in to hear his labour of love, "An Audio History of the Mid-Century Newfie Joke." Daedalus has always been a history buff but never fancied himself a historian. Amazing how Canadians here in 1996 reach back with yearning to any odd little fragment of the past.

With a light heart and a full bank account, he is off to work in the rented electric mini-car. On the way, his part-time secretary calls him from the university, on the wrist telephone that most Canadians wear. It is strictly for short-range communications, ideal for exchanging messages, or dodging the telephone calls one doesn't want.

"A man from Revenue Canada is trying to reach you," she says.

"Tell him I've taken a student class to the Moon," Daedalus says, and rings off abruptly.

Five minutes later he is renting time on one of the 500 consoles in Enrichment Centre #15. For four hours — surrounded by students, housewives, businessmen and teachers pursuing their own jobs, studies or hobbies at other consoles — he marks audio examination tapes, dictates comments into the file for playback to his students, and records an audiovisual lecture to be delivered in January over the microwave network to a class in Calgary.

Work over. Daedalus punches a code call to his home telephone, causing the automatic system to turn on the oven. Tonight he will enjoy an old fashioned hot dinner, for tonight is special. His reconstructed history program is finally finished, and waiting in the computer bank. Tonight, on his home console, he will indulge in "A Talk with Great-Grandfather."

Reconstructed history is Canada's newest educational/ recreational craze. It is simple in theory, so simple that the Canadians of 1974 visualized it. Naturally, in those primitive years, they lacked the expertise to produce it. Now, with an enormous information bank on every conceivable subject and with computer speeds in the order of 40 nanoseconds (40 billionths of a second), it is relatively easy to reconstruct almost any period and person from history, complete to habits, food, dress, environment and events. Hire an author-researcher to concoct a scenario, turn it over to a brilliant programmer, put it all in the wondrous computer and "talk" to people of the past. One poses simple questions on the keyboard and gets answers on the video screen, answers that the subject from history would logically have given.

Naturally, it works best with well-known figures — Winston Churchill, Mackenzie King, Marilyn Monroe, people whose lives were intimately documented in olden times. But one can, as Daedalus has done, hire an author-researcher to build a personalized program. So Daedalus, amateur historian, has ordered a reconstruction of his maternal great-grandfather, the man and his little world of Toronto, 150 years ago.

Daedalus settles at his console; flicks on a wall-holograph view of Toronto, 1846, for mood; plugs into the system and "talks" to great-grandfather Charles McVitty. He feels a trifle silly at first.

"How is the weather today?" he types awkwardly.

"Cloudy, getting warmer," the screen replies. "The streets are almost bare. Bad weather for sleighing."

"What did you buy the family for Christmas?"

"Button shoes. Butter churn. Cameo brooch."

Daedalus, warming up to the situation, decides on a trick. He'll see if the computerized program really *is* authentic.

"Are you going to telephone your brother in Montreal tonight?"

There is a pause. The screen blinks out:

"I do not understand 'telephone.'"

"Are you going to call brother John in Montreal?"

"I do not understand. It is a four-day journey. I will not call on him before Christmas."

An eerie feeling creeps over Daedalus. This is all make-believe of course, but the old man — dammit, the *computer* — is beginning to sound real!

"Do you not know that people will talk over wires, before you die?"

"That is impossible."

"Have you heard of the telegraph?"

"There was a thing called 'electric magnetic telegraph' in the City Hall today."

"What is it?"

"I did not see it. They say that words went through the air to Hamilton."

"Are you not pleased? Excited?"

"No. I think it is a trick. Such things are not possible."

Daedalus suddenly snaps off the console, flicks his Polaroid window glass to "open" and stares unseeingly into the night. That old man, McVitty, could not dimly imagine the changes that were going to shake his lifetime. But. . .can anyone? *What lies ahead for you, John Daedalus?*

For 20 years men have predicted an electronic instrument that would permit one human mind to transmit to another, brain to brain — a step below universal ESP. Already they are experimenting with such devices in laboratories. A few people, here in 1996, can actually make them work. Will his niece and nephew and all Canadians of tomorrow *think* their messages around the world?

Exhilarated and a little frightened, Daedalus darkens the window glass, turns the wall-holograph to soothing starlight and falls asleep at the threshold of the 21st century.

# Chronology

*1846*
— First Canadian demonstration of electric telegraph in Toronto city hall (July 24–25).
— Canada's first telegraph messages, between Toronto-Hamilton over lines of Toronto, Hamilton & Niagara Electro-Magnetic Telegraph (Dec. 19). Line later popularly (but not officially) known as Toronto, Hamilton, Niagara and St. Catharines Electro-Magnetic Telegraph.

*1847*
— Toronto/Montreal telegraph service inaugurated over Montreal Telegraph line (August 3).

*1849*
— New Brunswick Electric Telegraph opens (Jan. 1).
— Pony express carries first despatches from Halifax to Digby for relay to Saint John, N.B. telegraph (Feb. 21).
— Nova Scotia Government Telegraph completed (Nov. 9); carries first European despatches (Nov. 15), ending pony express.

*1851*
— Nova Scotia Electric Telegraph takes over government telegraph lines.

*1852*
— Montreal Telegraph under Hugh Allan buys out Toronto, Hamilton & Niagara.
— Newfoundland Electric Telegraph completed between St. Johns and Carbonear (March 6).
— F. N. Gisborne lays North America's first cable between Cape Tormentine, N. B., and Carleton Head, P.E.I. (Nov. 22–23).

*1856*
— New Brunswick Electric Telegraph leased by American Telegraph Company (Feb. 1).
— Newfoundland/Cape Breton cable laid (and relaid in 1857); Newfoundland telegraph pole line completed.

*1858*
— On second attempt, Atlantic cable landed at Trinity Bay, Nfld.; first messages cross Atlantic, Aug. 16; cable breaks, Sept. 4.

*1860*
— Nova Scotia Electric Telegraph leased to American Telegraph Company.

*1865*
— Western Union telegraph line reaches New Westminster.
— Collins Overland Telegraph begins line construction north from New Westminster to link North America with Europe via Russia.
— Another Atlantic Cable attempt fails.

*1866*
— Victoria connected to B.C. mainland via cable and telegraph (Apr. 24).
— Anglo-American Telegraph Company founded; sets up operations in Nfld.
— Atlantic Cable successfully laid across ocean to Heart's Content, Nfld. (July 27). Broken cable from earlier attempt is retrieved and mended. Collins Overland Telegraph to Russia is abandoned.
— Western Union takes over American Telegraph leases in Nova Scotia and New Brunswick.

*1868*
— Dominion Telegraph Company founded (reorganized three years later).

*1871*
— Montreal Telegraph opens 54 new offices in Nova Scotia.
— Canadian government takes over British Columbia telegraph lines, including remnant of Collins Overland, as B.C. joins Confederation (July 20).
— First telegraph lines link Winnipeg and eastern Canada via U.S. (Nov. 20).

*1874*
— Alexander Graham Bell describes idea for telephone to his father in Brantford (July 26).

*1875*
— Bell constructs world's first telephone in Boston; transmits speech sounds.
— Canadian government telegraph built between Livingstone, Man., and Battleford, Northwest Territories.

*1876*
— Government telegraph completed from Selkirk, Man., to Hay Lakes near Edmonton.
— Bell patents telephone in U.S. (March 7); transmits first intelligible speech, room to room, in Boston (March 10).
— World's first definitive telephone tests (one-way transmission) are held in Canada: Brantford to Mount Pleasant, Ont., two miles (August 3); Brantford to Bell homestead (August 4); world's first long-distance call, Brantford to Paris, eight miles (August 10).

*1877*
— Bell obtains Canadian telephone patent (August 24).
— Descriptions of telephone published in *Scientific American* help stimulate experiments in Nova Scotia; Prof. J. E. Oram, Windsor, and H. S. Poole, Halifax, contrive working models. Same magazine articles inspire William

Wall, mechanic, to install telephone hook-up at coal mines near Nanaimo, B.C.
— Nova Scotia's first commercial telephones brought to Caledonia Mines, Glace Bay, by Bell's father-in-law, Gardiner Hubbard (July–August).
— Alexander Graham Bell turns over Canadian telephone interests to his father (75 percent) and to Charles Williams, Boston manufacturer (25 percent).
— Melville Bell conducts three-way telephone experiment in Hamilton (Aug. 29) for Hugh C. Baker, Charles D. Cory, T. C. Mewburn and Mrs. J. R. Thompson. Service begins for these Hamiltonians with leases dated (Oct. 18).
— Bell leases phones to Prime Minister Alexander Mackenzie (Nov. 9) but backdates lease to September 21, calling it "first" in Canada.

### 1878
— Cyrille Duquet, Quebec City, patents telephone (Feb. 1).
— New Brunswick's first phones leased to G. & G. Flewwelling, Hampton (March 1).
— Horace McDougall, Winnipeg telegraph agent, receives Manitoba's first two telephones from East; connects his home and telegraph office.
— Postmaster-General John Delaney and meteorologist John Higgins of St. John's install Newfoundland's first phones (March 20).
— R. B. McMicking demonstrates Victoria's first two phones (March 22).
— Montreal Telegraph Company becomes agent for Edison telephones (May).
— Canadian government telegraph completed between Fort William and Selkirk (August).
— Thomas and James Cowherd open Canada's first telephone factory in Brantford.
— World's ninth telephone exchange, and first outside the United States, opens in Hamilton (July).
— 19 Cowherd telephones shipped to Hamilton exchange (December).

### 1879
— Dominion Telegraph Company becomes agent for Bell telephones (February).
— Alexander Melville Bell tries to sell his Canadian company to Dominion Telegraph and others. Finding no Canadian buyers, the Bell family insists that the National Bell in the U.S. buy the Canadian company.
— Hamilton District Telephone Company builds Canada's first commercial long distance line (Hamilton to Dundas).
— Toronto gets Canada's first telephone directory (June).
— Dominion Telegraph installs telephone exchanges in Halifax and Saint John.
— Ottawa gets its first exchange.

### 1880
— The Bell Telephone Company of Canada gets its charter (April 29).
— W. J. Jeffree's Clothing Establishment and W. J. Pendray's Soap Factory install Victoria's first commercial telephone hookup (Jan. 21).
— Victoria and Esquimalt Telephone Company becomes B.C.'s first (May 8).
— Great North Western Telegraph Company founded in Winnipeg, May 7.
— Niagara Falls telephone convention adopts "Hello" as standard salutation (September).

— First public pay phones in Bell Central exchanges. Payment to attendant.
— Canadian Pacific Railway telegraph construction begins, for train dispatching.

*1881*
— Horace McDougall sells Winnipeg telephone system to Bell (Feb. 21). First Winnipeg telephone directory has 42 subscribers. First switchboard arrives from east via U.S., on train and Red River cart.
— Duquet forms Quebec and Levis Telephone Company.
— Erastus Wiman and Western Union interests take over Great North Western Telegraph Company. GNW then takes over Dominion Telegraph and Montreal Telegraph, to monopolize telegraphy in Canada.
— First phone for public use outside Bell Central offices opens in Lancefield's Stationery shop, Hamilton, Ont. Payment to attendant.

*1882*
— Bell opens manufacturing shops, forerunner to Northern Electric (later Northern Telecom Ltd.)

*1883*
— NWMP use first telephones in Regina.
— Canadian Pacific begins commercial Telegraph service.

*1884*
— New Westminster and Port Moody Telephone Company gets charter.

*1885*
— Prince Edward Island founds own telephone company (July 5).
— Anglo-American Telegraph Company opens telephone exchange in Newfoundland.
— Exchange opens in Tilley's Bookstore, Granville (later Vancouver), November.

*1886*
— All-Canadian telegraph system completed. First message goes from New Westminster, B.C. to Canso, N.S., in three minutes (Dec. 20) and on to England via cable.

*1887*
— Peter Lamont opens Saskatchewan's first telephone exchange in a bookstore at Hamilton and South Railway Streets, Regina (October 26).
— Bell Telephone sells majority holdings in Nova Scotia and New Brunswick to Nova Scotia Telephone Company (Nov. 28).

*1888*
— New Brunswick Telephone Company founded.

*1889*
— New Brunswick Telephone Company takes over telephones in that province.

*1893*
— Coin box (5-cent) installed for use with public telephone in Joseph Lee's drugstore, Toronto; payment by honour system.

*1895*
— Romaine Callender, Brantford inventor, demonstrates his automatic telephone in New York (January 23).

*1897*
— Dr. J. F. Demers, Saint-Octave-de-Métis, builds telephone line from his home to local railway station.

*1898*
— Demers forms La Compagnie de Téléphone de Métis. In February 1900 he buys up La Compagnie de Téléphone de Bellechasse (founded 1893).

*1899*
— Yukon telegraph service extended from Dawson to Bennett.
— Northern Electric produces push-button pay phone (connections made only after 5-cent deposit); first goes into Nicolle's Drug Store, Montreal (Aug. 14).

*1900*
— Ottawa gets Canada's first common battery system (April 13); no batteries needed in home telephones.
— Canadian-born Reginald Fessenden, working in U.S., achieves world's first wireless voice transmission over one-mile distance (Dec. 23).

*1901*
— Telegraph connection completed between Yukon and southern Canada (Sept. 24).
— Whitehorse gets Canada's first successful automatic telephone exchange.
— Marconi receives first wireless signal, from England, at Signal Hill, St. John's (Dec. 12).

*1902*
— Jointly owned government telegraph cable links Canada, Fiji, New Zealand and Australia across the Pacific.
— United Towns Electric Company of Carbonear, Nfld., opens small telephone exchanges.
— Canadian Northern Telegraph Company founded.

*1904*
— Vernon and Nelson Telephone Company acquires assets of New Westminster and Burrard Inlet Company, and the Victoria and Esquimalt Company; then changes its name to British Columbia Telephone Company Limited.

*1905*
— B.C. Telephone Company acquires Nanaimo Telephone Co., and Kootenay Lake Telephone Co.
— City of Edmonton establishes edmonton telephones (Jan. 1).
— Parliamentary Select Committee in Ottawa investigates Canadian telephone industry.

*1906*
— Grand Trunk Pacific Telegraph Company incorporated.
— First long distance line, Winnipeg-Regina (Nov. 6).
— Reginald Fessenden achieves first two-way Morse transmission across the Atlantic; receives first voice transmission from across the ocean; makes world's first radio broadcast (December 24) between New England and Caribbean.

*1908*
— Manitoba and Alberta governments buy Bell telephone interests.

*1909*
— Saskatchewan government buys Bell telephone interests.

*1910*
— Nova Scotia Telephone Company buys telephone company of Prince Edward Island.

*1911*
— Maritime Telegraph and Telephone Company purchases all assets of Nova Scotia Telephone Company.

*1915*
— Canadian Northern Telegraph Company takes over most operations of Great North Western Telegraph Company. CN, CP and Grand Trunk now operate the only major telegraph companies in Canada.

*1916*
— Montreal speaks to Vancouver over newly completed U.S. transcontinental line.

*1917*
— Vacuum tubes, improving long-distance transmission, introduced to Canada.
— Canadian Northern Railway (and telegraph company) becomes Crown Company.

*1919*
— United Towns Electric of Newfoundland acquires Anglo-American Company (briefly held by Western Union) and founds Avalon Telephone Company.
— Canadian Marconi transmitter, XWA, begins radio broadcasts in Montreal (December).

*1920*
— Canadian Northern Telegraph Company becomes Canadian National Telegraph Company.
— Grand Trunk Pacific Telegraph transferred to management of Canadian National.

*1921*
— Newfoundland's first long-distance line runs from St. John's to Carbonear.
— Telephone Association of Canada formed.

*1923*
— Canadian National's newly established radio department transmits broadcasts to moving trains (July).
— Royal Canadian Corps of Signals exchanges northern Canada's first wireless messages, Dawson to Mayo (October 20).

*1924*
— Canadian National acquires Western Union telegraph lines in B.C.

*1925*
— RCCS Aklavik radio station opens (Oct. 6). Northwest Territories and Yukon Radio System now includes Aklavik, Dawson, Mayo, Fort Simpson, Fort Smith and Edmonton.

*1927*
— First trans-Canada radio network broadcast over telephone and telegraph lines celebrates Canada's Diamond Jubilee (July 1).

*1928*
— Canada attends Imperial Wireless and Cable Conference, setting stage for supervision of international telecommunications.
— CNT acquires ownership of Grand Trunk Pacific Telegraph Company.
— Temiskaming Telephone Company becomes Northern Telephone Company.

*1929*
— CNT acquires Western Union lines in Maritimes.
— British Columbia Telephone Company sets up a subsidiary, North-West Telephone Company, to become world's first radiotelephone firm (March 20). First link (June) connects Powell River on mainland with Campbell River, Vancouver Island.

*1932*
— Trans Canada Telephone System inaugurated. Earl of Bessborough, Governor-General of Canada, speaks to each Lieutenant Governor in the nine provinces (January 25).

*1939*
— Telephone service begins between Canada and Newfoundland.

— Royal Train, carrying King and Queen on first royal visit to Canada, is equipped with switchboard and internal telephone system.

*1942*
— Commonwealth Telegraphs Conference in Australia recommends complete review and study of communications systems throughout British Commonwealth, aiming for wireless and cable improvement and coordination.

*1943–1944*
— Quebec City is "wired" for historic meetings of Winston Churchill, Franklin Roosevelt, Mackenzie King and other wartime leaders.

*1948*
— Commonwealth Telegraphs Agreement signed; Commonwealth Telecommunications Board established, membership includes Canada.
— World's first microwave for commercial and voice transmission: Prince Edward Island to the mainland (Nov. 19).

*1950*
— Canadian Overseas Telecommunication Corporation (now Teleglobe) founded. Corporation takes over assets in Canada of Cable and Wireless Limited and Canadian Marconi Company, including cable stations at Harbour Grace, Halifax and Bamfield, B.C., and connecting landlines. As a result, COTC operates telegraph cables across the Atlantic and Pacific and to Bermuda; radiotelegraph services to the U.K., Australia, Barbados, New York, St. Pierre and Miquelon; radiotelephone services to U.K. and West Indies.

*1951*
— COTC installs direct radio-teletype circuit to Bermuda.

*1955*
— Québec-Téléphone emerges from line of companies traced back through Le Corporation de Téléphone et de Pouvoir de Québec (1927), to earliest companies founded by Dr. Demers.
— Canada gets direct radio-telegraph circuit to Germany (November).

*1956*
— Canada gets direct radio-telegraph link to France (May).
— First trans-Atlantic telephone cable brought into service (September 25) jointly owned by COTC, British Post Office and American Telephone and Telegraph Company.
— Trans-Pacific radio-telephone calls now go directly from Vancouver to Australia and New Zealand (rather than via San Francisco) (November).
— CN/CP launch Telex in Canada.
— COTC introduces international Telex into Canada (December 3).

*1957*
— Mid-Canada Defence Line completed, with Bell Canada, representing Trans-Canada Telephone System, as project agent.
— Direct radio-telegraph service, Canada to Japan (June 27).
— Radio-telephone service between Vancouver and New Zealand (December).

*1958*
— Toronto gets Canada's first direct distance dialing system (May 25).
— Tropospheric scatter radio relay system opened for telephone service from Quebec to Knob Lake, Sept Isles, Goose Bay, Schefferville.
— Direct radio-telegraph circuit, Canada to Rome (April).
— Trans-Canada microwave system inaugurated (July 1).

*1959*
— Radiotelephone service extended to St. Pierre and Miquelon (November).

*1961*
— CANTAT, a multi-channel multi-purpose cable is opened between Canada and Britain (December 19); Queen Elizabeth chats with Prime Minister John Diefenbaker.
— Direct telephone, telegraph and Telex services now available between Canada and Argentina, via radio (November).

*1962*
— Telex and radio-telegraph service to Peru.

*1963*
— ICECAN, cable system between Canada, Greenland and Iceland now in service with extensions to Britain and Europe.
— COMPAC, the Commonwealth Pacific Cable System, multi-channel multi-purpose cable now in service over 8,000 miles from Canada to New Zealand and Australia via Hawaii and Fiji (December 2).

*1964*
— CN and CP build transcontinental microwave.

*1967*
— CN and CP completely integrated into CN/CP Telecommunications.
— Canada's first electronic switching telephone office installed in Montreal.
— First telephone with an all-Canadian design, Contempra, introduced.
— Station-to-station calling introduced between Canada and Britain.
— SEACOM, Southeast Asia Commonwealth Cable inaugurated (March 30) making a 23,000 mile link between Britain, Canada and Southeast Asia.

*1972*
— The Canadian Telecommunications Carriers Association, a nonprofit organization, founded to represent the industry: carriers of any kind of information that can be transmitted electronically. Telephone Association of Canada

terminated and its membership included in new Association.

— Anik I satellite launched (Nov. 9); world's first geostationery, domestic communications satellite.

*1973*

— Trans Canada Telephone System introduces "Dataroute," world's first nation-wide digital data system.

— Anik II launched (April 20).

*1975*

— Anik III launched (May 7).

*1976*

— Canada launches world's most powerful Communications Technology Satellite, government sponsored (January 17).

# Bibliography

## Unpublished Sources

Bell, Alexander Graham, *Letter*: to federal minister of marines and fisheries, 1899, suggesting study of Marconi wireless for Sable Island; Public Archives of Canada.

Bell, Alexander Melville, *Letter*: offering sale of Bell Telephone company, 1879; Bell Canada Archives.

Bernstein, Otto, *Manuscript*: "The Beginning of Fairview Mutual"; Public Archives of Alberta.

Black, William, *Manuscript*: "The Radio Contribution of Canadian National Railways"; CN Telecommunications.

Boss, Reginald, *Manuscript*: Autobiography; New Brunswick Telephone Company.

Bossé, J. Fr. X., *Letter*: Municipal telephone rights, 1898; Quebec Telephone.

Britnell, G. E., *Manuscript*: "Public Ownership of Telephones in the Prairie Provinces, 1934"; Robarts Library, University of Toronto.

Bulkley, Charles, *Papers*: Public Archives of British Columbia.

Connelly, W. E., *Manuscript*: "History of Communications"; Teleglobe Canada, Montreal.

Conway, E., *Papers*: PABC.

Cowherd, James, *Letter*: Production of Canadian telephones, 1881; BCA.

Duquet, Cyrille, *Record*: of patents; BCA.

Easson, Robert, *Manuscript*: "The Telegraph in Canada"; CNT.

Fessenden, Reginald, *Papers*: PAC.

Fowler, George, *Letter*: re compensation for inhabitants of St. Lawrence river land used by telegraph semaphore, 1815; PAC.

Gisborne, F. N., *Letter*: to Adolphe Caron re awards for telegraph operators, Riel Rebellion; PAC.

Gisborne, Francis, *Letter*: re his father; PAC.

French, Lt. Col. G. A., *Letter*: re Indian interference with telegraph lines, 1875; Public Archives of Saskatchewan.

Howe, Joseph, *Letter*: to F. N. Gisborne, 1867; Public Archives of Nova Scotia.

Huck, W. H., *Memorandum*: Department of Defence Production assessment of Mid-Canada Line, 1959; Private.

Johnston, Alex, *Report*: Marconi's choice of Glace Bay site; Maritime Tel and Tel Archives.

Kee, C. A., *Manuscript*: "History of New Brunswick Telephone Company"; NB Tel.

Kemp, George, *Manuscript*: "Diary of Marconi Experiments, December, 1901"; Canadian Marconi Company.

Lanham, E. H., *Manuscript*: "A Brief Story of the Growth, Evolution and Expansion of Telephone Systems"; Northern Telcom.

Macaulay, Rev. W., *Papers*: Public Archives of Ontario.

MacIsaac, Cpl. J. *et al.*, *Logbook*: RCCS, Ennadai Lake, 1949–54; RCCS Museum, Kingston, Ont.

Marconi, G., *Telegram*: to Wilfrid Laurier, "Laurier Papers, Vol. 246"; PAC.

McQuay, Robert, *Manuscript*: "Brief History of Early Telegraph in Maritimes Colonies"; New Brunswick Museum, Saint John.

McMicking, Robert, *Letterbooks*: PABC; British Columbia Telephone Company archives.

———, *Manuscript*: "Telegraph in B.C., 1898"; BCTA.

Minto, Lord Gilbert, *Memorandum*: of discussions with Marconi, January, 1902, Minto Papers Vol. 4; PAC.

Morisson, Charles F., *Manuscript*: "Collins Overland Telegraph"; PABC.

Oakley, Beatrice, *Manuscript*: "History of Early Edmonton"; Edmonton City Archives.

Oppenheimer, D., *Letter*: to William Van Horne, 1889; Canadian Pacific Archives.

Patterson, C. R., *Manuscript*: "Transportation and Communications in the Canadian Prairie West, 1867–1905"; PAS.

Pearce, William, *Manuscript*: Postal Communication in the Three Prairie Provinces; PABC.

RCCS, Edmonton, *Manuscript*: "A History of the Northwest Territories and Yukon Radio System"; CN Tel, RCCS Museum.

Sise, C. F., *Letterbooks*: 1880–1906; BCA.

Sykes, R. O., *Memorandum*: to shareholders of Bearspaw Mutual; PAA.

Van Horne, William, *Letterbooks*: PAC.

———, *Telegram*: to his wife, Canadian Railway Museum, Delson, Que.

Wilkinson, Elfleda, *Manuscript*: B.C. telephone history; BCTA.

*Lease*: of telephone to Alexander Mackenzie, 1877; BCA.

*Manuscript*: "Quebec Telephone (de ses origines à nos jours)"; Quebec Tel.

*Papers*: Sudbury Area; PAO.

*Records*: Canadian Independent Telephone Company, 1896–1926; Ontario Public Search Office.

*Report*: Meeting authorizing Montreal Telegraph, Montreal Board of Trade, 1846; PAC.

*Transcript*: Mission Control proceedings, Anik III launch, 1975; Kennedy Space Center, Florida.

# Public Documents

*Debates of the House of Commons*, 1905, p. 2682.

*Journals of House of Assembly*, Nova Scotia, No. 83, 1850.

Memorandum of Agreement between G. Marconi and Government of Canada, 1902, *Privy Council Official Records*, Vol. 145.

*Proceedings of Select Committee of House of Commons on Telephones in Canada*, 1905 (2 vol.)

*Report of the Canadian Pacific Railway Commission Evidence*, Ottawa, 1882 (3 vol.)

*Sessional Papers*, Canada Legislative Council, No. 1, Vol. 5, 1846.

*Sessional Papers of Canada*, No. 10A, 1883; "The Dominion Telegraph Service in Manitoba and the North-West Territories."

*White Paper on a Domestic Satellite Communications System for Canada*, Queen's Printer, Ottawa, 1968.

# Newspapers and Periodicals

**Bell News**, Bell Canada, Montreal, 1964, 1974.

**The Blue Bell**, Bell Canada, Montreal, 1926–46, 1956.

**British Columbian**, New Westminster, 1865.

**British Colonist**, Toronto, 1846–47.

**Bulletin**, Edmonton, 1881–84, 1908.

**Canadian Electrical Review**, Toronto, 1892.

**Canadian Illustrated News**, Montreal, 1874.

**Canadian Magazine**, Toronto, 1932.

**Canadian Monthly and National Review**, Toronto, 1876.

**Canadian National Magazine**, CNR, Toronto, 1924, 1944.

**Citizen**, Ottawa, 1938, 1964.

**CNR Reporter**, CNR, Montreal, 1968, 1974.

**Coastguard**, Shelburne, N.S., n.d.

**Daily Press**, Timmins, 1947.

**Daily Telegraph**, Quebec, 1877, 1880–81.

**Echo**, Manitoba Telephone System, 1921–45, 1950, 1958.

**Electrical Engineer**, New York, 1889, 1892.

**Electrical Review**, New York, 1883–85–86.

**Electrical World**, New York, 1887.

**Examiner**, Toronto, 1846–47.

**Expositor**, Brantford, 1931.

**Financial Post**, Toronto, 1944.

**Financial Times**, Montreal, 1923.

**Free Press**, London, 1881, 1953.

**Gazette**, Montreal, 1887.

**Globe**, Saint John, 1901.

**Globe**, Toronto, 1846, 1881, 1901, 1905.

**Grumbler**, Toronto, 1858–65.

**Herald**, Halifax, 1910, 1946, 1950.

**Le Soleil**, Quebec, 1910.

**Leader**, Regina, 1883, 1906.

**Leader-Post**, Regina, 1934, 1942, 1955, 1962.

**Mail**, Toronto, 1881.

**Mirror**, Toronto, 1846.

**Monthly Bulletin**, Maritime Tel & Tel, 1917, 1927–28, 1933, 1936–37, 1945, 1948.

**New Times and Reporter**, Halifax, 1879.
**News**, Toronto, 1906.
**Ontario Times**, St. Thomas, 1881.
**Planet**, Chatham, 1880.
**Province**, Victoria, 1896.
**Public Ledger**, St. John's, 1852–54, 1857.
**Royal Gazette**, St. John's, 1846, 1851–54.
**Saskatchewan Herald**, Battleford, 1878, 1881–84, 1908.
**Saturday Night**, Toronto, 1959.
**Spanner**, CPR, Montreal, 1950.
**Spectator and Journal of Commerce**, Hamilton, 1846.
**Star**, Montreal, 1914.
**Star**, Regina, 1928, 1936.
**Star**, Toronto, 1933, 1940, 1946.
**Sunday Dispatch**, Columbus, Ohio, 1941.
**Telegram**, Toronto, 1907, 1926, 1946.
**Telephone Journal**, Toronto, 1936.
**Telephone News**, NB Tel, Saint John, 1933–39.
**Telephone Talk**, BC Tel, Vancouver, 1930–1947.
**Telephony**, Chicago, 1908.
**Times**, Prince Albert, 1882–84.
**Times**, New York, 1904.
**Watchman**, Montreal, 1898.
**Witness**, Montreal, 1891.
**World**, Toronto, 1896, 1905–07.

# Published Sources

Anderson, Frank W., *Regina's Terrible Tornado*; Calgary, n.d.
Anonymous, "The Original Projector of the Atlantic Telegraph," Boston *Ledger*, Nov. 13, 1858.
———, "Telegraph Pioneer in Newfoundland," St. John's *Daily News*, Dec. 31, 1943.
Arctander, J. W., *The Apostle of Alaska*; New York, 1909.
Braithewaite, Max, "Year of the Killer Flu," *Maclean's*, Feb. 1, 1953.
Bird, Michael J., *The Town That Died*; London, 1962.
Bolger, F. W. P., *Canada's Smallest Province*; Charlottetown, 1973.
Bridle, Augustus, *Sons of Canada*; Toronto, 1916.
Brown, Ronald, *Telecommunications — The Booming Technology*; New York, 1970.
Bruce, R. V., *Bell and the Conquest of Solitude*; Boston, 1973.
Budenski, Gladys, "Dial a Ghost," *The Big Country News*, June 6, 1971.
Burrows, Acton, *The Canadian Pacific Railway Telegraph*; Winnipeg, 1880.
Carter, Samuel III, *Cyrus Field: Man of Two Worlds*; New York, 1968.
Cashman, Tony, *Singing Wires*; Edmonton, 1972.
Collard, Edgar Andrew, *Call Back Yesterdays*; Toronto, 1965.
Collins, Perry McD., *A Voyage Down the Amoor*; New York, 1860.

Collins, Robert, *A Great Way to Go*; Toronto, 1969.

——, "The Way You'll Live in 2000 AD," *The Canadian Magazine*, Jan. 18, 1969.

——, "Remember When Radio Was the Rage?", *Maclean's*, Aug. 15, 1953.

Connelly, Dolly, "The One World of Perry Collins," *The Beaver*, Summer 1971.

Campbell, Dr. Murray, *The Postal History of Red River, British North America*, Historical Society of Manitoba, 1951.

Creighton, Donald, *John A. Macdonald, The Young Politician*; Toronto, 1952.

Deaville, A. S., *The Colonial Postal System and Postage Stamps of Vancouver Island and British Columbia, 1849–1871*; Victoria, 1928.

Denison, Merrill, *Canada's First Bank* (Vol. II); Toronto, 1967.

Dibner, Bern, *The Atlantic Cable*; New York, 1964.

Drake, Earl, *Regina — The Queen City*; Toronto, 1955.

Dufferin, Marchioness of Dufferin and Ava, *My Canadian Journal, 1872–78*; London, 1891.

Dunsheath, Percy, *A History of Electrical Engineering*; London, 1962.

Field, Cyrus, *The Atlantic Telegraph*; London, 1856.

Field, Henry M. *The Story of the Atlantic Telegraph*; London, 1893.

Fergusson, Dr. Bruce, *The Mantle of Howe*; Windsor, N.S., 1970.

Fetherstonhaugh, R. C., *Charles Fleetford Sise, 1834–1918*; Montreal, 1944.

Galbraith, J. S., "Collins at the Colonial Office." *B.C. Historical Quarterly*, July–August, 1963.

Grant, Sir James, "Gisborne Memoriam," *Transactions of the Royal Society of Canada*, 1893.

Green, Ernest, "Canada's First Electric Telegraph," Papers and Records of Ontario Historical Society, 1927.

Grindlay, Thomas, *A History of the Independent Telephone Industry in Ontario*; Toronto, 1976.

Guillet, Edwin C., *The Story of Canadian Roads*; Toronto, 1966.

——, *Toronto, From Trading Post to Great City*; Toronto, 1934.

Ham, George, H., *Reminiscences of a Raconteur*; Toronto, 1921.

Harlow, A. F., *Old Wires and New Waves*; New York, 1936.

Hawley, Mrs. J. P., "The First Telegraph Office in Napanee," Historical Society, Napanee, Ont., 1909.

Healy, W. J., *Winnipeg's Early Days*; Winnipeg, 1927.

Howay, F. W., *The Overland Telegraph Scheme*; Victoria, 1914.

Hutton, Eric, "What You Don't Know About Howe," *Maclean's*, July 2, 1956.

Innis, Harold A., *A History of the Canadian Pacific Railway*; Toronto 1967.

Jefferson, Robert, *Fifty Years on the Saskatchewan*; Battleford, 1928.

Jolly, W. P., *Marconi*; London, 1972.

Jones, Donald, "Scottish minister's son helped change our culture," Toronto *Daily Star*, Dec. 6, 1975.

Kane, Paul, *Wanderings of an Artist*; London, 1859.

Kee, C. A., "The Story of the Saint John Exchange," New Brunswick *Telephone News*, October 1948.

Kennedy, Howard Angus, "A War Correspondent in 'The '85,'" from *The Story of the Press*, Canadian North-West Historical Society Publications, Battleford, 1928.

Keyser, Walter, "The Introduction of Bell's Telephone in London, Ontario, 1875–1880"; Bell Telephone Archives, 1946.

Leacock, Stephen, *Leacock's Montreal*; Toronto, 1948.

Leech, P. J., "The Pioneer Telegraph Survey of B.C.," *B.C. Mining Record*, August 1899.

Macdonald, J. Stuart, *The Dominion Telegraph*; Battleford, 1930.

MacKay, Douglas, *The Honourable Company*; Toronto, rev. ed. 1966.

Mavor, James, *Government Telephones: The Experience of Manitoba, Canada*; Toronto, 1917.

McAfee, Rev. T. A., "Diary of George Weldon," Regina *Leader-Post*, Apr. 25, 1931.

Middleton, J. E. *The Municipality of Toronto, A History*; Toronto, 1923.

Mill, J. S., *Principles of Political Economy*; London, 1857.

Morgan, T. J., *Telegraphy and Telephony*; 1963.

Mulvaney, C. P., *The History of the North-West Rebellion of 1885*; Toronto, 1885.

Muir, Gilbert A., *A History of the Telephone in Manitoba*, Historical and Scientific Society of Manitoba, 1964–65.

Murray, John, *A Story of the Telegraph*; Montreal, 1906.

Myers, Elgin, "A Canadian in New York," *The Canadian Magazine*, 1893.

Neuberger, R. L., "The Telegraph Trail," *Harper's Magazine*, October, 1946.

Nichols, M. E., *(CP) The Story of the Canadian Press*; Toronto, 1948.

Orpperrman, Joseph, *Pole Line to Alaska*; Edmonton, 1945.

Parker, J. M., "A Defeated Success," *Overland Monthly*, July 1888.

Patten, William, *Pioneering the Telephone in Canada*; Montreal, 1944.

Porter, Mackenzie, "Canada recruits the man who won the war," *Maclean's*, Aug. 1, 1952.

Quinpool, John (J. W. Regan), *First Things in Acadia*; Halifax, 1936.

Raby, Ormond, *Radio's First Voice: The Story of Reginald Fessenden*; Toronto, 1970.

Raddall, Thomas H., "Nova Scotia's First Telegraph System," *Dalhousie Review*, 1947–48.

Reed, James D., *The Telegraph in America*; New York, 1886.

Regan, John W., *The Inception of the Associated Press*; Collections of the Nova Scotia Historical Society, 1912.

Reville, F. Douglas, *History of Brant County*; Brantford, 1920.

Rich, E. E., *Hudson's Bay Company 1670–1870, Vol. III*; Toronto, 1960.

Robinson, Howard P., *The Founding of the New Brunswick Telephone Company* (as told to Sen. G. P. Burchill), 1974.

Ronaghan, Allen, "The Telegraph Line to Edmonton," *Alberta Historical Review*, #4, Autumn, 1970.

Scadding, Henry, *Toronto of Old*; Toronto, 1966.

Smith, Donald A., *At the Forks of the Grand 1793–1920*; Paris, Ont., 1951.

Stevens, C. R., *History of the Canadian National Railways*; Toronto, 1973.

Thompson, R. L., *Wiring a Continent*; Princeton, N.J., 1947.

Usher, Jean, "Duncan of Metlakatla," from *The Shield of Achilles* (edit. by W. L. Morton); Toronto, 1968.

Vaughan, Walter, *Sir William Van Horne*; Toronto, 1926.

Wade, M. S., *The Overlanders of '62*; Victoria, 1931.

Wade, Mason, *The French Canadians*; Toronto, 1955.

Wiman, Erastus, *Chances of Success: Episodes and Observations in the Life of a Busy Man*; New York, 1893.

Whidden, D. G., "Nova Scotia's Telegraphs, Landlines and Cables," Wolfville *Acadian*, 1938; PANS.

Whymper, F., *Travel and Adventure in the Territory of Alaska*; London, 1868.

Woodhouse, T. Roy, "Hamilton's First Telephones"; address to Head-of-the-Lakes Historical Society, Hamilton, Nov. 11, 1955.

Woodsworth, Charles J., *Canada and the Orient*; Toronto, 1941.

Wright, L. M., "Bactrians in B.C.," *Beaver*; spring 1957.

Young, Filson (ed.), *Trial of Hawley Harvey Crippen*; Toronto, 1919.

# Pamphlets and Brochures

"A Technical Description of the Canadian Domestic Satellite Communications System"; Telesat Canada, Ottawa, 1974.

"An Experiment in Conference TV"; British Columbia Telephone Company, 1974.

"An Outline of the History of CP Telecommunications"; Canadian Pacific, Montreal, 1972.

"Anik: Experience with a Domestic Communications Satellite Service to the Public"; Telesat Canada, Ottawa, 1974.

"Communications in the North"; CN Telecommunications, Toronto.

"Five Years of War: The Contribution of Canadian National"; CN Telecommunications, Toronto.

"Global Telecommunications: Implications for the Canadian Carriers"; address by Jean-Claude Delorme, Teleglobe Canada, Montreal, 1975.

"History of the Telephone in Saskatchewan"; SaskTel, Regina.

"Instant World, A Report on Telecommunications in Canada"; Information Canada, 1971.

"Moloch or Aquarius?", by Gordon B. Thompson; "the", issue 4, 1970, Bell-Northern Research, Ottawa.

"New Developments in Telephony"; address by G. F. MacFarlane, British Columbia Telephone Company, 1975.

"People of Service: A Brief History of Manitoba Telephone System"; MTS, Winnipeg.

"Telephony in the Nor'West," from *The SGT publication*, SaskTel, Regina.

"The Future of Communications," by A. G. Lester, Child Memorial Lecture, 1970; Bell Canada, Montreal.

"The Greening of the Wired City," by G. B. Thompson; Bell-Northern Research, Ottawa.

"The Replacement of Travel by Telecommunications," J. H. Kollen and John Garwood; Bell Canada, Montreal, 1974.

"The Vital Link"; Canadian Telecommunications Carriers Association, Ottawa, 1974.

"Winged Words Over a Century"; Canadian National Railways, 1946.

# Index